Walks in

Walks in Wild Yellowstone

A Summer of Solo Backpacking in
Yellowstone National Park

Cliff Murray

ISBN-13: 978-1500424961
ISBN-10: 150042496X

Library of Congress Control Number: 2016901485
CreateSpace Independent Publishing Platform,
North Charleston, SC

O for a muse of fire

William Shakespeare

Spirit that form'd this scene, these tumbled rock-piles

Walt Whitman

And 'mid these dancing rocks at once and ever it flung up momently the sacred river

Samuel Taylor
Coleridge

*Never did sun more beautifully steep in his first splendour, valley, rock, or hill;
Ne'er saw I, never felt, a calm so deep!*

William Wordsworth

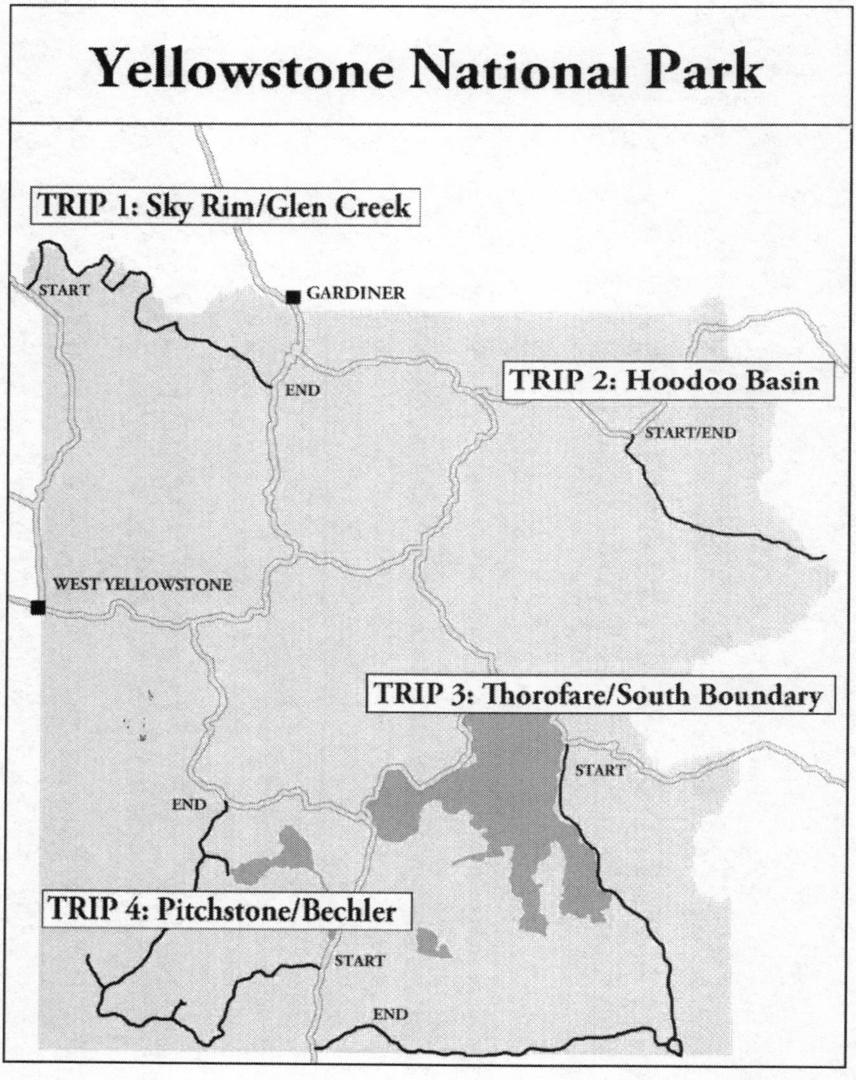

Yellowstone National Park

TRIP 1: Sky Rim/Glen Creek

START

■ GARDINER

END

TRIP 2: Hoodoo Basin

START/END

WEST YELLOWSTONE

TRIP 3: Thorofare/South Boundary

START

END

TRIP 4: Pitchstone/Bechler

START

END

Prologue

This is a book I always wanted to read, a book about experiencing the wild backcountry of Yellowstone National Park. For more years than I care to remember, I was stuck—or felt stuck—in a high-rise office in Dallas, Texas, working as a corporate attorney. During those long days of soulless work, I often dreamed of chucking it all and moving to the wild Rocky Mountains. Somewhere closer to nature, where there was more to life than ambition and the pursuit of superfluous wealth.

But one has to make a living, and corporate law provided a good living, if not a good life. So I kept working. And saving, and dreaming of wild places, places such as Yellowstone. Until the time came for me to make a literal escape, I hoped to make do with a literary one, and I searched for a book that would transport me out of the city and into the Yellowstone backcountry. Surprisingly, few such books exist.

About the park itself there are plenty of books, many quite good. But most of these have a singular focus, on history or geology or some aspect of park policy. They helped put my earlier Yellowstone trips into a richer context, but they always left me in the big city. I needed a book that would get me out of there. A few came close— sort of—but these were disjointed collections of essays or old magazine stories, or they spent most of their pages somewhere outside the park.

Where was the book to immerse me in deep Yellowstone? At a campsite on the banks of the Yellowstone River in the wildlands above the lake. Or near waterfalls in the park's southwest corner. Or in the park's high country, overlooking broad valleys undefaced by roads and buildings. If such a book existed, I couldn't find it.

There is a saying that if you search for a book you avidly want to read, and find it doesn't exist, then it's your responsibility to write it. Could that be my answer for the Yellowstone book? Surely not— who was I to write a book about Yellowstone? There are many people who have spent more time in the park than I have, who have worked there or been going back year after year for much of their lives. And there are people who know more about Yellowstone than I do, who have invested years in exploring and studying various aspects of the park.

But none of them had written that book.

So maybe that was my answer.

But there was another problem: how was I to write about experiencing the wilds of Yellowstone while stuck in a city a thousand miles away? Perhaps I could spread things out—make one backpacking trek per year. Even that seemed unrealistic. Working at a large law firm, it's difficult to schedule long vacations, and venturing beyond the grasp of e-mail and cell phones—even for a few days—was, to say the least, frowned upon. (Actually, there was a lot of frowning at that firm, but that may have been just me.)

Still, I pored over Yellowstone trail maps, following backcountry routes to remote destinations. My eyes were always drawn to four areas: the Sky Rim in the park's northwest corner, Hoodoo Basin in the northeast, Thorofare in the southeast, and the Bechler in the southwest. Treks to these areas are considered life trips by many hikers, and rightfully so. They include some of the park's deepest wildlands. And each offers a different kind of experience: high ridgeline trails along the Sky Rim; fascinating geological formations in the Hoodoo Basin; a wild, expansive valley in the Thorofare, almost thirty miles from the nearest road; and majestic waterfalls in the Bechler. Someday, I told myself, I'd get out there and see those places, though it always felt like a pipedream.

And then came the Great Recession. As the economy tightened, my firm's business slowed and billable hours dropped. Layoffs soon followed. Support staff was hit first and hardest, and every few weeks groups of people simply disappeared—no longer with the firm. While my coworkers worried about being let go in the worst recession in recent memory, I began to dream.

What if . . . ?

When the firm got around to laying off attorneys, I was ready. I told one of the partners in my section to put my name at the top of the layoff list. Proving the old adage you should be careful what you wish for, I was soon set free from the corporate rat race.

Soon after, I left the big city and moved to the wilds of Montana. And suddenly all those pipedreams about backpacking deep Yellowstone were within reach. Even better, instead of making mad-dash escapes, trying to cram in one trip per year—if work permitted—there was time to do all four in one summer. This added a sense of continuity, even poetry. Now the progression of hikes would match the flow of the seasons, as both moved across the Yellowstone landscape. And each trek would build upon the last. When all were complete, they would amount to a single large journey, one greater than the sum of the separate hikes.

Scattered across the Yellowstone backcountry is a series of designated campsites, most connected by trails. For overnight stays at any of these, you need a permit. These are easy enough to get from any of the park's backcountry offices, but what can be difficult is getting the campsites you want. Or any campsite at all in popular areas near lakes, choice fishing streams, and almost all of the Bechler region.

The odds improve if you reserve sites in advance. This is done by sending a form listing your first, second, and third choices of campsites for each night of your trip to the Yellowstone Central Backcountry Office. There's a small fee for this convenience, which was twenty-five dollars per trip in 2012. Park staffers begin processing requests in April of each year, handling those that arrive by March 31 in random order. Those that come later are done in the order received.

To ensure mine would get in with the first batch, I mailed them on March 23. The first confirmation came via e-mail on April 5, and another arrived the following day. By April 10, I had all four. In most cases I got my first choice of campsites, though my second appeared a few times and my third twice. This was no disappointment. My selections were little more than guesses to begin with, and there was a chance my third choice would be as good as my first, if not better. All that mattered was the plans were in place, and the four treks into remote Yellowstone, which I had dreamed of making for so many years, were finally about to begin.

Throughout the summer, I told myself, I'd keep records on everything, from planning and preparation to journals of the hikes. When the last trek was completed, it would all go into a book. And when the book was finished, I'd offer it back across time to my former self—the one stuck in a noisy apartment in the big city—and to everyone else who dreams of being in Yellowstone but finds themselves somewhere too far away.

This, finally, is that book. Perhaps it will encourage some others to publish their own Yellowstone stories. I sincerely hope it does. Yellowstone is such a wonderful place. We could certainly use more good books about the experience it offers.

So let's go backpacking. Leaving road traffic and crowds far behind, we'll cross mountains, meadows, and rivers, where the only sounds we'll hear are the whisper of water and wind, the creaking of tree branches, and the songs of birds. Our nights, many miles from the artificial light of civilization, will bring a rich and natural darkness, enlivened at times by the calls of owls, coyotes, and wolves. It will be a dream of a summer. Far away from the hustle and bustle we'll walk in wild Yellowstone, and immerse ourselves in the pure spirit of nature.

Trip Locator
(More detailed map on following pages)

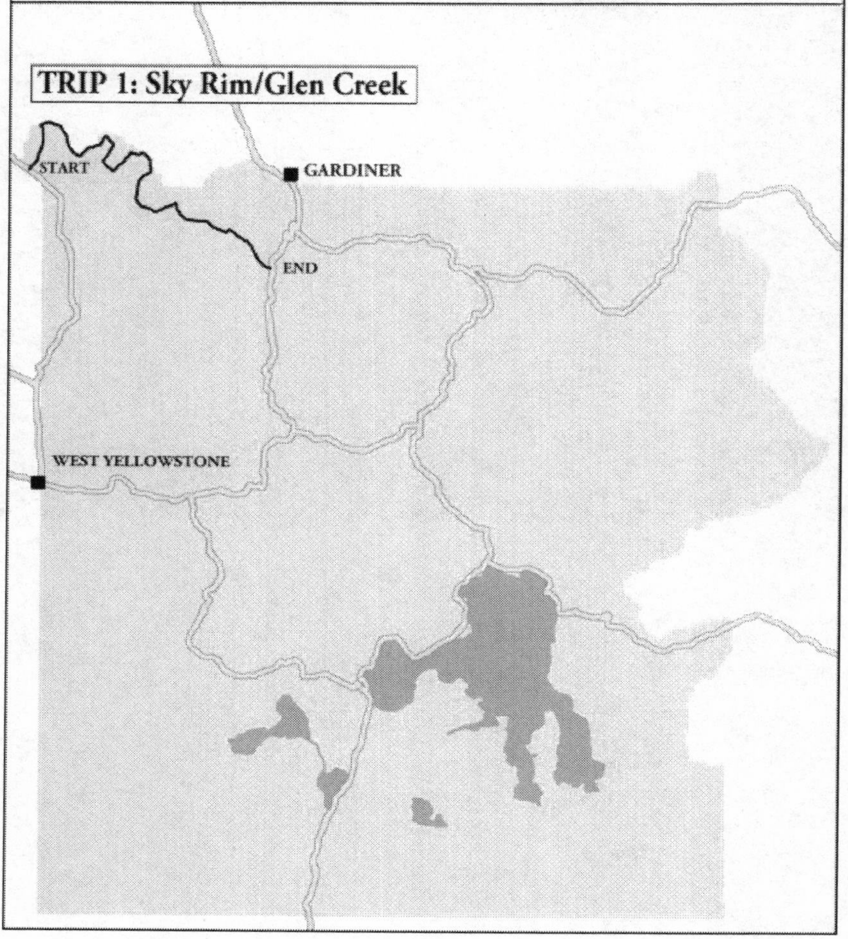

TRIP 1: Sky Rim/Glen Creek

START

■ GARDINER

END

WEST YELLOWSTONE

Trip 1
Sky Rim—Glen Creek
July 22-28, 2012

Trip Overview

- START: Dailey Creek Trailhead on Highway 191
- Sky Rim Trail to Shelf Lake
- Crescent Lake Trail to High Lake
- Sportsman Lake Trail to Sportsman Lake
- Climb over Electric Pass
- END: Glen Creek Trailhead a few miles south of Mammoth Hot Springs

Duration: Forty-one miles in seven days.

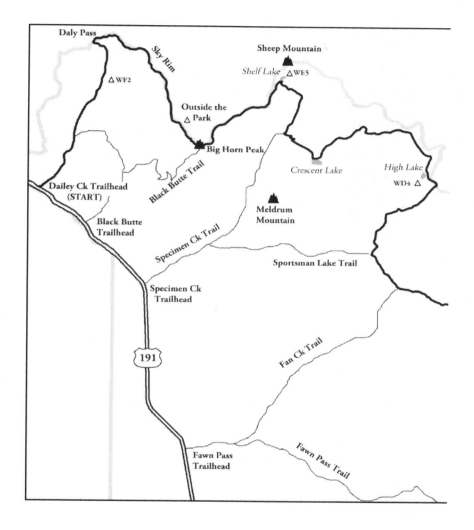

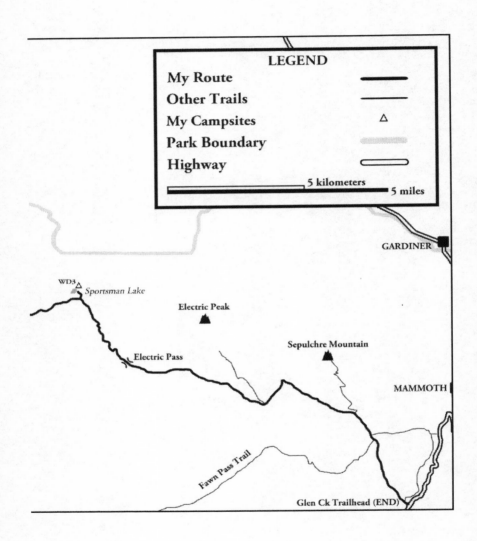

Day 1. From Home to Dailey Creek, Campsite WF2

My backpack is stashed in the back of my girlfriend Mari's Subaru as we wind our way through Gallatin Canyon, headed south. It is Sunday, July 22, a bright, clear day of early summer. The morning air is rich with a sense of beginnings.

Our destination is the northwest corner of Yellowstone National Park, where Mari will drop me off for the first of my four backpacking trips. Seven days from now I'll emerge forty-one trail miles to the east, at a different trailhead on a different road, a few miles south of Mammoth Hot Springs. Mari and I traveled there yesterday to drop my car at the ending trailhead. In backpacking parlance, this is known as setting up a shuttle.

At Mammoth we also stopped to get my backcountry permit (the e-mail I received in April was only a confirmation of the campsite reservations). The park was as busy as one would expect on a July Saturday, with groups of various sizes milling about the general store, hotel, and visitors center. Dodging the crowds, I hurried into the backcountry office and presented my reservation to the uniformed ranger. I also showed him a permit for a short backpacking trek I'd made two weeks ago, a tune-up trip to ensure my gear and fitness were ready for this longer outing. This was to let him know I'd already seen the instructional DVD hikers are required to watch before heading into the backcountry. The taciturn ranger appeared relieved at not having to sit through the program another time.

As the printer churned out my permit, the ranger intoned in an official manner that, due to recent dry weather, wood fires are prohibited in the park. He then handed me the permit, set in a zippered plastic cover with a twist-tie for attaching to a backpack,

and a card to leave on my car's dashboard while parked at the ending trailhead. Almost as an afterthought he added, "You may run into some stock up there." And that was it.

The elevation at Dailey Creek Trailhead is 6,733 feet, low for Yellowstone, where the average is near eight thousand. Because much of the Sky Rim is above nine thousand feet, there's a bit of climbing in my future. Most of it will come tomorrow. On this first day out, when my pack is fully loaded and my hiking time shortened by the drive to the trailhead, I've scheduled an easy trek: three and half miles, with a gradual climb of seven hundred feet.

The initial route heads up the broad valley of Dailey Creek. The terrain is open sagebrush grassland with an abundance of wildflowers freshly in bloom. A uinta ground squirrel lounges on a boulder near the creek, soaking up the midday sun.

The trail meanders to the northeast, skirting the base of Crown Butte before bending northward. A high ridgeline marks the horizon ahead. It's the western half of the Sky Rim. From the valley floor it seems high and distant. And appropriately named.

Dailey Creek Trail

The highway is now a mile away and a few hundred feet below. A tiny tractor-trailer flows silently by, its noise muted by distance and masked by a gentle breeze rustling sage and grass. A northern flicker calls from across the valley. When it falls silent, the only audible sound other than the breeze is the rattle of an unseen grasshopper in the nearby grass.

Where the route intersects the trail from Black Butte Creek, two uniformed park rangers approach, each with a set of elk antlers strapped to their back like huge skeletal wings. We exchange hellos, and the senior ranger explains they are gathering material for an interpretive program. I recognize the other ranger as one I met on my tune-up trip two weeks ago. It was on a socked-in, rainy day, when low, drizzly clouds covered the valley. Undeterred by the elements, she was out swinging a single-bit axe to clear a log fallen across the route. I saw her again toward trip's end. This time she was jogging the trail in shorts and t-shirt.

"You're hard-core," I said.

"I try," she answered with a modest grin.

Now, having already heard of my backpacking plans for the summer, she is interested in my route. She asks to see my permit, not so much in an official capacity as in the interest of a fellow hiker. I do a half-turn so she can see the permit attached to the back of my pack. She reads off each campsite in an approving tone, pausing toward the middle to ask her partner, "Is the bear pole up at High Lake?"

"I think they just got it up," he answers.

This raises the question of why a bear pole wouldn't be up at this time of year. Do some of them fall, or are they taken down for some reason? Before I can ask, the senior ranger speaks again. "Make sure you hang your food at night," he says.

"I always do," I say.

"Good," he says. "We hammer that pretty hard, because if a bear gets into someone's food, it will become habituated and then have to be euthanized."

"I'd hate to be responsible for getting a bear killed," I say, quite sincerely.

He grins. "Well, we don't want you to get hurt, either." The grin fades. "But if you don't hang your food, it's a pretty hefty fine. You probably already heard this in the backcountry office, but your route passes through the Gallatin Bear Management Area. Just make sure you stay on the trail as you go through there."

"I will," I say, leaving out that the ranger in the backcountry office didn't mention BMA restrictions, or much of anything else.

"I'll be working at the Sportsman Lake cabin in a few days," the younger ranger says. "Maybe I'll see you out there."

"I'll look for you," I say. We exchange best wishes and go our separate ways, them toward the trailhead and me toward my first campsite.

As the trail continues its gentle climb, the creek narrows and swings away to the west, leaving drier ground with taller, bushier sage. Wildflowers still abound, sticky geraniums, shrubby cinquefoil, yarrow, and plenty of wild dandelions. Farther up, the slopes on either side begin to close in, pushing the creek toward the trail. A swallow flits about over the water, making tight, graceful arcs. Another appears behind it and higher above. After pausing in midflight to hang in the breeze, it dives into the cover of the creekside brush.

I stop and stand and take in the setting, trying to absorb the wildness of the moment and reminding myself I need to slow down. Having come from the city, after days of rushing about getting last-minute supplies, I am not yet in tune with the wilderness, and more likely to miss nature's subtler moments. Until I become mentally and spiritually settled, I'll need to make a conscious effort to reduce my pace, look around more, and resist the tendency to charge on to the next destination.

Where is that childlike sense of wonder nature brings? It has been dulled, perhaps, by too much time in the city, too many years spent chasing a living. But it's not gone. It just needs time in wild nature to reawaken. Okay, here it is . . .

Walking more slowly and with a curious eye turns an ordinary hike into a contemplative amble. This is something I learned almost too late. Twenty, perhaps even ten, years ago, younger and more ambitious, I would have planned these trips much differently, with longer hiking days to more distant campsites. With longer hikes, I would've reasoned, I'd see more of the park. Now, years of experience in both backpacking and life have shown excessive ambition makes you see and experience less. If you're always charging ahead with eyes trained on the path in front of you, thinking only of reaching a goal, you'll surely get there, but it will be late in the day when there's too little light to enjoy it.

I continue on at a moderate amble. Alert and in the moment, I tend to see more, and it all feels right. This is why we backpack—not to rack up miles, but for meaningful time in a wild, natural setting. The magic is often found in smaller moments, when we take time to pause and look, not only at majestic views of mountains and waterfalls and large animals, but also at birds, insects, and wildflowers, the tight bends of a creek, the interplay of forest and meadow, and rocks given new colors by lichens and time. These subtle noticings all flow together to bring a deeper connection with nature. It's the feeling of renewal so many seek.

In the trailside foliage, a tiny fluttery movement draws my attention to what appears to be a black-and-white butterfly. It is actually a green lattice moth. Rising slowly and erratically from a patch of blossoms, it flits with the jerky motions of a miniature bat. When a sustained gust hurtles down the valley, bouncing tall grasses in fluid waves, the moth disappears in a mass of flowers. Just beyond, on the low banks of Dailey Creek, three dark-eyed juncos hop about as though oblivious to the turbulence above them.

The valley continues to narrow through its gentle climb, and the sage grows shorter and more widespread. Patches of forest creep down the slopes and across the valley floor, obscuring the view. In such places it's important to stay alert for bears.

Yellowstone is home to both grizzly and black bears, and while bear maulings are rare, they have happened in Yellowstone. A few quite recently. The cause is often human error, when a person does one of three things you should never do in grizzly country: surprise a bear at close range, approach one guarding a kill, and, perhaps worst of all, get too close to a sow grizzly that has a cub. There is also a fourth thing, but it usually comes after you and the bear have already seen each other: you should never run from a bear. It is thought to trigger predatory instincts, and may cause them to give chase. Grizzlies can sprint up to forty-five miles per hour for a hundred yards or more. No human can outrun that.

Still, the presence of bears is not something to fear, as long as we respect them and take precautions to avoid confrontations. To keep from surprising unseen bears while hiking, it's best to make noise when the terrain restricts your view. Bears don't want conflict any more than we do, and they usually run away when they know humans are about. But they can't smell you if you're downwind, and they may not hear your footsteps if the sounds are masked by wind or a flowing creek. A good practice is to make noise loud enough to avoid a surprise encounter—talk, clap, sing, whatever you're comfortable with. And always carry bear spray as a last resort, and keep it handy at all times. Mine stays on the hip belt of my backpack when I'm on the trail, and in a cargo pocket of my pants at other times.

Four fatal bear attacks occurred in the Yellowstone area in the summers of 2010 and 2011, including two inside the park. In the first, a couple hiking the Wapiti Lake Trail were frightened by the sight of a grizzly sow with cubs and started running. The grizzly gave chase and caught and mauled the husband, who died of his injuries. Because the grizzly's actions had been defensive, park rangers left it in the wild. The second fatality was on the Mary Mountain Trail, but because the victim was hiking alone, no one knows what happened. According to the official report, the victim registered at a park campground the day before the attack, and when an employee tried to give him the standard bear safety talk, he said he didn't need it because he was a grizzly bear expert. The next day he hiked alone in prime grizzly habitat without carrying bear spray—a very un-expert thing to do. When his partially eaten body was found, there were bite marks on his hands, arms, and back. Though park biologists couldn't determine which bear killed him, DNA evidence found at the scene revealed that one of the bears that fed on his body was the grizzly that had killed the first hiker. Because of this, park rangers euthanized that bear.

These attacks were on my mind when I went for my permit for my tune-up trip. Yellowstone rangers have long recommended hiking in groups instead of alone. Groups have more eyes to watch for danger, they're more noisy and less likely to surprise a bear, and bears are reluctant to charge a large number of people. Wondering if the fatalities had changed the recommendations into something more prohibitive, I asked the ranger in the backcountry office if they ever restrict solo hiking in the park.

"We advise against hiking alone," he said, "but we don't come right out and say you can't do it."

Fair enough.

A small sign marks the spur route to campsite WF2, which sits across a small, unnamed creek at the edge of a long meadow. At the forest edge is the site's cooking area, a fire ring of blackened stones surrounded by a few logs for sitting. Two nearby trees are spanned by a food pole fifteen feet up, each end secured with heavy rope.

In grizzly country it is important to hang all food, and anything that might smell like food to a bear, in a tree a hundred yards from your tent. This way, if a bear's powerful sense of smell draws it to the food, it won't be led to where you are sleeping. The bag should hang at least ten feet above the ground and four feet from the nearest trunk. This is easy to do in Yellowstone, where most campsites have bear poles.

With a moderate throw of my quarter-inch nylon rope, the coiled end sails over the horizontal pole and unwinds in bouncing dangles on the opposite side. When the rope is tied to the food bag—a cinchable waterproof number—I hoist it up and tie the loose end to a nearby tree.

Without my noticing, the day has turned suddenly dark, and the sun has gone missing behind a mass of dark clouds. The time is 4:30, about right for a summer storm. Time to set up the tent before things get wet.

Shouldering my pack, I set out across the meadow. Unburdened by a week's worth of food, the pack is considerably lighter. Though I forgot to weigh it before leaving home, it was probably just under forty pounds. In addition to food and clothes, it carries a tent, ground pad, and sleeping bag. Such items would make ultralight backpackers scoff from under their space blankets and tarp-like shelters, which keep out weather but not bugs. Though I envy their twenty-five pound pack loads, I'm not willing to go so far in the sacrifice of comfort.

These days, in fact, I'm more likely to go in the opposite direction. As I've aged into my late forties, my pack has gained more items brought solely for comfort. Among the most recent is a compressible pillow, something I would've never considered in younger days, when my only headrest was a clothes bag set atop my hiking shoes.

It's not just me, apparently. A recent online search for a thicker ground pad turned up several reviews along the lines of "As I've gotten older, comfort has become more important to me, and I've loved having this thick ground pad on my trips." Perhaps there's a correlation between pack weight and age—for some of us, at least. My philosophy is you can pack all the luxuries you want, as long as you're the one carrying them.

A fair distance from the bear pole, across a meadow of ankle-deep grass innocent of any path, are a few clear spots. They would make good tent sites if they weren't at the base of a line of standing dead trees on the forest edge. If a storm were to blow through, as one is threatening to do now, a strong gust could snap or uproot one of these and drop it right across your tent. I keep walking. Toward the meadow's far end, two large trees stand in the open. In the shaded area between them the grass grows low and thin. Home for the night.

As the first rumbles bounce across the darkened sky, the tent goes up, the rain fly extra tight. A powerful gust hurtles in from the west, sending kinetic waves through the grasses and wildflowers. This time, instead of only passing through, the wind remains. The earlier calm is replaced with crashing gusts that sound like a seashore.

When the rain begins, I crawl in the tent and lie listening to the showers and wind. In the forest nearby a tree falls, in a progression of sounds from an initial *crack!*, through a crash of breaking branches, to a thunderous impact of trunk against ground. As the wind rages, a few more trees fall, none dangerously close to camp. Little rain falls, however, and even less finds its way to the ground beneath the large sheltering trees. Soon the sun is shining again, in a mostly clear sky with only a gentle breeze. Mountain weather.

Back at the food area, the rain has given rise to a new odor. The first impression is the smell of wet dog, but it morphs into the barnyard odor of horses. This makes more sense. Domestic dogs are prohibited on national park trails, but some people choose to see Yellowstone from the back of a horse. The odor fades as sunlight dries the new-fallen moisture.

The departure of rain and wind leave a peaceful midsummer evening in the wild. As the sun dips low to the northwest, partly obscured by a bank of distant clouds, the air turns comfortably cool. The nasal call of a nuthatch rings out of the forest, along with a partial utterance of a chickadee, which calls out a single *Chickadaaaah!* To these are added the distant chatter of Steller's jays and the nearby chittering of a red squirrel.

After dinner I go to re-hang the food in the dim half-light that follows sunset. The raising is more difficult this time, as the rope's rough texture grabs the rain-softened wood of the pole. I give the bag an upward shove with one hand and quickly take up the slack with the other, using the bag's momentum to get it to its former height.

Lying in the tent in the deepening darkness, I think ahead to tomorrow's hike. When filling out my campsite requests in March, I hoped to spend the next two nights at Shelf Lake. This would allow a free day, to hike Sheep Mountain or just sit and enjoy the wild setting on a mountain lake. But I got only one night at Shelf Lake— the one after tomorrow night. For tomorrow I received my third choice, which was any spot of my choosing on the national forest land that borders the Sky Rim.

I've come to see this as better than what I'd requested. Instead of an extra night at Shelf Lake, I'll camp high on the Sky Rim. The views up there should be striking, especially at sunset. The only challenge will be the absence of water on the high ridges. I'll need to carry an extra supply tomorrow, enough to last through the afternoon, night, and until I reach Shelf Lake the following day. At just over two pounds per liter, the added weight will be noticeable, but the distance won't be great.

With Shelf Lake only nine and a half miles from here, I'll split the difference and go four or five miles tomorrow, depending on the terrain and, possibly, the weather. Consulting the map with the light of a headlamp, I look ahead to a spot near the halfway point, where the contour lines show a wide unnamed hill about a mile short of Big Horn Peak. It has a large flattish section that stretches far outside the park boundary. That should work nicely.

I put the map away, turn off the light, and lie listening to the sounds of the night. Another dead tree crashes in the forest, a bit closer than the ones before. From this spot well out of range of precarious snags, the sound is invigorating.

As silence envelopes the valley, my thoughts drift back to the rain shower. While there were no visible flashes, lightning is always possible in these summer mountain storms. And because most of tomorrow's hike is along the high spine of an exposed ridge, I'll need to keep an eye on both the sky—for gathering clouds—and on the terrain—for routes down from the crest—in case a storm suddenly arises. More importantly, I'll get an early start and hope to have camp made by early afternoon, before rain clouds typically form.

With that decided, I relax in the darkness, which is now complete. All is right with the world, on this first night of the first trip in a Yellowstone summer. The air is still filled with a sense of beginnings.

Day 2. WF2 to the Sky Rim

Morning arrives peaceful and golden, the sky clear but for a few wispy clouds high overhead. As much as I'd like to linger in the tranquility of the new day, I'm also eager to move on and see what's ahead.

Soon the tent is packed and the gear loaded, everything except the food, which still hangs from the bear pole across the meadow. I head in that direction. An energy bar makes a quick breakfast, washed down with the last of my water. Nearby, two red squirrels chase about on the trees holding the bear pole, descending in frenetic spirals. Having not noticed me seated on the ground, they come bounding down the log that serves as my backrest. Scarcely two yards away they stop abruptly and scamper in a flurry of alarmed chittering back to the treetop. Branch-hopping, they disappear into the forest.

In the new silence a faint rumble of motorcycles drifts up from the highway, perhaps three miles away as the raven flies. It's not exactly a wilderness ideal, but this is only the first morning and I'm headed farther in. It's my cue to get moving.

All that's left to do is load up on water from the tiny creek that flows past the food area. According to a note on my permit, this water source may be dry at times, but today it runs at a decent trickle. Though narrow and shallow through much of its course, in steeper places it falls over rocks, where it's easily caught in a water bag.

So far upstream and in a remote part of the park, the water is likely pure enough to drink untreated. But there's also a chance it contains *giardia lamblia*, a microorganism that causes diarrhea, cramping, and dehydration. Though the presence of *giardia* is often attributed to aquatic mammals such as beavers and muskrats (the resulting illness was once called beaver fever), we now know it is spread through the feces of many animals, including humans. To avoid nasty complications, I always filter water from streams or lakes.

Today I take seven liters, putting two into bottles and leaving the rest in the water bags. This should be enough—four liters for today and another three for tomorrow's hike to Shelf Lake.

When I finally hit the trail, it's not quite as early as planned, but not late, either. With less than five miles to hike, I should still make camp by midafternoon, even without hurrying.

The trail starts in open forest, climbing more steeply than yesterday. In a thick stand of firs, where visibility is limited, I talk aloud to myself to let the bears know I'm here. Rather than repeating "Hey, Bear!" as is often recommended, I take a more conversational approach, speaking to myself as I would to a hiking partner.

"It's pretty dense in here," I say. "Don't want to surprise any bears." Pretty mundane stuff. If the grizzlies don't run away, perhaps they'll be too bored to charge.

The forest opens again on a series of small meadows, each filled with masses of wildflowers accented by early golden light. The diffuse glow adds a gentle vibrancy to the rainbow of petals, and the scene is enlivened further by butterflies flitting softly between blossoms. Two gray jays glide with seeming-effortless flight to examine the bare limbs of a fallen tree. Finding nothing of interest, they rise to a low branch of a nearby lodgepole.

The burble of water rises from the base of a wooded slope where Dailey Creek still flows, even at this elevation. It is something backpackers are more likely to notice when carrying extra water, wondering if the added weight is really necessary. While it's best to play it safe when approaching dry stretches, you'd rather not carry seven liters past a creek within easy reach.

No regrets, so far—getting water here would require descending a steep, brushy slope. No, thanks. A bit farther on, the trail crosses a tiny stream trickling down from the ridge. One could resupply here in a pinch, but it would take a long while, scooping one trickle-filled cup at a time. It was the right call to load up at camp.

As the route climbs toward the Sky Rim, the meadows become larger. Each is filled with a spectrum of wildflower colors: reds and oranges of paintbrushes, dandelion yellows, blue lupines and bluebells, and a violet expanse of sticky geraniums. (For those looking for Roy G. Biv, the green is in the foliage, and the indigo, as with most rainbows, takes some imagination.) To all these are added soft shades of white from cow parsnip and white geraniums. Above it all is a swirling constellation of bees, flies, and butterflies, all patterned in colors to match various petals.

Adding sound to the springtime setting are squawking Clark's nutcrackers, buzzing mountain chickadees, and the shriek of a distant flicker. Not to be missed, a ground-hunting robin flies up from the trail with a single cluck. Tying it all together is the trickle of mountain water from the unseen creek.

At the top of a brief but aerobic climb is Daly Pass, where the national park boundary is marked by a large square post painted white but for a red top. On it is mounted a white metal sign like an elongated license plate. In black letters it says:

> Yellowstone National Park
> Boundary Line
> Hunting Prohibited

My course turns to follow the park boundary north and east, ascending the crest of an open ridge. The wind blows unimpeded across the high terrain, whipping about in powerful gusts.

The ridge narrows with elevation, and one section, while not exactly a knife-edge, is fairly close. The crossing is made adventurous by a bare, eroded patch that slopes down to the south. Beyond it is a grassy shoulder dotted with low-growing wildflowers, delicate-seeming plants on such a high ridge exposed to the vagaries of Yellowstone weather.

A short distance downslope, sitting atop a large boulder, is a golden-mantled ground squirrel. Tan and brown with a white stripe on its side, these squirrels are often mistaken for chipmunks. Though chipmunks are smaller, the key difference is chipmunks have stripes on their cheeks, while the stripe on a golden-mantled ground squirrel ends on its shoulders.

At the base of the final rise to the start of the Sky Rim is a set of switchbacks. Nearing the top, they skirt a large outcropping of conglomerate rock, an aggregation of stones ranging from pebbles to small boulders all united in a single mass by a natural cement. (Some geologists would consider this breccia instead of conglomerate. The main difference is the rocks that make up conglomerate are rounded, while those in breccia are more angular. These fall somewhere in between, lending credence to the adage that one geologist's breccia is another's conglomerate.)

I pause to study the huge agglomerations, wondering how they came to be on top of a ridge. Conglomerates, composed as they are of other stones, typically form some distance below the terrain that supplied the individual rocks—in streambeds or valleys. How they ended up here is a riddle that hints at the rich geologic history of Yellowstone.

For most visitors, Yellowstone's geology tends to come piecemeal, if it all, without a unifying glimpse of a larger picture to put the pieces into perspective. We often hear of the Yellowstone hot spot and its most recent caldera, and of the petrified tree near Tower Junction, or, perhaps, of the glaciers that carved the Lamar Valley. What is often left unclear is how all these and other elements combined to sculpt the landscape we see today. For this, a brief overview is helpful.

From about five hundred million years ago—with geology it's always "about" or "approximately" because geologists rarely agree on timing—until seventy million years ago, the Yellowstone region was a broad, flat terrain near sea level. (Imagine—Yellowstone without mountains, canyons, or geysers, just a lowland near the coast.) During that long period the land was intermittently covered with water, first by coastal ocean, later by an inland sea that spanned the center of what would become North America. As these waters came and went they deposited layer upon layer of sediment, which would one day harden into limestone, sandstone, or shale.

Toward the end of this period, as the tectonic plate holding North America drifted west, it collided with other plates underlying the Pacific Ocean. Because ocean plates are denser, these sank beneath the continental slab, and the grinding collisions caused western North America to buckle and rise. This began a period of mountain building that started eighty million years ago and lasted for twenty-five million years. During that time those old layers of sedimentary rock—the limestone, sandstone, and shale deposited by earlier waters—and some of the older rock beneath them, were thrust upward and eastward, casting up mountains and ridges across much of the Yellowstone region.

From fifty to forty million years ago, large chains of volcanoes arose in the northern and eastern parts of the region. They cast up high conical peaks that formed much of the Gallatin Mountains and the Absaroka range (pronounced ab-SOR-ka, in spite of the spelling). Periodic eruptions triggered powerful debris flows—slurries of mud, ash, and rocks that moved downhill with the consistency of wet cement—snapping trees and covering whole forests. The buried trees didn't rot (due to a lack of oxygen), and over time the slow seepage of mineral-rich groundwater filled gaps in the wood with silica, which eventually hardened into petrified wood. Over millions of years of volcanism, new soils formed on top of old debris flows, and new forests grew, only to be buried in turn by later debris flows from later eruptions. As a result, layers of petrified forests stretch across much of northern Yellowstone.

About thirty million years ago, due to the movement of tectonic plates, parts of the western United States began to be stretched apart. This created numerous faults in the region, and as the pulling continued, some blocks of terrain dropped along fault lines to form valleys. Others rose to build mountains. Together they formed what is known as Basin and Range topography, long north-south-trending mountain ranges separated by broad valleys. When there was movement along the fault lines, it often came in powerful earthquakes, where the land on one side jumped upward or downward in relation to the other. This is what happened during the Hebgen Lake earthquake in 1959.

A little over two million years ago the Yellowstone hot spot arrived in the region, moving in from the southwest at a rate of about one inch per year. Most geologists attribute the hot spot's shifting location to the southwestward movement of the North American plate, though some believe the hot spot is also moving. Either way, there's no doubt the hot spot is moving relative to the earth's surface. It has left a long line of eroded calderas behind it, stretching westward across the Snake River Plain to the point where the hot spot began in southwestern Idaho.

A hot spot is an area where superheated rock and magma rise from deep in the earth's mantle to within a few miles of the surface. As the Yellowstone hot spot moved into the region, it caused the land to bulge upward, increasing elevation by as much as seventeen hundred feet. Since its arrival, the hot spot has caused three cataclysmic eruptions in the Yellowstone region: 2.1 million years ago, 1.3 million years ago, and 640,000 years ago. After each eruption, when huge volumes of magma had been blasted from the underground chamber, spreading layers of ash over much of North America, the roof of the chamber collapsed in the hole, leaving a giant caldera.

Since the last hot spot eruption, smaller volcanic events called lava flows have mostly filled in the old calderas, with a bit of help from erosion. A few smaller eruptions have also occurred, including one about 174,000 years ago, which blasted the large crater that now forms the West Thumb of Yellowstone Lake. The last lava flow occurred seventy thousand years ago, when enough molten rock flowed from fissures in the ground—known as vents—to form the massive Pitchstone Plateau in the southwest part of the park.

In addition to the volcanism over the last two million years, Yellowstone has periodically been covered by ice caps. Some of these reached eleven thousand feet above sea level and buried all but the highest peaks. During these periods, huge glaciers—flowing masses of ice sometimes thousands of feet thick—moved over the landscape, plucking up boulders and dragging them across the land's surface, scouring and reshaping the rock below. When the glaciers melted in warmer periods, they dropped their boulders and left ridges of rocky debris in the valleys. The most recent glacial period ended about thirteen thousand years ago.

While all these events were intermittently shaping the Yellowstone landscape, another force was constantly at work. It was erosion, slowly scratching away at the mountains, even as they were being pushed into the sky, and dropping sediment into the streams and valleys.

Erosion is the key to understanding how this mass of conglomerate came to be high on this peak. These mountains are part of the Gallatin Range, cast up by volcanoes some fifty million years ago. Though it can be difficult to imagine today, some of these peaks were once towering volcanic cones. An eruption from one of them caused a debris flow (known as a lahar, a word that's just fun to say) that was later cemented by ash and superheated mud to form this conglomerate. Then, over the tens of millions of years between then and now, those towering cones of high volcanoes slowly eroded into shorter, rounded peaks, leaving a riddle set in conglomerate left on high.

After a last bit of climbing, the trail reaches the rounded summit and the official start of the Sky Rim Trail. In a grassy spot high above the surrounding terrain, I pause for a sit-down snack break, reclining against my pack in the warmth of the late morning sun. A swallow-tailed butterfly, braving the near-constant wind, flutters up from the lower slope. As it dips toward a mass of wildflowers a sudden gust casts it up and backward. Flapping erratically, it plunges into a more distance patch of blossoms.

With the map oriented to match the lay of the land, I scan the upcoming route. For the most part, it follows the crest of the highest ridge, where the terrain falls away on both sides in a more dramatic way than contour lines can show. My eyes follow the route as far as possible, scanning its ups and downs, of which there are many. From my current elevation of 9,118 feet, the trail drops to 8,872 to cross a gentle saddle before climbing back to 9,223. Then, after a gentle dip to 9,192, is a climb to 9,564. The pattern continues for the length of the Sky Rim, topping out at 9,930 and ending at Shelf Lake, 9,150.

I put the map away and settle against my pack, staring across the high terrain and trying to take in the immensity of the setting. Mountains rise in all directions, some small with distance. They are backed by more mountains, in a fading expanse that recedes to the horizon to blend with faraway clouds.

Some time later, I snap out of my mountain reverie and glance at my watch. After noon already? Have I been sitting here that long? Time to get moving.

At the start of the Sky Rim Trail a pair of black plastic sunglasses lies forgotten on the ground. They are useless to me with my prescription eyewear, but I put them in my cargo pocket so they no longer mar the natural beauty.

Toward the bottom of the first descent the forest returns, with trees dense enough to make you almost forget you're on a high ridge. Following the best line of travel, the path drifts below the crest. Curious of the views above, I leave the trail and make a quick ascent, emerging at the edge of a steep open slope covered with odd formations of coarse gray rock. Standing nearby is a large petrified tree stump, fully upright and perhaps five feet tall. Beyond it, spread across the ridge, are more stumps, small masses of tan that stand out from the charcoal-gray rocks.

Intense fascination pulls me toward the largest one, and I reach out my hand to touch it. Though the visual cues—the long grains of shiny yellow and brown—suggest polished wood, the tactile sensation is one of cool stone. It's difficult to fully comprehend that, some fifty million years ago—long before the Yellowstone hot spot was even a gleam in the region's Idaho—this stony mass was a living tree. Way back then, during the chain of eruptions that were casting up these mountains, the tree was buried by volcanic debris. Then slowly, over time, it altered, changing from wood into stone. This has let it endure for tens of millions of years, to emerge again when erosion chiseled away the rock that buried it.

After wandering the ridge for a long while, I return to the trail and find it blocked by a fir tree fallen across the route. A gap between upright limbs allows a narrow passage to the trail beyond, where the forest thins and sweeping views return. Down the slope are more petrified stumps, set low to the ground among oddly shaped columns of dark volcanic rock.

Near the trail, bits of petrified wood dot the ground. A few of these I pick up for closer examination, then return them to their rightful place. There's no temptation to pocket even one. Not only is it illegal to take such specimens from a national park, it is also morally wrong. Each item we find out here, however large or small, whether a pebble, a bit of petrified wood, an antler, even a feather, forms a part of this landscape. The theft of even one such item would diminish the land. And for what? The piece stolen from Yellowstone would only sit on a shelf or in a box somewhere, forgotten and collecting dust. This would diminish it. No, these things should be left out here where they belong.

There are treasures we can take home with us, however, things more durable and valuable than trophies and souvenirs. They are the memories of passing through this wonderful place and seeing bits of volcanic rock and petrified wood left where nature and history have put them. These treasures never collect dust. Instead, they take root in our soul and remain with us the rest of our lives.

We can pick them up at any time with only a thought. At other times, when we are especially lucky, the memories will rise on their own, filling our consciousness and bringing us back to Yellowstone. That's something no stolen trophy can do.

The route continues through more ups and downs on the ridge crest. It's easy to see how this high divide separates two watersheds, one flowing into the park toward Dailey Creek, the other out to Tom Miner Basin. It's fitting that this dividing line is also the park boundary.

This was not always the case. Back when Yellowstone National Park was established in 1872, few people had seen enough of this land to assess where the boundaries should be. As a result, the park came into existence as a large rectangle drawn haphazardly on a map, with no regard to, or even understanding of, the lay of the land, the flow of its waters, or the migrations of wildlife.

As first drawn, the northwestern corner of Yellowstone was four miles south of here, meaning this area was not originally part of the national park. Then, in the early decades of the twentieth century, there were calls to enlarge the park, and redraw the boundaries to match the topography. One proposal sought to add this area, shifting the old boundary northward to follow this watershed divide. Others sought to add the headwaters of Pebble Creek to the northeast, the Lamar River to the east, and the Yellowstone River to the southeast.

Though these shouldn't have been controversial—the proposed additions were already federal lands—some were fiercely opposed. The opponents were mainly commercial interests—cattle grazers and hunting outfitters—who didn't want an expanded national park curtailing their profitable use of public lands. As commercial interests do, they enlisted the aid of vote-seeking politicians, who raised enough of a ruckus to defeat some, though not all, of the expansion proposals.

Among those that passed was the inclusion of these lands bound by the Sky Rim, in 1929. In addition to putting this part of the boundary on hydrographic lines, it also gave better protection to the petrified forests that now lie within the national park. Other expansions, to include the Pebble Creek and Lamar River headwaters, also passed. But the one seeking to take in the headwaters of the Yellowstone River, south of the park in the wild Thorofare, was defeated. We'll visit that area during the third trip of the summer. Perhaps we'll see if this has made any difference.

After a bit more hiking, the route approaches the summit of Specimen Ridge, which shares its name with the high ridge bordering the southern Lamar Valley. Both allude to their petrified tree specimens, which date back to the fiery days of the Absaroka volcanoes.

This Specimen Ridge tops out at over ninety-five hundred feet, the highest point of the trip so far. From its elevation a short stretch of the Yellowstone River is visible twelve miles to the northeast, through the window of Tom Miner Basin. Not far beyond, dark clouds trail rain showers across the high Absaroka peaks. No lightning yet, but the clouds will bear watching. For now, at least, the Sky Rim and the surrounding lands are under a clear sky.

Moving on, the trail crosses two snow patches that linger in the protective shade of a north-facing slope. Across one of these is a light path where a few hikers have made a slushy traverse, following an approximation of the buried trail. I take the same path and continue on, passing two more icy patches on the next ridge.

Through this part of the hike the dark clouds move closer, crossing into the sky overhead. It seems early for storms, but with the time I took looking at petrified stumps and taking in mountain views, it is getting toward late afternoon. As more turbulent clouds build and fill the entire sky, it becomes time to find a campsite. Though I'm not halfway to Shelf Lake, not quite, this is close enough under these conditions. Any level-ish spot a short distance down one of these ridges will do. The only requirement is that it be outside the park.

After crossing a ridge too steep for camping, the route reaches a short section of open slope. Fifty yards below, on the national forest side, is a narrow but level area near the base of several small trees. Another huge tree, with long, thick branches perfect for a bear hang, stands alone a safe distance farther down. This is probably as good a campsite as I'll find before the storm hits. As the clouds continue to darken, I leave the open ridge and make the short descent.

When the tent is up, I take the food bag and rope down to the makeshift food area. The slope is steeper than it looked from above. Once the rope is in place on the tree's lowest branch, I eat a quick dinner while storms build in the valley below. A gray mass of rain screens the opposite peaks and flows across toward me. As it climbs the base of my ridge, I hang the food and climb to the tent, getting inside just before the storm hits. Though there will be no sunset views tonight, the sensation of lying in a rain-pattered tent high on a remote ridge is a nice alternative.

As evening falls, the showers continue, becoming more intermittent in the deepening darkness. I remain in the dry tent, reading with the light of a headlamp. Soon after dark, a fierce wind streams over the ridge crest, audibly whipping the trees above. Only a short distance below, the tent remains undisturbed. Another wonderful night in Yellowstone.

Day 3. Sky Rim to Shelf Lake, Site WE5

The day begins with another rain shower, but the sky clears soon afterward. I linger over breakfast at the food area, watching as the sun warms the surrounding ridges with golden light. In sheltered spots on north-facing slopes, patches of old snow glisten in the early rays.

With breakfast I drink a liter of water to ensure my hydration is up for the hike to Shelf Lake, which includes a strenuous climb of Big Horn Peak. This drops my supply to a single liter, reinforcing the rule about carrying water across dry stretches: always take more than you think you'll need. With a little over four miles to reach Shelf Lake, I may be a little thirsty when I get there, but it won't be a problem. The upside is my pack is much lighter than it was at the start of yesterday's hike, having shed the weight of six liters of water, about thirteen pounds.

Back on the ridge crest the route heads south, still following the park boundary. Two mule deer bucks, their antlers coated in velvet, climb onto the low saddle behind me. Moving slowly and warily, they cross the exposed ridge, their coats shining orange in the morning sun.

Halfway up the next climb, the trail disappears in the grass. I continue upward, following the common advice about route-finding on the Sky Rim: stay high. In other words, if the trail disappears, head for the highest terrain, which is what this route does as it follows the park boundary along the high divide. Halfway through the climb, powerful sustained gusts whip the air with a hoarse roar. Leaning into the headwind and the climb, I reach the summit. The high point is marked by a small cairn, a stack of stones hikers build to mark travel routes.

The peak is a wide, grassy expanse dotted with blue patches of lupines. This is where I had hoped to camp last night, had it not been for the storms. As the map foretold, there's an abundance of level terrain stretching far outside the park, though it could be a long walk to find a tree for hanging the food. Also, in this ferocious wind, you'd need extra tent stakes to keep your house from blowing away.

The route continues southward, still without benefit of a trail. There's no doubt about the course of travel, which is now marked by a line of white boundary posts, widely spaced. As I refer to the map to confirm this, a sudden, intense gust nearly snatches it from my hands. With visions of my map swirling high above the steep cliffs and across the valley, I quickly refold it and stuff it deep in my cargo pocket.

The trail eventually reappears in the form of a light path along the ridge's spine. A few trees are now mixed in with the boundary markers, suggesting one might find good camping here. After a descent to a high saddle, the route reaches the base of the climb to Big Horn Peak. From a patch of forest comes a low gurgling sound, which turns out to be a small herd of bighorn sheep. All ewes and lambs, they graze calmly near a snowfield. Two rams, which tend to stay aloof on higher terrain until the fall rut, are visible on the slopes far above.

What is not visible is any sign of a trail up the steep climb of Big Horn Peak. When the path I'm following reaches the steep pitch, it makes a tentative start at the climb but quickly disappears. Another map check confirms the route. Through binoculars the tiny form of a trail sign appears at the top of the slope. If it marks a junction, it doesn't include a trail from down here.

Near the sign are two fuzzy white dots that, through ten times magnification, resolve into mountain goats. These animals, through no fault of their own, have become unwitting players in an above-the-scenes drama in Yellowstone.

Non-native to all of Wyoming and parts of Montana east of the Continental Divide, mountain goats were introduced in the Madison and Absaroka Mountains at various times between 1947 and 1959. That was back when many people believed, as some still do, that while nature made a decent start, human assistance was still necessary to improve the land for better recreation. Along these lines, some enterprising Montana wildlife managers decided nature should've put mountain goats in this high country, so local hunters would have another type of trophy for their cases.

As often happens when humans try to manage nature, there were unintended consequences. The goats spread, drifting across the high Gallatins and Absarokas and into Yellowstone National Park. The first breeding populations in the park are thought to have established in 1990, and just as they did outside the boundaries, goat populations inside the park continued to grow. Now they're competing with native bighorn sheep for high-terrain grazing, and taking a toll on the delicate alpine plants.

Yellowstone scientists are studying the situation to figure out what, if anything, they should do about the goats. The options include everything from doing nothing to taking steps to eradicate goats from Yellowstone. It's a sticky problem. Many tourists like seeing goats, when they can, and it's not the goats' fault they are here. They are native to mountains only a few hundred miles to the west, and they might have eventually gotten here on their own, following mountains and high ridges along the Continental Divide—if it weren't for all the highways, fences, and development in between.

But the fact remains that they didn't, and their presence in Yellowstone may be a threat to bighorn sheep, which are native to this ground. A thorny situation, indeed. To further complicate matters, the National Park Service's authority stops at the park boundary, meaning they can only deal with goats found inside the park. Meanwhile, just across the arbitrary line, Montana continues to manage goat populations for a sustainable harvest by hunters.

With no better route up the steep six-hundred-foot climb to the summit of Big Horn Peak, I go straight upslope, following the line of white boundary posts. The herd of bighorns has moved to higher ground ahead of me, where the grassy terrain gives way to rocky ledges. When my direct route takes me within thirty yards of them, the ewes look merely annoyed, but the lambs show expressions of bewildered alarm. As they scatter, one scrambles up a nearly vertical cliff, dislodging a large rock that nearly strikes a lamb below it. Hating to cause them such stress, I turn sharply away and walk side-hill a good distance before turning upslope again.

Though six hundred feet doesn't sound like much of a climb, the steepness is what makes this one challenging. According to one of the Yellowstone hiking guidebooks, this is the steepest official trail in the park—except that there's no trail. Though the ground is covered with grasses and forbs, which make for stable footing, it is still a long, strenuous ascent. My steps slow to a deliberate pace best described as trudging. Or perhaps plodding.

Whew!—If you're going up this thing, you'd better wear your work clothes.

On a normal backpacking year, I wouldn't have started with such a strenuous route. I would have begun instead with a moderate outing on more level terrain, with perhaps a mountain pass at the end. But this year, when planning to do four Yellowstone trips in one summer, it was clear Sky Rim had to be first.

My first inclination had been to start with the Thorofare, the first half of which is a flat route along Yellowstone Lake and up a gentle valley. But that trek includes some big water crossings, fords of the upper Yellowstone River, Thorofare Creek, and the Snake River. In early summer those waters run high and fast, and trying to ford can be dangerous, especially when traveling alone. Such crossings are better left for mid-August or later, when water levels are down.

The Bechler trip had similar concerns, with four fords of the Bechler River, which can be challenging even into late summer. Also, early summer is peak season for mosquitoes and biting flies, and the wet, marshy areas around Yellowstone Lake and the Bechler can produce plague-like numbers of both. Even with DEET, swarms of biting insects are likely to chase you into your tent, where you lie trapped amid a fervent whine of pestilence. During such buggier times, it's better to be in higher terrain.

The route to the Hoodoo Basin also includes a ford, of Cache Creek, as well as a climb of over two thousand feet in the first few days. So it became clear the Sky Rim was the place for me to start. Also, I liked the idea of beginning in the park's northwest corner and doing the trips clockwise. It just felt right.

Starting with the Sky Rim wouldn't pose a problem as long as I was in good enough shape. This would take some work. Now into my late forties, I'm beyond the days of hitting the trail with no preparation and walking myself into backpacking shape over the first few days. So, to prepare for the Sky Rim, after a winter of cross-country skiing and weight training, I began hiking in early spring, when the trails near my home were mostly clear of snow and ice. Through June and into July the hikes increased in length and difficulty until I could comfortably hike ten miles with two thousand feet of elevation gain and loss while carrying a heavy pack.

The work is paying off now, out here on the steep flanks of Big Horn Peak. Trudge, trudge, trudge. Plod, plod, plod. Pausing for a breather, I turn to look for the sheep. They are in the same area, now far below, and have returned to their grazing, some in the sun, others in shade. Actually, only the older ones are in the shade. Perhaps the youngsters haven't figured out yet how the sun works, or maybe they're enjoying the warmth.

At the top of the climb, I am tired but not exhausted. The tiredness quickly fades as I turn to take in the top-of-the-world views in all directions. To the north and west, my eyes follow the Sky Rim back to its humble beginnings on the low ridge at Daly Pass. It now seems a world away, the start of two days of hiking without seeing another person. I chalk this up to the remote and strenuous route.

The trail sign I saw from below does in fact mark a junction. From here the Black Butte Trail heads down to a trailhead a mile and a half south of where my trip began. In the other direction, Shelf Lake is only three miles from here.

The route crosses the high, grassy expanse of Big Horn Peak, where the few shrubby trees have been twisted and flattened by wind. On the far side, things get more interesting.

Leaving the grass, the trail descends on a rocky ledge to a knife-edged crossing to the next peak. Though not especially long, the path is narrow, and on either side the land falls away in dramatic plunges. It's a terrain that's more than merely steep, and better described as precipitous. Though that word is often overused in mountain country to create dramatic effect, it's one that applies here. Adding to the fun, parts of the trail are dusted with tiny, ball-bearing stone fragments (watch your footing!), and a forceful crosswind hurtles between the peaks.

Even so, the crossing is easier than it looks. After a brief open stretch that feels quite exposed, a mass of rock rises to form a low wall on the trail's north side. It slopes upward toward the opposite cliff and the next summit, the highest peak in the area. According to popular usage, this higher summit is Big Horn Peak, a designation supported by the National Geographic map, which names only one mountain in this area: Big Horn Peak, elevation 9,889. Logic suggests the name should adhere to the highest point. But on the topographical map published by the U.S. Geological Survey (known informally as a USGS topo map), this higher summit is labeled Wickiup Peak, with an elevation of 9,930. On this map, Big Horn Peak, still with an elevation of 9,889, is shown as the wide, grassy expanse back across the knife-edged pass.

From the high summit the trail switchbacks down through grassy terrain to the ridgeline route to Shelf Lake. It is now early afternoon, and under a clear and sunny sky, heat waves shimmer above the rocks ahead. I stop and take my last sip of water. No worries now, with the lake less than two miles away. But still, I should have brought one more liter.

Though the trail has dropped from its maximum height, it still towers above the surrounding terrain. Masses of wildflowers grow along these high slopes in sprays of yellows and reds, above which mountain bluebirds float in the breeze. Farther along, the trail holds a mass of bear scat. It's not especially fresh, certainly not still steaming (it's a bit of a Yellowstone cliché to claim to have seen steaming bear scat). But steaming or not, it's a reminder that bears use these trails for ease of travel. After pausing to scan the slopes and ridges for brown or black masses, I continue on, talking a little more loudly to myself where visibility is limited.

"It's pretty open up here," I say, "but I don't want to surprise any bears. Especially a mama griz with cubs. Nooooooo mama beeeeeeaaaaaaar."

After seeing that mound of scat dropped right on the trail, talking seems less than adequate. Perhaps I should do something more, but what—loud singing? Nobody wants to hear that. I file the thought away for later, for when I find a pile of fresher scat, if I ever do.

Beyond another ridge and a few low hills, the route veers down toward Shelf Lake. It's a moderate descent, to what promises to be an idyllic campsite on a high mountain lake. I've been looking forward to camping here since March, expecting it to be one of the highlights of the trip.

Shakespeare is often misquoted as having written, "Expectation is the root of all heartache," though the line appears nowhere in his complete works. He did write something similar, however, in *All's Well That Ends Well*: "Oft expectation fails and most oft there where most it promises." Here at Shelf Lake, my expectation has failed miserably.

When planning my stay at this mountain lake in the Yellowstone backcountry, I envisioned a peaceful camp near tranquil waters. Unfortunately, the lake today is crowded with young teenagers from at least two groups—it's difficult to tell from all the scattered gear and the shouting kids running up and down the lakeshore and splashing about in the water.

One group is set up at site WE7, on the west side of the lake, while the other is based amid several rows of backpacks strewn between the trail and the water. Either they've just vacated the other campsite here—my site for the night—or they're camped at one of the sites down Specimen Creek and have day hiked up here for a swim. This proves the necessity of the park's permit system. As much as we'd like to camp wherever we want, without the permit requirements, places like this would be trampled beyond recognition. They may be anyway, from the looks of things.

Bypassing the gaggle of packs, I make my way along the lake's eastern shore toward site WE5, hoping to get beyond the loudest of the shouts. Unfortunately, it is a small body of water. Instead of a quiet stay at an idyllic mountain lake, my time is punctuated by screams of "Cannonball!" Might as well be camped at the Madison campground. Or a city pool.

This is not to say the kids are wrong. They have a right to be here as much as anybody. It's just a matter of differing approaches to the backcountry, whether one sees it as a sacred place, a playground, or something in between. Those of us in the minority know that, when differing approaches collide, the loudest wins.

The tent goes up beyond the far end of the lake in the faint hope more trees and shrubs will filter some of the noise. The hope goes unfulfilled. One of the kids produces a ukulele and plays through the only three chords he knows, banging out a repeated sequence with a rhythmic variety in inverse proportion to its duration.

A look at the map puts things into perspective. Because Highway 191 runs southeast from the park's corner on its way to

Specimen Creek, this lake—which is thirteen tough trail miles from the Dailey Creek Trailhead—is only eight miles from the highway on the Specimen Creek Trail. And any backcountry lake within a day's hike of a highway is likely to be a popular spot.

Now the kids are throwing rocks into the water and screaming back and forth across the lake. The two adults with them, an older middle-aged couple, don't seem to mind the noise. Perhaps they're used to it.

With the influx of humanity, now is an appropriate time to consider the human history leading up to the formation of Yellowstone National Park.

From artifacts found in and around Yellowstone, we know humans have been in the area for at least eleven thousand years. They arrived some time after the last big glaciers and ice sheets receded, around thirteen thousand years ago. While little is known about the earliest peoples, in recent centuries the land that would one day become Yellowstone was traveled by (to name only a few) the Crow, Blackfeet, Shoshone, Bannack, Salish, Nez Perce, and a distinct band of Shoshones who resided here full time: the Sheepeaters.

The first whites were trappers, and the first for which we have a record—which is not necessarily to say the first who was here—was John Colter. Colter was a member of the Lewis and Clark Corps of Discovery from 1804 to 1806. On the long journey home, after all the hardships of crossing mountains and portaging prairies, when all that was left was an easy downstream float to St. Louis, Colter asked the two captains for a discharge. He wanted to return to the wild mountains with two trappers the party had met. Having given good service, and the expedition nearly over, Colter was granted his release. After staying through winter, he tried to head eastward again the following summer, but this time he met fur trader Manuel Lisa, who persuaded him to return yet again.

In the fall of 1807, Colter, who was then thirty-five, set out on a five-hundred-mile trek in search of neighboring tribes in hopes of establishing trade. The journey extended through fall and into winter, with Colter traveling on foot or snowshoes. He began at a trading fort at the mouth of the Bighorn River, some sixty miles downstream (northeast) of present-day Billings, and he reportedly passed through what was not yet Yellowstone. Though few details are known of his route—maps of the region were sketchy, at best—historians believe Colter's journey took him along the west side of Yellowstone Lake, across the Yellowstone River near Tower, and through the valleys of the Lamar River and Soda Butte Creek. Historians are less certain, though, about which direction he traveled, whether he moved generally north or south.

Colter finally made it back to civilization in 1810, and while in St. Louis he met with William Clark, his old captain. Clark was at work building a map of the West, a map that had huge swaths of blank spots. He listened as Colter told of his travels, and he used the information to fill in some of the blanks.

Later, more trappers arrived in the Yellowstone region, driven by commercial interests. Beaver pelts were in high demand for making fancy men's hats, which were then in fashion in Europe and the eastern United States, and they brought hefty prices. Driven by fashion's whims, the Rocky Mountain fur trade continued to grow, and trappers fanned out up the streams and valleys across the West. According to Aubrey Haines, the park's first official historian, who wrote the landmark two-volume history, *The Yellowstone Story*, trappers were likely in this area every year after 1826, all the way up to 1840, when changes in fashion ended the profitability of killing beavers. We know Jim Bridger was here in the 1830s, as was Johnson Gardner. In 1835, Osborne Russell, one of the few literate trappers to leave a record, made his first of five forays, as told in his charmingly rustic *Journal of a Trapper*.

Two decades after the collapse of the fur trade, prospectors began finding gold in the Yellowstone region. In 1863, they found it near what is now Virginia City, Montana, about forty-five miles northwest of the park, and in 1864, they struck it near present-day Helena, about a hundred and twenty miles north. Soon, prospectors were fanning farther afield, searching every creek, crevice, and gulch in hopes of finding a new Sutter's Mill. Unlike the trappers before them, who favored gentle streams where beavers built their dams, the prospectors went higher, searching canyons, gulches, and ravines, looking for quartz veins as indicators of possible gold strikes.

In 1863, a civil engineer named Walter DeLacy led a motley band of prospectors up the Snake River (from south of

Yellowstone) and across Pitchstone Plateau to Shoshone Lake, neither of which had yet been named. They then turned up what is now DeLacy Creek and crossed to the Lower Geyser Basin. Though they didn't find precious metals, DeLacy used his travels to make a map of the region. In 1869, he would go to work for the Montana Surveyor General, one Henry Washburn, and his knowledge of the region's topography would come in handy.

More prospectors came in the following years, often with DeLacy's map in hand. Some crossed Two Ocean Pass, south of the present park, and traveled up the Thorofare, past Yellowstone Lake, and down the Yellowstone River to the north. Others moved in the opposite direction, heading up the Yellowstone River and turning east up the Lamar Valley to reach the Absarokas. Some made a successful strike east of the current park, one that would eventually lead to the establishment and growth of Cooke City. Still others came from the west, traveling up the Madison River and the Firehole to reach the geyser basins. From there they turned northeast, taking what is now the Mary Mountain route across to the Yellowstone River, where they found a trail made by horse thieves trafficking stock between Montana and Idaho. It wasn't exactly undiscovered country by then.

Like the trappers before them, prospectors returned from the mountains with stories of strange wonders, of volcanoes, geysers, and petrified forests. This fed a growing curiosity among the general public, especially the more prominent citizens, who knew the value of getting in front of a trend. As a result, after millennia of Native American presence, and decades of poking around by trappers and prospectors, came several groups called—with no apparent sense of irony—the explorers.

Heading down to the lake for more water, I stop as two hummingbirds buzz along the shore at grass-top level. After pausing to examine a cluster of paintbrush, they float away in the forest. Without my binoculars, which are back at the tent, it's difficult to be certain, but a few buff-colored flashes suggest they were rufous hummingbirds. The brief natural interlude helps get me regrounded.

In the evening the ukulele makes an encore appearance, another incessant banging of the three-chord progression. I regret not bringing an MP3 player with earbuds. Normally, it would be a travesty to choose recorded music over wilderness sounds, but this setting ain't exactly wild.

The noise subsides, finally, with the fading of the light. Darkness brings a ponderous peace under a starless sky obscured by clouds. At some point overnight, a sprinkling rain falls, tapping gently on the tent fly. Tomorrow is a new day.

Day 4. Shelf Lake to High Lake, Site WD4

In the morning I hurry about breaking camp, eager to put this site behind me. As the last of the gear goes into the pack, the older middle-aged couple from across the lake wanders right into my campsite.

"We're just out taking a walk around the lake," the man says. He adds that they are leading a scout group camped at the other site, as though, perhaps, I hadn't noticed. "We have this site reserved for tonight," he continues, "so we wanted to come over and check it out."

"You can have it," I say, putting on my pack. If they don't understand the rudiments of camp etiquette at their age, there's nothing I can tell them.

Leaving Camp Ukulele behind, I set out at a fast pace. The peaceful hike puts me in a better frame of mind. Getting back to center.

The initial route is all downhill, making a steepish descent along the forested headwaters of the North Fork of Specimen Creek. It's the first sound of running water since Dailey Creek, two days ago. The forest is active with bird life, with calls of Clark's nutcrackers and Steller's jays ringing from the high canopy. From the ground near the trail, a northern flicker takes off in a flash of red wings and white rump.

The elevation profile of today's route is typical of high terrain hiking. A quick descent of fifteen hundred feet in two miles is followed by a climb of slightly more than fifteen hundred over six miles, capped with a short drop to my next camp, at High Lake. The setting there is supposed to be exquisite, but in light of recent experience, all supposed-to-bes are now suspect. Like Shelf Lake,

High Lake is within a day's hike of a trailhead—though it's ten miles in—and it also has two campsites.

The route descends with the flow of the creek, and with decreased elevation the forest becomes denser, darker green, and more shadowy in the early light. Where visibility is limited I resume my scintillating bear talk, commenting on the trail, the creek, the trees. Long stretches of forest are interspersed with flowery meadows, walled on either side by grassy slopes awash in wildflower cascades. On the rocky bluffs above, the stones are the color of charcoal, with lighter grays mixed in, accented here and there with lichens of yellow-green. A few mosquitoes are mixed in as well, though not enough to require DEET.

Looming above the forest ahead are two high ridges, marking the mouth of an intersecting valley. It is the next leg of my route, where the climbing will resume to regain the elevation this trail has given up.

At the junction, a sign says High Lake is 5.9 miles away, past Crescent Lake, at 1.4. Shelf Lake is now 2.1 miles back; and the Specimen Creek Trailhead is six miles to the west. The new route begins with a crossing of the North Fork of Specimen Creek, about calf deep and ten feet across. A short distance upstream is a log set across the watercourse, but it looks old and rotten, likely to break under the weight of a hiker with a pack. This means the first stream ford of the trip, though a small and easy one on a firm stream bed. Even at the center, the creek doesn't flow with much force.

The trail doesn't waste time before it starts climbing, making a purposeful ascent through a wet valley fed by springs and the outlet of Crescent Lake. Tiny streams trickle across the trail in places, or run down it in short, shallow rapids, or flow across to drop through gaps in boulders set on the outer edge. Yellowstone's trail crews have done good work here.

Two boys approach, the first maybe twenty years old and his companion around twelve. Though hiking quickly, they observe good trail etiquette and pause for a chat. The older, quite mature for his apparent age, does all the talking.

"We camped at Crescent Lake last night," he says. "Now we're headed for Shelf Lake." In an apologetic tone he adds, "We had a late start and didn't get on the trail until a few minutes before one o'clock."

They are eager to move on, so we exchange farewells and part. A short distance ahead, two middle-aged women approach. Without slowing down they ask where I'm headed, speaking in friendly tones but clearly focused on covering ground, likely to catch up with the two boys ahead of them. I step out of the trail to let them pass, answer their question as briefly as possible, and wish them a nice trip. They return the courtesy from a short distance down the trail.

Scattered about in the mud, mixed in with the prints of the recent hikers, are a few old horseshoe tracks, calling to mind what the ranger back at Mammoth said: "You may run into some stock up there." These tracks are pretty old, though, so maybe not today.

Still climbing. The elevation gain is now evident from the amount of blue sky appearing through the trees and the way the peaks behind me, which towered above the trail junction, have fallen closer to eye level. Just ahead is Crescent Lake, which sits in a wide bowl at the base of towering cliffs. My plan had been to take the short spur route to the lakeshore for lunch, but the junction is crowded by a large number of kids sitting on the ground in a loose group spread across both trails. Some are sitting in the main trail, until one of the closer kids, seeing my approach, tells them to move. Making a quick change of plans, I keep walking, weaving my way through the group, with a quick hello to the youthful group leader sitting in their midst.

After a brief but aerobic climb, lunch is observed at an unnamed pond a short distance above Crescent Lake. It's a small body of water, clear with a slightly brown tint, like the appearance of strong tea. Blue dragonflies and damselflies skim the surface, and a brown duck floats near the opposite shore. A bit beyond, a robin works the mud on the bank. Mosquitoes are thick here, as one would expect, requiring the trip's first application of DEET.

Back on the trail, several trees have recently fallen across the route. With no good way around them, the passage requires a bit of slow-motion gymnastics, stepping and swinging over several thick trunks while dodging needled branches. The added exercise accentuates the growing afternoon heat under a cloudless sky. Perhaps there will be stars tonight, for a change.

The trail soon disappears in a stretch of sparse forest covered with tufted grass. Occasional orange, diamond-shaped markers are attached to trees along the route, but many of these are sun-faded or affixed to dead trees long since fallen. In a trail-less stretch, I choose what appears the most likely route, keeping an eye out for downed markers. These appear infrequently, either off to the side or behind me.

More people approach, this time four students from Montana State University. They are out studying the native bighorn populations along the Sky Rim, trying to assess the effect mountain goats are having. Their trek also began at Dailey Creek and covered the Sky Rim, but instead of descending to Shelf Lake, they stayed on the ridgeline, taking an off-trail route to the divide above High Lake. On their way out now, they have a campsite reserved at Crescent Lake for tonight, but they figure they'll bypass it and hike all the way to the trailhead. This is a common experience in backpacking: once you're within hiking distance of the final trailhead, it's hard to stop and set up camp.

In the higher terrain the route remains sketchy, marked in places by a faint path or an occasional orange diamond standing or lying nearby. A gray jay floats to the ground in pursuit of some insect, taking three bounding leaps to catch it. Too bad it's not after mosquitoes. They are in abundance up here, whining around my face and ears. The source of their numbers soon comes into view, a small pond near a bend in the trail.

Near the high point of the hike is a divide separating the watersheds of the North Fork of Specimen Creek and the East Fork. Spread across the high expanse is a skeletal forest of large dead trees, some standing and some on the ground. Though most of the grayed branches have long been barren, more recent victims hold onto masses of red needles, clustered in groups of five. Only two species of trees in Yellowstone grow needles in clusters of five: limber pines and whitebark pines (Lodgepole pines, the most common conifer in Yellowstone, grow needles in clusters of two.) While the ranges of whitebark and limber pines do overlap, whitebarks tend to grow at higher elevations, like on this divide.

These dead trees are victims of a widespread die-off of white pines across the Northern Rockies. The cause is a combination of factors, including white pine blister rust (caused by an introduced fungus), a long-term surge in mountain pine beetle populations, and the effects of climate change.

Blister rust, a deadly disease for which North American white pines have little resistance, took a circuitous route to reach Yellowstone. Native to Asia, the fungus made its way into Europe in the 1850s, where it infected pine seedlings in nursery stock. Around the turn of the twentieth century, some infected trees were sold to foresters in the United States. From these rootholds the fungus spread, infecting white pines across the country and reaching Yellowstone around mid-century.

Mountain pine beetles are native insects that have long been a part of Rocky Mountain ecosystems. Over the centuries, periodic spikes in beetle populations occurred naturally, killing large swaths of trees. Those outbreaks didn't last for long, historically. Severe winters killed many of the beetle eggs and overwintering larva, reducing populations and limiting their long-term effects. But these days, due to the effects of climate change, winters are not as cold, and more beetles survive from year to year. And they prefer to attack trees that are under stress, perhaps due to blister rust or a lack of water.

The loss of so many whitebarks is expected to have far-reaching effects across much of the Rocky Mountains. Whitebarks, which often grow in the high country, once provided shade to parts of the snowpack, slowing the spring melt and preserving the moisture. And their pine nuts have historically been an important food source for several species, including grizzly bears. Grizzlies, who must build up fat stores before going into hibernation, eat all the high-fat pine nuts they can find. As the trees have continued to die, bears have had to find other things to eat. Some people like to point out that grizzlies are omnivores and are capable of finding other food sources (even before whitebarks began to die off, there were years of light cone production.) While this is true, long-term shifts in feeding patterns can ripple throughout the ecosystem, affecting the abundance and scarcity of other food sources and other species.

The trail descends to the head of a high valley that's alternately covered with inky-green forests and yellow-green meadows. No sign yet of High Lake, but the map suggests it's beyond the next line of trees. The trail becomes more distinct as it crosses a long meadow, an open green swath that flows with the topography, wrapping around elevated stands of trees, turning and stopping in pockets, breaking and rejoining.

Glimpses of a shiny, watery surface flash through the forest, and High Lake appears, nestled in a wide grassy bowl. The lake's surface is calm and reflective, holding an inverted image of blue sky, white clouds, and the opposite forest. It's a beautiful scene with a feeling of high remoteness, one it gets both from the lay of the land and the hiking required to get here.

Approaching the lake, the route passes the spur trail to the other campsite, set back in the forest a good distance from the trail. Three tents are scattered behind the trees, but no people are in sight, or— perhaps even better—hearing.

High Lake

At the lake's southern end, another spur route leads to site WD4, which is nicely screened from the main trail. The cooking area has water on two sides, the lake to the north, and to the west, the lake's outlet channel. It doesn't appear to be flowing, judging from the clear water and its smooth surface. It looks more like a pond, in fact, with several large tadpoles scooting along the muddy bottom with wiggling tails.

Though the campsite is the most beautiful of the trip, so far, it is also the most littered. Scattered under the food pole is an array of discarded food wrappers and balled-up bits of paper towels. I recall this is the site the ranger mentioned on my way in, asking her partner if the bear pole was up. As it turns out, not only is it up, but it's *way* up—at least twenty feet above the ground. My rope is more than long enough to work, but because the pole is quite close to the best tent sites—which are toward the lake and separated from the water by a small stand of trees—I decide to bypass it and hang my food in the forest.

Across the meadow is a large tree with a limb reaching out in the open. After tying the rope to a rock for weight, I toss the rock over the limb. Or try to. The rock sails high, bounces off another limb, and falls to the ground with a taunting thud. On the next try it clears the right limb and pulls the rope down the other side. The makeshift bear pole is set.

With camp made, I stand looking across the lake and taking it all in. Near the far shore, floating on the still water, is a single waterfowl. It's too far away for a positive identification, but from the shape of its head and the indistinct white on its wing, it could be a female Barrow's goldeneye.

The group at the other camp remains quiet, though voices carry across the water intermittently. They seem good neighbors, the best you can hope for at a lake with two campsites. Less neighborly are the mosquitoes, which are numerous and tenacious. Time for more DEET.

The sudden arrival of storm clouds shortens the sunny evening, as dark, billowing masses crowd every horizon. By seven, the sky is a solid charcoal gray. Still, no rain falls. As the daylight fades behind the thick cloud cover, I settle into a spot near the forest edge from which to watch the meadows and outlet stream for wildlife. Right at dusk, when wild animals are more active, a round of screaming and laughter erupts from across the lake. No point in waiting for wildlife now. I crawl inside the tent and read.

In 1869, a newspaper in Helena, Montana, announced a planned exploration of Yellowstone, to be undertaken by local prominent citizens, complete with a military escort. When the escort was later canceled due to perceived Indian unrest, all the would-be explorers backed out. All but three. In late summer, David Folsom, Charles Cook, and William Peterson—three more or less regular guys—traveled up the Yellowstone River and into the present-day park.

They carried the map Walter DeLacy had published four years prior, and they followed ancient Indian trails and the advice of prospectors who had recently been in the area.

Their travels took them to Tower Fall (not yet named), where they crossed the Yellowstone River and headed up the Lamar (then known as the East Fork of the Yellowstone). Leaving the river, they climbed Mirror Plateau and crossed to the Grand Canyon of the Yellowstone. From there they headed upstream (south) to Yellowstone Lake, and then crossed the divide to the geyser basins. When they returned home, they quietly got on with their lives. Not being prominent citizens, like those who had backed out of the expedition when the escort was canceled, they worried that if they spoke of the wonders they'd seen, they would be called liars.

During the following winter, Folsom took a job with the newly appointed surveyor general of Montana, Henry Washburn. One of his new coworkers was Walter DeLacy, author of the well-used map. Working together, DeLacy and Folsom revised the old map, adding terrain features observed by Folsom, Cook, and Peterson.

The new map was finished in 1870, just in time to aid the next attempt by prominent citizens to see Yellowstone, the famous Washburn Expedition. The group also benefited from the diary Folsom and Cook kept, and as much first-hand information about terrain and route-finding as Folsom could give them. Among his advice was a recommendation to take a more direct route from Tower to the Yellowstone falls, instead of going up the Lamar and across Mirror Plateau.

The Washburn Expedition set out in the summer of 1870. It was a group of leading Montana citizens—lawyers, tax collectors, merchants, bankers, and politicians (some fell into several of those categories). Unlike Folsom, Cook, and Peterson, they brought a staff of two packers and two cooks, and they had a military escort led by Lieutenant Gustavus Doane.

As the Folsom party had, the Washburn group went first to Tower Falls. Then, heeding Folsom's advice, they turned south, climbed the peak they would name Mount Washburn, and descended to the lip of the Grand Canyon of the Yellowstone. They then circled Yellowstone Lake, and near the lake's southern end Truman Everts, a fifty-four-year-old lawyer, got himself lost. It's a misstep for which he is still known, favorably or otherwise. (As academic historian Richard Bartlett, who also wrote an excellent two-volume history of Yellowstone, put it, "Everts not only was no outdoorsman, he appears to have been singularly lacking in common sense.") From the lake's West Thumb, the Washburn party crossed to the geyser basins and descended the Madison River, eventually returning to Helena six weeks after their departure.

According to a persistent myth, the idea of making Yellowstone a national park began with the Washburn Expedition. Nearing the end of their journey, as the story goes, the party's members sat around a campfire on the Madison River and were overcome with uncommon impulses of altruism. They agreed then and there that the region should be set aside, never to be defiled by private ownership, and preserved solely for public use.

It's a nice story, with all the elements to appeal to people who love Yellowstone—foresight, selflessness, appreciation of nature, and a desire to do what was right. The problem is there's no evidence it happened. Though the Washburn Expedition began and ended in 1870, the first report of the campfire story didn't appear until thirty-five years later, after Yellowstone had been a national park for thirty-three years.

In the early 1900s, when it was clear the first national park had been a successful idea, various people began stepping forward to take credit. Conspicuous among them was Nathaniel Langford, who, in 1905, published what he claimed was his diary from the 1870 journey, which contained a detailed account of the campfire story. For decades, his account was accepted and even embraced. A historical placard was erected at the site of the campfire, and rangers recounted the story in talks and reenactments.

Then historians looked more closely at the documentary record, trying to confirm Langford's account. They read journals kept by the Washburn Expedition's other members, but found no mention of a lofty conversation around a campfire. When they went to check Langford's published account against his original, handwritten diary, they found that this one diary, alone among a lifetime of journals Langford preserved, had gone missing.

It was a convenient absence. While the story's supporters couldn't prove conclusively that the conversation actually happened, historians also couldn't prove that it didn't. We were supposed to take Langford's word for it. These days, with nothing else to support the campfire story, and the dubious way it came to light (decades after the fact and purportedly based on a diary that no longer existed), the myth has fallen out of favor. The story's many holes, and the ensuing fight with park boosters, some of whom wanted to preserve the myth even if it wasn't true because it made for good copy, are discussed in detail by two Yellowstone historians, Paul Schullery and Lee Whittlesey, in their thorough and thoroughly readable *Myth and History in the Creation of Yellowstone National Park*.

Yellowstone historians also found that Langford, in addition to his skillful self-promotion, was also being paid to promote the business of the Northern Pacific Railroad. In 1870, when the Washburn Expedition was being put together, the railroad was busily expanding westward, having reached only as far as Duluth, Minnesota. Building a rail line across great distances requires capital, and lots of it, and the Northern Pacific sought to raise money through the sale of bonds. To sell bonds successfully (in the 1870s, just as today) you need a good story, one that will hook potential investors, a surefire moneymaking scheme that will ensure the bonds will be a safe and profitable investment.

What the Northern Pacific needed was some attractive destination way out west, one that would draw hordes of paying customers from the east. Because the only other means of cross-country travel in those days were stagecoaches—brutal and brutally slow in comparison to railroads—if an attractive destination, such as a new national park, existed out west, the railroad would have a monopoly.

Soon after the Washburn party's return, Langford was at work converting his trip journal into a lecture presentation. On the payroll of Jay Cooke, financier of the Northern Pacific Railroad, Langford would go on a speaking tour publicizing the wonders of Yellowstone. He made his presentation in Washington, D.C., New York City, and Philadelphia, where he spoke to a select group gathered at the home of Jay Cooke.

At the presentation in Washington, D.C., Langford's audience included, in addition to the Speaker of the U.S. House of Representatives, the head of the U.S. Geological Survey, Ferdinand Hayden. A bit of an opportunist, himself, Hayden recognized that, with all the new interest in Yellowstone, Congress might be willing to fund an official exploration. One led, of course, by the head of the Geological Survey.

Congress was willing (though at least partly due to behind-the-scenes influence of the Northern Pacific), and in the following year—the summer of 1871—the Hayden expedition headed west. In addition to Hayden, the group included a cadre of scientists, topographers, and photographers, all of whom would compile and present a more complete picture of the Yellowstone region. Added to the group later was another, unofficial, member, a guest working in the interests of the Northern Pacific Railroad, the painter Thomas Moran.

Based in part on the reports and the black-and-white photographs produced by the Hayden expedition—and, significantly, the beautiful and colorful paintings done by Moran— Yellowstone National Park came into being on March 1, 1872. Aiding its creation was more influence from the railroad, including a letter Hayden received in late 1871, written by a high-ranking employee of Jay Cooke. It stated that "Judge Kelley [a long-term Congressman from Pennsylvania—Jay Cooke's home state—who also had interests in the Northern Pacific Railroad] has made a suggestion which strikes me as being an excellent one, viz. Let Congress pass a bill reserving the Great Geyser Basin as a public park forever. . . . If you approve this would such a recommendation be appropriate in your official report?"

The group across High Lake has been silent for a while, so just before dark I go out for another look around. The meadows and water show no signs of movement, but the sky is a gray mass of roiling clouds. As the remaining light dims, I head back to the tent.

From out on the darkened lake some waterbird makes a wavering call. It's a pleasant sound that adds depth of feeling to the natural setting. It is soon replaced by the jangle of a cowbell, which is somewhat less pleasant. Having neither seen nor heard any horses today, I wonder if perhaps the other campers have set up some sort of cowbell wind chime to frighten bears away. You never know what people will do. The jangling and clanking continue intermittently overnight. At least it's not a ukulele.

Day 5. High Lake to Sportsman Lake, Site WD3

The mystery of the cowbell is solved by a round of early morning whinnying. Apparently a stock party arrived late yesterday. Still, it's a peaceful morning at High Lake, with a radiant sun in a clear sky. I sit and stare across the calm water and the surrounding meadows, hoping to absorb some of the spirit of wild Yellowstone.

It's a bit of a struggle, still trying to quiet my mind and get in tune with the wilderness. Two nights sharing backcountry lakes with loud groups hasn't helped, in addition to all the moving around with breaking camp and hiking on to make a new one every day. Normally, I plan a layover day in the first few days of a backpacking trek, time to pause and settle into the natural setting, both mentally and spiritually. That had been the plan for this trip, originally, when I asked for an extra night at Shelf Lake. Fortunately, things worked out differently.

Still, I don't feel I'm really *here* yet, not fully in the moment in the wild. The trip seems to be passing too quickly. It's almost as though I'm missing something.

This isn't to say it hasn't been a good outing. It's always beneficial for the spirit to be in wild nature. In contrast to city life, among buildings, pavement, traffic, and noise, all of which tend to constrain and constrict, being among forests, meadows, rivers, and mountains can free and augment the soul, sometimes in imperceptible ways.

Just being here, open to what nature has to offer, brings a sort of spiritual renewal. It just takes time for the peace to settle, like a seep that feeds a mountain spring, filtered pure by the land. If nothing else, this trip will prepare my mind and spirit for the deeper wilderness of the next two treks. Both of those are in less-traveled parts of the park. Perhaps that's how I should look at this first outing, a week in nature with time for scattered thoughts to settle as the cup is refilled.

Soon I'm back on the trail for what should be an easy day, a hike of seven and a half miles, with only a five-hundred-foot climb toward the end. All the rest is downhill. The initial route crosses mature forest, veering outside the park for a short distance before returning a half-mile below High Lake. From a signed junction, the Mill Creek Trail travels northeast, away from the park and down toward Cinnabar. My route turns southwest, descending the East Fork of Specimen Creek.

Up here near its headwaters, the creek is narrow and not at all deep, though its flow is swift. The watercourse and the trail both meander through open forests and long meadows. Some of the forested parts are old and dense, with thick stands of trees and large logs lying scattered among the brush. In the limited visibility my bear talk resumes. This time, instead of speaking to myself, I address a hairy woodpecker working the bark of a leaning snag.

"Hey, Hairy," I say in passing. "Seen any bears?" Having been on the trail for five days, this doesn't feel at all strange.

A tiny stream intersects the route ahead. While moving to step across, I freeze in mid-stride as a small rodent comes swimming toward me, traveling quickly with the water's flow. Perhaps four inches long, not counting the tail, it zips past where I was about to plant my foot. In my surprise and lurching effort to lengthen my stride, I don't get much of a look at the tiny animal. A short distance downstream it leaves the water and disappears under a boulder.

As the sun moves higher and shortens the shadows, the warming air fills with a sweet aroma of pine forest and sun-heated soil. It's a familiar sensation of Rocky Mountain summers, one I associate with backpacking. Sensing it again for the first time in a long while, I inhale deeply.

Beyond the last ford of the East Fork of Specimen Creek, the trail leaves the forest for a wide green expanse, a meadow braided with streams that wind and tumble and flow together on their way to lower terrain. Not far beyond is a trail junction. The sign says Sportsman Lake is 4.3 miles to the east, and High Lake is 3.4 miles behind me. To the west, the Specimen Creek Trailhead is only 6.7

miles away. I feel a twinge of tension at being so close to a highway in the midst of a wilderness trip. Time to move on.

After another mile and another trail junction—this one with the Fan Creek Trail—the route enters the Gallatin Bear Management Area. BMAs, as they are depicted on maps, are places designated by the Park Service as high-density grizzly habitat. In a laudable attempt to reduce human-bear conflicts, and give grizzlies some undisturbed spaces to be wild bears, the areas come with travel restrictions for hikers. These can vary from one BMA to the next, and here in the Gallatin BMA, off-trail travel is prohibited between May 1 and November 10. This includes pretty much all of backpacking season in Yellowstone.

Philosophically, BMAs should really be called Human Management Areas (HMAs), because it's not bears that are being managed. Any management being done is to keep people from traipsing over critical habitat when the bears need it most. I don't mind such restrictions. It's good that a few areas are set aside for grizzlies, who need wild land and lots of it. It's not just the bears that benefit. Many others species do, too, as well as the land itself.

At the ford of the North Fork of Fan Creek, my travels are joined by a cohort of mosquitoes, and I walk along in the midst of a mobile cloud, like Pig-Pen. While I pause to apply DEET, another small rodent, this one with the roundish shape of a vole, scampers across a patch of bare ground and under a rotted log. I step closer for another look, and it darts across the trail, disappearing in the brush.

Back on the route the climbing begins, through dense forest broken by wide, grassy meadows. Higher, the adjacent slopes crowd in, pushing the trail toward an unnamed west-flowing tributary of Fan Creek. As the trail continues its climb, the stream's splashes and cascades diminish to a trickle and then silence. Higher still, instead of a stream is a marshy, wildflowery meadow. Bits of blue sky shine through low gaps in the forest ahead, indicating the pass is near.

As the terrain levels and begins a gentle descent, the whisper of trickling water rises again, this time from an east-flowing stream bound for Sportsman Lake. High gaps in the trees offer views of Electric Peak, which looms only six miles away. Farther down, the dirt of the trail holds greenish-brown cobbles of fresh horse manure. It's something I'd rather not see after two nights at noisy campsites.

Leaving the forest, the route descends a ridge burned in the 1988 fires. The open terrain allows sweeping views. Sportsman Lake appears below, in a green marsh beneath towering cliffs on one side and the base of Electric Peak on the other. It's a beautiful setting. After switchbacking down, past jumbles of bleached logs and stands of vibrant fireweed, the trail passes the Sportsman Lake Cabin. It is unoccupied, locked, and shuttered.

My campsite for the next two nights is WD3, which the map shows on the lake's opposite shore. On the way there, the trail skirts WD2, where several two-person tents are set up among the trees and brush. Just beyond is a metal sign with an arrow indicating WD3 is to the left. It doesn't agree with the map, but sometimes campsites get moved. Turning that direction, I follow the trail as it circles back to the site with the tents. This can't be right.

A woman appears, and I feel guilty for intruding. She doesn't seem to mind. "Hello," she says in a friendly voice.

"Hi," I return. "Sorry about passing through your camp. The sign said WD3 was in this direction, but I don't think that's right."

"I think it's over there," she says, pointing across the lake. "There were some backpackers camped over there last night."

That's where the map shows it, so the sign was wrong. I thank her and turn to go.

"You may run into my husband on the way out," she says. "He's supposed to be bringing in a group of clients any time now."

"Okay," I say. "Thanks."

I return to the junction and check the sign again, to make sure I didn't misread it. Nope, the arrow for WD3 points to the left, right into WD2. It should point up, indicating the site is straight ahead. As I walk in that direction, just as the outfitter woman foretold, three people on horseback approach. I step into the tall grass to let them pass. After exchanging friendly greetings, we go to our respective camps.

Site WD3 is set in open forest on the rocky north shore of Sportsman Lake. At the food area, the act of tossing the rope over the bear pole is made challenging by the need to repeatedly swat at a swarming horde of biting flies. Their bites are like fire, as though they're ripping bits of flesh from my legs. Once the food is up, I tear into my backpack and change from shorts into long pants. It's a bit late—my legs are already oozing blood in several places. But the combination of long pants and sleeves, and a bit of DEET, is effective, and the flies cease to be a nuisance.

When the tent is set up in the forest above the lake, I walk the site to check the lay of the land and take in the views. Electric Peak shines with a golden glow in the afternoon sun, and the entire scene, the massive mountain and the blue sky above it, faintly shrouded by thin, misty clouds, is reflected in the lake's smooth surface.

Electric Peak reflected in Sportsman Lake

By late afternoon, the clouds have thickened and darkened, and rumbles of thunder bounce across the high ridges. As the wind builds, the wide valley becomes a natural arena, with gusts screaming from one side and thunder answering from the other. When the rain begins, I am back in the tent, watching through a narrow gap in the tent fly. As the storm settles in, the sky shifts from charcoal dark to light gray and back again, as rain comes in waves. This is no passing storm.

The writers of the law that brought the park into existence—the Yellowstone Organic Act—knew it was unlikely to pass if it came with a price tag. So they proposed a park that could financially support itself. Operating funds would come from future fees paid by future concessionaires out of future income collected from future tourists. This was based on a belief the railroad would soon reach the park and bring crowds of eastern tourists, who would pay to be housed and transported around to see hot springs and waterfalls.

What it overlooked was that, in 1872, the Northern Pacific Railroad hadn't gotten farther west than Fargo, Dakota Territory. The following year it reached Bismarck, where operations were sunk by the insolvency of its investment bank, Jay Cooke & Company. The rails wouldn't move any closer to Yellowstone for the next six years, and wouldn't reach the park until 1883.

So Yellowstone National Park came into existence with no budget. No money to pay a superintendent or caretakers, and no means of protecting wildlife and natural wonders from poachers and vandals. Not surprisingly, Nathaniel Langford secured an appointment as the first superintendent of Yellowstone. This was, of course, an unpaid position. During his five years in office, Langford visited the park only twice, and one of those was as a guest of Hayden's second expedition to Yellowstone, in 1872.

With no one around to protect the place, tourists showed up with axes and guns. They chopped off pieces of thermal formations for souvenirs, and they blasted away at wildlife for food or just wanton pride of destruction. Far worse than the tourists, hide-hunters were also at work, killing thousands of elk as well as other ungulates (hoofed mammals) for the price of their pelts.

In retrospect, the government's plan to fund Yellowstone through concession fees might actually have worked. During Langford's superintendency, there were numerous applications from people offering to build and operate hotels, stores, and toll roads in the new park. Had any of these been approved, they would have provided some operating income. But Langford rejected every one.

Some historians believe Langford was stalling on behalf of the Northern Pacific, whose plans didn't end with rail transportation.

Not even close. What the railroad envisioned was a monopoly over all services in Yellowstone. They would transport wealthy vacationers into the park on their trains—on rail lines they expected to build right up to the most popular areas, including the geyser basins—put them up in resorts the company would build in the park, and drive them around on tours in company-owned coaches. They would make money at every turn, once the rails reached the park. They just needed more time.

Whether Langford was actually stalling or was merely neglectful, he was removed from office in 1877 and replaced by Philetus Norris. Norris worked hard to be an effective superintendent, staying in the park for long periods and working to stop vandals and poachers. When Congress finally got around to appropriating funds for Yellowstone's management, starting in 1878, Norris put the money to work, building a park headquarters and a network of primitive roads. These were the forerunner of today's Grand Loop. (As an interesting aside, Norris's road-building efforts were interrupted at one point when the local bank holding the appropriated funds became insolvent. An investigation assigned part of the blame to neglect by the U.S. Bank Examiner, who had failed to properly audit the bank's books. The bank examiner was none other than Nathaniel P. Langford.)

Norris's efforts would eventually get him on the wrong side of a variety of local boosters—gateway towns, developers, and the railroad—all of whom saw the park as a potential cash cow. Due to their political maneuvering and machinations, Norris was ousted in 1882. This led to dark times for Yellowstone. The next three park superintendents, either through incompetence, dishonesty, or more political machinations, were largely ineffective in protecting the park.

The storm passes and the clouds fade, but the daylight remains muted by an early dusk under high western cliffs. I spread my raingear at the base of a tree near the lake and sit watching for wildlife. According to the guidebooks, these meadows are good for seeing moose and elk.

It is a peaceful evening. The lake's surface is smooth and glassy, except where fish strike floating insects. Along the outlet stream is a marsh of tall grasses, home to numerous young waterfowl at this time of year. Adult ducks fly in and out occasionally, but lines of young ducklings often emerge to swim along the rushes.

High on the grassy slopes of Electric Pass, visible only through binoculars, a large elk herd grazes new grass among lingering snowfields. Spring has only recently arrived at that elevation, and because young, tender plants are more digestible and nutritious than old, woody ones, elk concentrate on them, as do other grazers. This results in a yearly progression that begins each spring in the valley bottoms, where most ungulates spend the winter. While the high ridges are still covered in ice, the valley floors begin the first green-up. As spring grows into summer, the green-up moves uphill like a wave unbound by gravity. Elk and other animals follow along, continuously grazing on young, tender plants and leaving the older ones, which have less protein and more indigestible fiber, on the valley floor. If those plants are still around when the elk come down in late fall, they will serve as winter food if the snow isn't too deep.

Down near the lake, the most striking wildlife sighting is a bat. It flits about erratically just overhead, before dipping to skim the water's surface for a drink. If bats eat biting flies, this one should be well-fed.

As daylight dims, I settle back and scan the meadow with binoculars. No moose, yet, but it's early. Then a loud ruckus of laughter and shouting erupts from the camp across the lake. Now it's too late. The noise continues intermittently throughout the evening, and then the outfitters turn their horses out to graze the meadow. This puts an end to the wildlife watching.

Day 6. Layover Day at Sportsman Lake

Morning comes windy and gray, but the clouds soon scatter and sunlight floods the marshy meadow. By midmorning, the stock party has packed and left. In the natural silence, the valley feels larger.

For the first day of this outing, there's nowhere I have to go. No need to break camp and move on—a day without a backpack. Not only is there nowhere I need to be, because of the BMA restrictions on off-trail travel, there's really nowhere I can go, other than on the trails, one of which I hiked yesterday and the other my route out tomorrow. It has the makings of good day, set in a beautiful, remote spot deep in the Yellowstone wilderness, with ample time to enjoy it.

Heading down to replenish my water, I find the lake and its outlet channel clouded with silt thick enough to gunk up my filter. A map check finds another stream about a quarter-mile to the north. Though it's partly fed from the same silty outlet channel, it is joined by a few tributaries flowing down from the ridge. Perhaps the water is cleaner there.

It turns out to be more than a quarter-mile to find a gap through the dense willows to reach the creek, but it's worth it. The water flows fast and clear, like a typical mountain stream.

Back at camp I find a comfortable spot overlooking the lake and meadow and sit against a log with my pack as a backrest. Across the lake, a band of yellow ducklings swims along a wall of marsh grasses. The tiny line breaks and reforms as they paddle across the still water.

Feeling at last the touch of nature's tranquility, I begin to settle into the solitude of wild Yellowstone. I had hoped more of my campsites would be like this, peaceful and natural. Though it didn't work out that way, this has been a good experience. One to make me appreciate wild solitude when I find it.

This is why we backpack, for time to enjoy such places as this, not to be always on the trail covering distance. You may see more of the landscape, however briefly, while hiking, but finding a natural setting and remaining in place, you *feel* more of the wilderness. It's a deeper experience.

Long days on the trail tend to dull the senses, and when you string too many together it can become routine. It's better to stop now and then and settle in. Remain still for a while, and you become part of the wilderness, not just someone passing through. Stay long enough, and you absorb the wild spirit, and it becomes part of you.

The glare of the midday sun sends me back to the tent for my sun hat. When I return, the hat can only shield me from raindrops, as storm clouds fill the western horizon and advance across the rocky bowl. Thunder rumbles over the mountains. When the real rain comes, I retreat to the tent to wait out a storm that's less dramatic than yesterday's. Instead of watching through the tent fly, I relax and read.

On this trip, instead of a heavy book or two as I've always carried, I've brought an e-reader for the first time. It's something I've resisted for years. E-readers smack of high-tech gadgetry, and gadgets steal our attention and deaden our skills. Part of the reason for backpacking is to get away from such things. I relented in this case because this is only an e-reader. It has no internet, music, games, or other time wasters. There is nothing on it but books. This makes it no different than carrying real books, except its negligible weight lets you fit your entire library in a backpack. In retrospect, it has been a good addition. It's also a reminder that technology can be okay—even on a wilderness trip—as long as it works for us and we don't work for it. Or let it waste our time.

The rain intensifies, falling in large drops that thud and splat on the tent fly. I lie back and listen as peals of thunder bounce across the darkened sky, trailing echoes like rockslides on distant mountains. The loudest crashes are over the slopes of Electric Peak. If this weren't a layover day, that's where I'd be right now, up there on the high, exposed ridge of Electric Pass.

As the storm grows, thunder comes from several directions, bouncing back and forth between mountains. Thunder in the east, thunder in the west, and thunder overhead, crashing, echoing, and flowing together like ocean waves. With the louder crashes, it's possible to follow their movement across the sky, until they trail off on distant horizons. Before one fully fades, another begins, building its own rumbling echoes.

This gives rise to a childlike excitement and an urge to pull on raingear and run outside to watch the storm. My responsible inner adult points out there's a shortage of clean, dry clothes. Besides, there's no need to rush. Many miles of backpacking lie ahead this summer. They will surely bring days when we'll have to hike in the rain.

Promise?

Without a doubt.

The damp air brings a chill, and the tent, which was almost too hot before, is now comfortably cool. This only lasts until the storm moves on and the sun returns, turning the air hot and muggy. I climb outside for a look around.

The campsite across the lake is still vacant, and it's already after three o'clock. Perhaps it will be quiet tonight. By four, the sky is black again, and a strong wind *whishes* through the trees. Soon I'm back in the tent putting on a fleece jacket and listening to more thudding rain.

In its plans to extend the railroad to some of the more popular destinations in Yellowstone, the Northern Pacific got as far as surveying routes inside the park. As for their goal of controlling all park business, they sought to disguise their planned monopoly by working through companies that appeared independent but were under the railroad's direct control. Foremost among these was the Yellowstone Park Improvement Company, whose general manager was a division superintendent for the Northern Pacific, Carroll Hobart.

From the get-go, the YPIC pushed to monopolize concessions in Yellowstone. Using political connections, they negotiated a sweetheart deal of a lease with an Assistant Secretary of Interior in 1882. Under the arrangement, the YPIC would get exclusive use of tracts measuring a full square mile at each of the seven most popular sites in Yellowstone (Mammoth, Old Faithful, Madison River, Soda Butte Springs, Tower, Canyon, and Yellowstone Lake). It would also give the YPIC the right to cut timber to power steam engines and for telegraph poles, and to grow vegetables and hay on park lands.

There was so much certainty the deal would go through, and such arrogance on the part of the YPIC, that, even before the lease was signed, they were already transporting construction equipment to Yellowstone. The deal was only averted through a stroke of luck, and nearly at the last possible moment.

As it so happened, General Philip Sheridan made a tour of Yellowstone in 1882. Afterward, he traveled to what was then the end of the rail line, twelve miles west of Billings, where he stumbled upon two steam-powered sawmills and a shingle mill bound for the park. "I regretted exceedingly to learn," he said later, "that the national park had been rented out to private parties."

Realizing the Northern Pacific was behind this, Sheridan pushed the Interior Secretary to prohibit railroads in the park. Then he added his voice to the rising outcry against park commercialization. As a result, Congress passed an act in 1883 restricting the Interior Secretary's authority to enter leases and nullifying previous agreements made by the department.

The YPIC ended up with a limited lease in 1883, but due to greed and mismanagement on the part of its general manager, Hobart, the company was soon bankrupt. When its assets went up for sale, they were bought by the Northern Pacific, of course, which still hoped to build their monopoly through other companies. Their hopes would be disappointed. They took another hit in 1907, when a competing railroad, the Union Pacific, reached the park's west entrance, and another less than a decade later, when private automobiles arrived in Yellowstone.

Meanwhile, back in 1882, railroad financier Jay Cooke took an interest in the mines near the park's northeastern boundary. He promised the locals he would build a railroad connecting them to rail lines in the east. In turn, the residents named their growing town in his honor: Cooke City, Montana.

But a rail line to that remote, mountainous area was easier promised than built. The only feasible route would have to extend from Gardiner, Montana, and cross the northern part of

Yellowstone National Park.

Still, the idea had supporters. They proposed amending the park's boundaries to carve out the lands north of the Yellowstone and Lamar Rivers and Soda Butte Creek. Even Yellowstone Superintendent Robert Carpenter—who saw his position as a platform for personal gain—supported the changes. In 1884, he traveled to Washington to lobby Congress in favor of the boundary adjustments. He and a group of coconspirators, who remained in Montana, had concocted a scheme in which they'd all profit. As the plan went, as soon as the boundary changes passed, Carpenter would telegraph an associate in Livingston, who would telephone friends in Gardiner, all of whom would immediately rush out and stake claims on the most valuable lands newly cut out of the park.

When the boundary adjustments appeared a done deal, Carpenter sent his telegraph. The next morning a mob of claim-stakers departed from Gardiner, followed by a crowd of curious onlookers who realized something was up. Among the claims staked that day were tracts in the names of C.T. Hobart, manager of the YPIC, and R.E. Carpenter, superintendent of Yellowstone National Park.

Fortunately, the boundary change hadn't passed. And the early morning land rush exposed the crooked scheme that had come so close to succeeding. As a result, the proposals to carve out the northern part of the park would never pass, and Carpenter was removed from office the following year. Not long afterward, he was seen in the Upper Geyser Basin, managing a hotel for the YPIC.

When the showers end in early evening, I emerge to a misty, shrouded world of subdued grays and greens. The air is calm and cool.

Back at the food area for a light dinner, I sit on a log watching the east end of the lake and the meadow. Above the trees across the lake, a thin wisp of wood smoke appears. It draws my attention to two people, backpackers apparently, working over a campfire at the other campsite.

They are quiet, at least. If it weren't for the smoke, I might not have noticed them. Still, knowing they are here makes the valley feel small again. Such is to be the nature of this trip, I conclude. The next will be better.

Day 7. Sportsman Lake to Trail's End

More rain overnight, another good excuse to sleep in. After breakfast and another water run, I am on the trail by midmorning. Today promises to be a big hiking day, starting out with a climb of two thousand feet. It's eight miles to my next campsite at 1G4, and another six to where my car waits at the ending trailhead.

Across the wide meadow, the route begins climbing steeply, but I'm feeling invigorated after a restful layover day, so it's a pleasant hike. Farther upslope, the steepness moderates and the forest thins, with old trees, young trees, lots of lodgepoles and firs. Patches of blue sky shine through the tree canopy in three directions, all except straight ahead, where there's only more climbing.

Leaving the forest, the trail enters an expansive old burn, where the few trees left standing are dead and limbless. Reforestation is slow in the high open, with only small firs growing in the protective cover of downed logs. A few young lodgepoles are also mixed in.

The shrill chatter of a chipmunk rings out from a mass of logs, sounding more distressed than the squeaks one usually hears. A flash of tan among the mass of bleached wood is followed by another, this one dark brown. Then a small elongated animal appears—a long-tailed weasel. It has a back of light brown, a yellow-tan chest, and a brown face. A black tip marks the end of its tail, and thick, bristly fur lines its paws.

We both stand motionless for a long while, regarding each other across the slope. Having disturbed it long enough, I move on, letting it return to its hunt, though the chipmunk is surely long gone or well hidden. At my movement, the weasel disappears among the lattice of logs and the slope looks as it did before.

Farther up, the route reaches the first of several snowfields. This one, small and dirty, melts in a series of trickles that join together and flow toward puddles below. Near the lingering pools are patches of wildflowers, browsed by an unlikely large bumblebee and several flies.

The climb continues, now switchbacking up the steep rocky slope, past more icy patches. I look uphill for any sign of the pass, but see only rolling, grassy slopes. To the north are growing storm clouds. I need to get up and over this ridge.

Near the top of the pass, among a mass of boulders, a family of yellow-bellied marmots lies basking in the sun. A youngster, much smaller than the others, crouches near the trail, watching me intently. On a flat boulder above it, draped spread-eagle, is a much larger adult. It can barely be bothered to look in my direction, moving only its eyes. I pause to glass the surrounding boulder field for signs of pika. This is their habitat, but if they are here, they have stayed quiet and out of sight.

The top of Electric Pass is a good spot for a lunch break, with views of the still-distant storm clouds. Though the elevation here is ninety-eight hundred feet, Electric Peak still towers high to the north, perhaps two miles away and another thousand feet above.

To the south, the ridges are lined with snowfields on north-facing slopes, all glistening in the midday sun. On this side of the pass the melting runoff drains toward the Gardner River, all that is not evaporated, absorbed, or lapped up by thirsty wildlife. I glass the ridge for any sign of the elk I saw from Sportsman Lake, but they are nowhere in sight.

Widespread poaching continued through the park's early years, along with vandalism of many natural features. In those lawless times, squatters set up homes and businesses in the Lamar Valley, bringing in cattle and horses, using mowing machines to cut hay, and putting up fences, corrals, and buildings, including at least one saloon.

After continued reports of the ongoing slaughter and destruction, Congress appropriated funds in 1883 to hire a cadre of assistant superintendents to protect Yellowstone. It didn't go as well as it could have, as most of the first appointments were based more on political connections than abilities.

The poaching worsened as market hunters, some of whom had recently helped slaughter the Great Plains bison nearly out of existence, set up bases of operations in the lands surrounding the park. They knew that, even inside Yellowstone, the most the government could do to poachers was escort them outside the park boundary and maybe confiscate any gear they had with them. They could come right back once the escort went away. And bison heads were selling for four hundred dollars apiece.

To address the lack of legal protections, Wyoming Territory passed an act, in 1884, that extended its laws into all parts of Yellowstone within territorial boundaries. Unlike the weak federal statutes, the Wyoming law had real penalties, with misdemeanors bringing up to a hundred dollars in fines or six months in jail. So far, so good. But the law had a fee-sharing provision that paid half of any fines to the officer or informer bringing the charges. This would cause problems.

To enforce the laws in Yellowstone, the Wyoming governor appointed two justices of the peace, one at Mammoth, the other in the Lower Geyser Basin, each assisted by a constable. The appointees were mostly undereducated frontiersmen, who had little experience with law, or interest in it. What they were interested in was getting their half of the fee-splitting arrangement.

The Yellowstone superintendent who succeeded Carpenter was David Wear, a go-getter who could have been effective had it not been for the mess left by his predecessors. Wear set about cleaning house with the assistant superintendents, eventually building an effective policing force. To protect against forest fires, he cracked down on abandoned campfires, imposing a hefty fine of fifty dollars on anyone caught leaving one burning.

His intended message was it's cheaper to extinguish your fire than to ride off and leave it. But the message heard by the Wyoming constables and justices—those working under the new fee-splitting law—was that any untended fire would earn them twenty-five dollars. The two lawmen in the Lower Geyser Basin came up with their own fee-sharing scheme, one based on volume. They brought flimsy charges on flimsier evidence, where even a bit of warm ground was taken as proof of a campfire insufficiently extinguished.

They had the misfortune of trying this with the wrong group in 1886. It was a party that included Judge Lewis Payson, a U.S. Congressman from Illinois, and Joseph Medill, editor of the *Chicago Tribune*. Despite a lack of evidence—the party had sufficiently doused and buried their campfire—the Wyoming justice handed down a guilty verdict, with a fine of sixty dollars, plus costs. When Judge Payson said he planned to appeal, the stymied justice offered to reduce the fine. He eventually reduced it all the way to one dollar.

This might have ended the matter, but then the justice asked Judge Payson for legal advice. At this, newspaper editor Medill called the justice a "damned old Dogberry" (in reference to the bumbling and misspeaking constable in *Much Ado About Nothing*, known for such lines as, "O villain! Thou wilt be condemned into everlasting redemption for this"). An account of the whole affair later appeared in the *Chicago Tribune*, along with an argument that national parks should be governed by national laws that were enforced by federal courts. Not long afterward, the application of Wyoming law to Yellowstone was repealed.

Because of this and other embarrassing cases of mismanagement in Yellowstone, the 1886 Congress debated what to do with the park. Some wanted to repeal Yellowstone's organic act and put the land back in the public domain. Others wanted to give it to Wyoming. Still others wanted to turn it over to the Army. Missouri Senator George Graham Vest, one of the park's most effective supporters, argued for keeping the park and its civilian management. In the end, Congress split the baby. It passed an appropriations bill that included the usual funding for park operations but left out any money to pay salaries, effectively firing Superintendent Wear and his ten assistants.

Before leaving office, Wear sent in a final report, declaring general lawlessness had already increased (the repeal of the Wyoming statute had emboldened poachers and other lawbreakers). He also reported three large wildfires raging out of control. With no other option, the Secretary of the Interior turned to the Secretary of War for help, and in August of 1886, the U.S. Cavalry arrived. Their mission was to protect the wildlife, forests, and thermal features of Yellowstone National Park.

The Army commanders—called acting superintendents because their stay was expected to be temporary, though it lasted for thirty-two years—were quite effective. They quickly set about fighting wildfires, which they, and nearly everyone else at the time, saw as threats to the forest. They also went after poachers, using creative tactics to avoid tipping off those in league with the bad guys: using secret patrols, avoiding the main trails, and communicating in code. Of their one legal recourse—removal from the park—they made effective use. Captured poachers were sometimes marched clear across Yellowstone and kicked out far from their base of operations, or they sat locked in cells while the soldiers worked the slow process of justice, sending messages to Washington, D.C., and awaiting replies.

Better laws finally came in 1894, with the passage of the National Park Protection Act, which contained real penalties for violators. (In connection with Yellowstone, this law is popularly known as the Lacey Act, which gets it confused with the Lacey Act of 1900, a law sponsored by the same Iowa Congressman, which prohibits trade in any fish, wildlife, and plants illegally taken, possessed, transported, or sold.)

The National Park Protection Act came about through a stroke of luck, though it began with the Army's excellent work in catching a notorious bison poacher. This was in the days when bison numbers were dangerously low and their extinction was a real possibility. On a late winter ski patrol, civilian scout Felix Burgess and a Yellowstone soldier discovered a hunter's camp near Pelican Valley. It held the scalps and hides of six bison but no hunter. On their way to check the broad valley, where one would expect to find a bison poacher, the two men heard six rifle shots. Out in the open terrain they saw poacher Ed Howell busily skinning one of five bison he had just killed.

But how to catch him? Howell was two hundred yards away, with commanding views all around, and he was armed with a repeating rifle, of much greater range than the single pistol shared by the would-be captors. Undeterred, the two men—who were traveling on what were effectively long cross-country skis—rushed across the long distance toward Howell. Fortunately, the poacher was so occupied with his skinning that he didn't notice them until Burgess was within fifteen feet of him. He was caught. His captors had to keep him from killing his dog for failing to warn him.

This is where the stroke of luck occurred. While taking Howell across the park, the party met a group that contained writer Emerson Hough, who wrote for a magazine headed by Yellowstone champion George Bird Grinnell. Hough fired off a story on the capture of a poacher inside Yellowstone, and its appearance led to a public outcry about protecting the park.

Within two weeks of Howell's capture, Iowa Congressman John Lacey had introduced an "Act to protect the birds and animals in Yellowstone National Park, and to punish crimes in said park." In less than two months it was law. In addition to putting Yellowstone exclusively under federal jurisdiction, the new law prohibited hunting in the park, and it directed the Interior Secretary to make rules and regulations to protect Yellowstone, "especially for the preservation from injury or spoliation of all timber, mineral deposits, natural curiosities, or wonderful objects within said park; and for the protection of the animals and birds in the park, from capture or destruction, or to prevent their being frightened or driven from the park."

Finally.

Though the Lacey Act owed its origins to the Army's good work in catching poachers, there would come a creeping realization that this was not a job the Army should be doing. While Yellowstone was once the only national park, in the early years of the twentieth century the number of national parks and national monuments was beginning to grow. And military attentions were being pulled in other directions, with soldiers based in Texas pursuing Pancho Villa into Mexico, and the growing buildup for World War I.

In 1916, the government formed a new civilian agency to manage national parks, and the Army turned Yellowstone over to the National Park Service. Only briefly, as it turned out.

When business owners in Gardiner, Montana, heard the soldiers were leaving, they worried about lost revenues, and they complained loudly to their congressional representatives. (This is an ongoing challenge for park managers, that gateway towns expect national parks to be managed for the benefit of local businesses, and they are quick to get politicians involved.) Swayed by the political pressure, Congress denied funding for the Park Service's work in Yellowstone, and soon the Army was back. They would remain until 1918, when the Park Service finally took over for good.

The storms remain far to the east, trailing gray smears across the Absaroka Mountains and flashing distant clouds with electric blues. From this high pass bathed only in sunlight, it is a wondrous sight.

Descent from Electric Pass

The initial descent is steep, on a trail covered with eroded rock fragments. A few hundred feet below, the route enters dense forest near a creek that splashes over moss-covered rocks. I resume my out-loud trail observations with more volume to rise above the cascading waters. In case the talking still isn't loud enough, I periodically smack flat rocks in the trail with the bottom of my hiking stick, making a resounding *clack!*

A few miles later, the trail makes a short, shallow ford of the upper Gardner River. From here it's just another mile to site 1G4, which I have reserved for tonight.

The reservation was solely to give me the option to climb Electric Peak tomorrow. Electric is the highest mountain in the northwest part of the park, and one of the more popular climbs in all of Yellowstone. Many consider it a must-do for hikers passing through the area, which is why I dutifully scheduled an additional day at the end of this trip for an ascent.

Now, I'm feeling more inclined to skip it. After so many nights camped near loud campers, a climb of a popular peak seems less attractive. Plus, today is Saturday, when more people are likely to be out. I'm not much for must-dos, anyway. You end up taking someone else's trip instead of your own.

When I reach the spur trail for site 1G4, which is set on a thin strip between the trail and the Gardner River, a young woman is standing near the food area. Seeing me, she becomes self-conscious and walks briskly away, following the river toward 1G3, only a quarter-mile downstream. I stay on the trail without slowing down. It's not even five o'clock yet, and the trailhead is only six miles away.

Site 1G3 is set right on the trail, and it's filled with a large group of backpackers busily setting up an assortment of tents. I feel better about my decision not to stop. They are all likely headed up Electric Peak tomorrow, and they will probably make a lot of noise tonight. My next trek, which begins in only seven days, promises to be a better wilderness experience. I'm ready to wrap this one up.

After fording the Gardner River a second time, the route turns northeast, passing the trail to Cache Lake before heading southeast again. A small wispy snake zips across the trail, showing a hint of stripes, which suggests a garter snake.

Farther along, now only three miles from the ending trailhead, I turn for another look at Electric Peak. Though it still dominates the view, it is already receding toward the horizon. Dense storm clouds gather above it.

The last of the route crosses the sage flats of Gardner's Hole. As I cruise along, several chipmunks dart across in front of me. One has a truncated tail mangled, apparently, by a less-than-successful predator.

Three young men approach from the trailhead, off to a late start at almost seven o'clock. Where could they be camping tonight? Over the next twelve miles from here to Sportsman Lake, there are only two campsites: the one occupied by that large group, and the one I have reserved.

After a friendly exchange of greetings, they excitedly tell me they are planning to climb Electric Peak tomorrow. "We stopped by the backcountry office to get a camping permit," one of them explains, "but they said all the sites were full." Apparently, they weren't to be deterred.

I tell them I have site 1G4 reserved for tonight, but am finishing my trip early. "There shouldn't be anybody there," I say, "but that won't help you if the rangers are out checking permits." (Permits are non-transferable.)

Already committed to camping somewhere illegally, they are excited to hear of an unclaimed site. The way I see it, because they are committed, it's better they stay in a designated campsite instead of trampling and flattening more wild vegetation. But they'll still get a citation if the rangers are out. We exchange best wishes and part.

Under a darkening sky filled with dense storm clouds, I maintain a brisk pace. Getting hit with no more than a few sprinkles, I reach the trailhead at seven-thirty. My vehicle sits just across the Grand Loop Road at the Glen Creek parking area.

I pause at the road's edge for a slow-moving car. Dusk is prime wildlife watching time, and the driver is cruising slowly, scanning the flats for bears, wolves, or anything moving. Seeing me approach in the dim light, she does a double take, as though I might perhaps be a bear.

Driving past, she realizes I'm just a backpacker bearing a week's worth of trail dust. The sighting is unusual enough, apparently. Her brake lights glow red as she turns to watch me cross the road behind her.

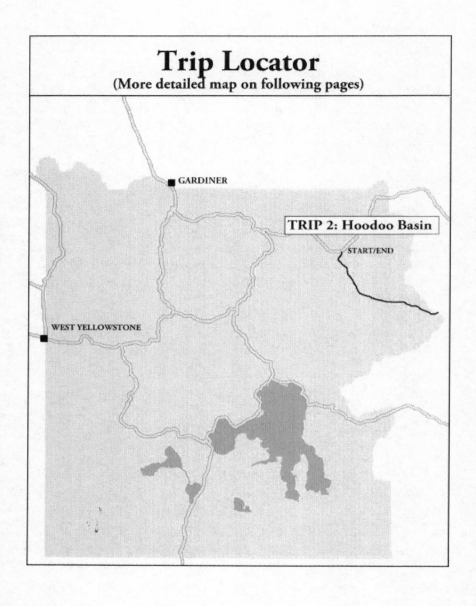

Trip Locator
(More detailed map on following pages)

GARDINER

TRIP 2: Hoodoo Basin

START/END

WEST YELLOWSTONE

Trip 2
Hoodoo Basin
August 4-10, 2012

Trip Overview

- START: Soda Butte Trailhead in the Lamar Valley
- Up the Lamar River to Miller Creek
- Up Miller Creek to the patrol cabin
- Climb to the Hoodoo Basin and camp near the park's eastern boundary
- END: Return to Soda Butte Trailhead via the same route

Duration: Forty-six miles in seven days.

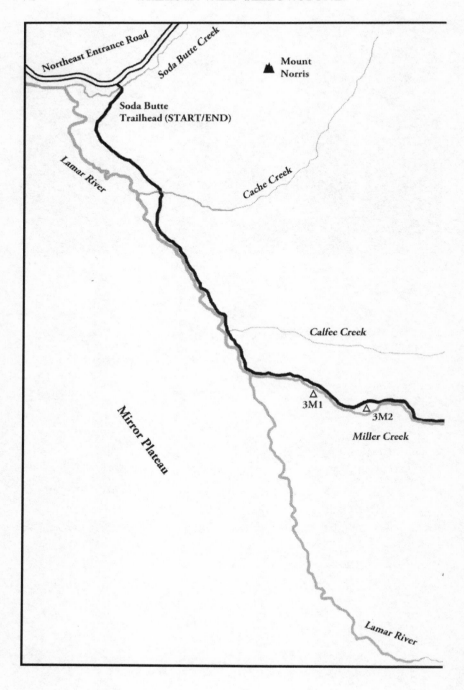

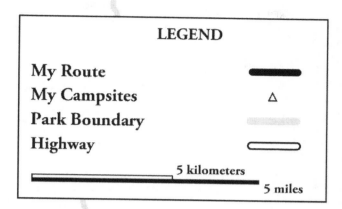

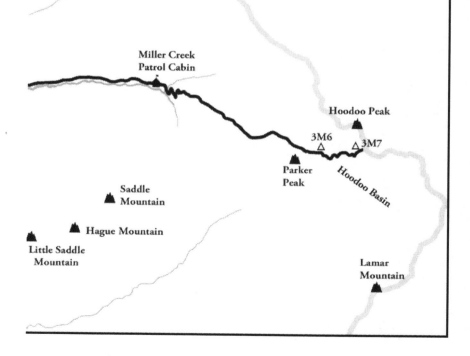

Preparation

This would be the only trek of the summer that started and ended at the same trailhead, meaning it wouldn't require a shuttle. As originally planned, it was to start on a Monday morning, when the roads and the trailhead parking would be less crowded. But ever since my campsite reservation arrived in April, I'd been rethinking the original plan.

The problem was it included just two nights in the remote Hoodoo Basin. This left only the intervening day to hike to the actual hoodoos, an area of striking geological formations of rocky pinnacles and spires. The more I thought about it, the more I realized two nights wasn't enough. It didn't seem right to hike twenty-one miles, including a climb of over two thousand feet, to reach a wonderful location, and have only one full day to see it.

Perhaps I could revise the permit and add another day or two in the high basin. Would any campsites be available? There was only one way to find out: take my reservation to the backcountry office and ask.

The Park Service will issue a permit up to forty-eight hours before the start of a trip, so I decided to go on Thursday. That way, if it were possible to start the trek two days earlier, I could pick up my permit and have all of Friday to pack for a Saturday departure. And if no campsites were available for a revised trip, I would stick to the original plan and get my permit on the way to the trailhead Monday morning.

At the Tower/Roosevelt backcountry office, I showed the ranger my reservation and asked if it was possible to make changes.

"Let's see," she said, setting a laminated copy of the National Geographic map of the Tower region on the counter. "What did you want to change?"

"Instead of starting on Monday," I said, "I'd like to go in on Saturday and spend the first night at site 3M1."

"Are you sure?" she asked, noting that 3M1 was over ten miles from the trailhead. "That's a long way."

It's the only time I've heard a ranger ask if a hiker may have been too ambitious in trip planning, something office-bound hikers, as well as those of us who are not as young as we used to be, have been known to do. While some hikers may be offended at having their abilities questioned, it's better to be offended than find yourself exhausted at the end of a long first day, realizing you can't make it to either your campsite or back to the trailhead.

"I just finished a long trek across the northwestern part of the park," I told the ranger. "The last day was fourteen miles, including the two-thousand-foot climb over Electric Pass."

Satisfied, she checked her computer and said site 3M1 was available Saturday night. So far, so good. After that, I hoped to camp in the Hoodoo Basin. The original reservation had me spending two nights at site 3M6, near the basin's western edge. Now I hoped to add two more nights, at 3M7, the only other campsite in the basin, near the park's eastern boundary.

The ranger checked her computer again. "Somebody is there the first night," she said, "but you can have it after that."

"How about 3M6 for the first night?" I asked.

"That's available," she said.

Done. She typed in the changes and printed the permit. I thanked her for all the help and headed home to pack.

Day 1. From Home to Miller Creek, Site 3M1

Early Saturday morning I'm headed east on Interstate 90 toward Livingston, when I'm passed by a group of six bikers. One of them signals a lane change by kicking out his right foot.

My route turns south on Highway 89, through Paradise Valley and toward the park's north entrance. As the landscape opens on a grassy expanse, I put in a CD of Philip Aaberg's *High Plains*. It's music to match the feel of the land, evoking rolling hills, wide valleys, and mountain streams. A fitting selection for a solo drive to the trailhead, it's helpful for easing one's mind into a mental terrain more in tune with the natural setting.

Inside the park, traffic is relatively light for a summer morning. Early wildlife watchers are already out with their spotting scopes and cameras, while more leisurely tourists are still at breakfast. At Tower Junction my route turns toward the Lamar Valley, a broad expanse of sage and grass, where the Lamar River flows westward to join the Yellowstone. Scattered across the lower valley, mature Douglas firs grow beside huge boulders. It's a recurring pattern on this landscape.

In contrast to the Gallatin and Absaroka Mountains, where the evident geology is volcanic, in the Lamar Valley it is glacial. Around fifteen thousand years ago, long after the Absaroka volcanoes had built their mountains, this valley was carved by mountain-sized sheets of ice. In those times, heavy snow fell in the Absaroka and Beartooth Mountains, piling up faster than it could melt. As huge snow masses grew both in size and weight, they compacted into ice and began flowing toward lower terrain in glaciers sometimes thousands of feet thick.

On the way down, the ice plucked up rocks and boulders in the high country and dragged them along, scraping and chiseling the landscape and shaping the valley. When warmer temperatures began melting the glaciers, about thirteen thousand years ago, the ice retreated back to the high country. As it thawed, it dropped its rocks and boulders on the valley floor, where they would one day seem so out of place to later observers.

These boulders, called glacial erratics, now perform an ecological role as nurse rocks. Young Douglas fir saplings don't grow well in the dry heat of full sunlight. This is why they often get their start in shaded forests of lodgepole pines. But in this open valley, the huge boulders provide shade and preserve moisture, forming microclimates where young Douglas firs can grow.

Other relics of the glacial era remain as well, in the many small pools called kettle ponds. These formed when huge masses of ice left by receding glaciers were buried under glacial outwash. As the buried ice melted, the overfill sank into the holes, which then filled with meltwater. Today these kettle ponds hold snowmelt and runoff for much of the spring and early summer, providing watering holes for birds and wildlife. Part of the poetry of nature.

At the valley's upper end is the trailhead for my route up the Lamar River. Actually, two trailheads lead to this route, one for stock parties and, half a mile farther, another for hikers. The advantage of the hiker trailhead, in addition to more parking away from the horse trailers, is that the hiker route crosses Soda Butte Creek on a footbridge. Just a bit downstream, the horses have to ford.

Today, the horse trailhead holds a large crowd, a mix of wildlife watchers and one sizeable group that's either preparing for a trail ride or has just finished one. A half-mile up the road, the hiker parking lot is also crowded—Saturday in peak season—but a single open space remains near the center, just past a piece of construction equipment, some sort of road sweeper. There's just enough room for me to pull in without getting too close to the large machine, hoping that whoever shows up to drive it on Monday can back it up in a straight line.

Outside, I scan the area to see what the crowd is about. Apparently, there's no single purpose. People are scattered in small groups, some looking through binoculars in various directions, a lone man sitting on the ground and staring across the valley as his two daughters play nearby, and several people walking in and along Soda Butte Creek with fly rods. The crowd's size falls short of the number of vehicles, suggesting several cars belong to hikers already on the trail, whether backpacking, day hiking, or fishing.

Near the trailhead is a signboard holding a notice that campsite 3L2, one of two sites along Cache Creek, is a bear frequenting area. I'm not camping near there, fortunately, though my route will take me right past it. While bears can be anywhere in Yellowstone—all areas are theoretically bear frequenting areas—it could be unsettling lying in a tent where campers had seen bears prowling about recently.

From the parking area the route descends to the wooden footbridge over Soda Butte Creek. Scattered on either side are an assortment of anglers. One is a fishing guide who is teaching a client to cast. As I cross above them, he describes how the fly should move as it travels over and in the water.

I set off across the open sagebrush grassland at a quick pace, trying to put distance between myself and the hubbub near the trailhead. A meadowlark appears atop a dense mass of sage. At my approach, it flies away in a flash of yellow and white, zipping above the gray-green foliage. Among the visible insects are butterflies, grasshoppers, and a fat Mormon cricket that waddles across the trail. Despite their name, Mormon crickets are a type of katydid. As part of this ecosystem, they feed on sage, grasses, and forbs—and sometimes other insects—and, in turn, they are preyed upon by birds, rodents, and sometimes coyotes.

A uinta ground squirrel spooks and runs skittering and tittering across the trail, recalling the one at the start of my Sky Rim trip. It's as though these ground dwellers are gatekeepers to the wilderness. But it cannot last. Though it's still early August, ground squirrels will soon retreat underground for nearly eight months of hibernation. They can't follow the greening wave to higher terrain as elk do, so ground squirrels stay near their burrows, nibbling plants while the growth is still young and nutritious. When the vegetation turns old and fibrous the squirrels will head underground, to sleep until new sprouts arise in the spring.

A quarter-mile to the south, a pronghorn stands motionless and statuesque atop a low ridge, backlit against a deep blue sky. My route continues southwest, farther onto the sage-covered plain dotted with dark shapes of perhaps a hundred bison. Some of these are drifting in my direction, toward the junction with the Specimen Ridge Trail. The huge bull leading the group walks with a purpose. It reaches the junction before I do, and pauses to graze near the trail sign. Another bison strolls up behind it and stops directly in the trail. It's as though they've seen me coming and have moved in to claim the territory first.

Park regulations—and common sense—require that we stay at least twenty-five yards from bison and other large mammals (a hundred yards from wolves and bears). Leaving the trail, I detour to the south. The large bull—I'd swear he knows where I'm trying to go—moseys along in the same direction, in a slow-motion head-'em-off-at-the-pass maneuver. The other bison follows. I pause again, giving them time to get wherever they want to go.

They amble a short distance down the trail and stop. Needing a larger detour, I head up the sandy ridge to the south. It turns out to be a bit of a workout, climbing through loose, bison-churned sand. From a higher ridge to the northeast, the lone pronghorn monitors my progress.

The top of the short climb takes me fifty yards from the lead bison. It's more than necessary, but these animals are still moving, so a bit of safety margin is in order. It's not too much to ask.

Though there were once tens of millions of bison in North America as recently as the early 1800s, less than a hundred years later they were nearly extinct. A count done in Yellowstone in 1901 found only twenty-three bison in all of the park. (Recall that bison poacher Ed Howell was captured in 1894, leading to the first real laws against poaching in the park.)

In 1902, Yellowstone purchased twenty-one bison from private owners. The females came from Montana and the males from Texas. These were kept in a captive herd, and later moved to what is still known as the buffalo ranch in the Lamar Valley. There they were kept like cattle: bred, inoculated, held in pens each winter, and fed hay raised on irrigated land near the ranch.

As their numbers increased, the bison were turned out to roam free in the park and replenish the native herds. In what is one of Yellowstone's greatest success stories, bison numbers continued to improve, even after the buffalo ranch was shut down in 1952. (The ranch is used today by the Yellowstone Association for educational programs, which I can say from experience are excellent.)

For some, the recovery of bison has been *too* successful. As their numbers have continued to grow—reaching five thousand in 2005—the bison narrative has changed from success story to one of Yellowstone's greatest current challenges. We'll delve more into that later.

More bison have drifted over to join the two leaders. They all amble to a trailside spot that holds three of the things bison love most: loose dirt, water, and widely spaced tree trunks. There, they are a picture of contentment. The lead bull scratches his colossal head and shoulders on the barkless trunk of an old snag, while his backup rolls in the loose dirt, swinging hooves high in the dusty air. As more bison wander in, the sounds of their deep-throated bellows rise above the wind. When two adults approach a small, muddy stream for a drink, a young calf trots hurriedly over to join them with a "me, too" manner. Two other youngsters linger beyond, eyeballing me warily and twitching their tails.

Thirsty bison

Now that the herd is stationary I should be able to get past. After following the ridge a good distance, I descend to the trail, looking continuously back at the bison. They remain in their area of grass, dust, and mud, lounging as bison do, and my detour is complete. Despite the extra workout at the start of a ten-mile hike, it was an enjoyable encounter, bison in their natural element instead of corralled on a roadway by idling cars.

The route crosses a wide, low ridge, where the sage thins and grass predominates. Swarms of grasshoppers spread like waves in front of me, but when I stop for a closer look, they disappear in the grass and dust as though never there. One, a tan-orange color to match the summer grass, attempts to hide in plain sight by sitting motionless on the trail. When I step toward it, it flies away in a flash of yellow.

Continuing on, I spook another ground squirrel, which disappears underground. In turn, I am spooked by the appearance of several dark shapes on the low flank of Mount Norris. (Those Bear Frequenting signs have a way of turning every unknown sight and sound into grizzlies.) Through binoculars, the shapes resolve into boulders.

As the trail climbs gently over the grassy flat, spread below is the green expanse of the Lamar Valley. A tiny ribbon of blue shines in a downstream bend.

At the junction with the Cache Creek Trail, a sign says Miller Creek is 6.2 miles ahead. Above the lettering, some idiot has carved a message into the sign's face: "Kerry K. (from Drew)." Alongside it is etched a wobbly arrow pointing toward campsite 3L1. I wish there were a way I could send my own message: "Drew (from Cliff): If you're going to split up your party, make sure someone in both groups has a map and knows the route. And stop defacing signs."

A short distance beyond, a hiking family appears, parents with three kids. "We're just out for a day hike," the father says. Looking at my backpack, he asks, "Where are you headed, and how long are you staying out?"

"I'm headed up to the Hoodoo Basin," I say. "About a week."

Blank stares all around. Before I can elaborate, the father says, "We saw that sign at the trailhead about the bear frequenting area. Maybe you'll see one." His expression suggests I'm supposed to be frightened.

"Maybe so," I say. "Out here, it's always a possibility."

We wish each other good trips and turn to go our ways.

"Stay safe," the mother says. Nice folks.

Beyond the edge of a low bluff, the waters of Cache Creek sparkle in the midday sun. On the descent to the floodplain, the trail branches and braids in a series of bison paths. At the bottom is a sign marking the spur route to site 3L1. Below it, a white plastic notice has been duct-taped to the post, bearing the outline of a grizzly, along with: WARNING BEAR FREQUENTING AREA. In smaller print it adds, "There is no guarantee of your safety while hiking or camping in bear country." My cynical lawyer side knows what this means: "If you get mauled, don't sue us."

The campsite sits about a hundred yards upstream, right on the creek. From here it appears to be a decent site, with easy access to water, but it's also within view of the trail and only three and a half miles from the trailhead. No tents are visible, but two people are walking near the creek. Perhaps they haven't made camp yet, so early in the day. Or maybe they're day hikers.

The streambed of Cache Creek is lined with rounded stones the size of oranges and cantaloupes. Some are larger. The water is no more than calf-deep and isn't flowing especially fast, but the large, smooth rocks, slickened by water, make for dicey footing. With a bit of concentration, I get across without incident.

The route climbs the opposite bluff, past the sign for site 3L2, which is also marked as a bear frequenting area. Farther south is a section of forest burned in 1988. Parts of it may have burned again more recently, judging by the deep black char on some of the logs. They stand out among the bleached bone-gray of the others. Where dead trees have fallen across the trail over the years, they have been sawn back several feet on either side by diligent trail crews. A few fresh cuts, underlain with sprinkles of sawdust, suggest some of this work has been done quite recently.

The logs exemplify one of the route-finding methods hikers can use when trails and markers disappear. If this trail were to fall into disuse over time, and it faded out of existence or was covered with plants, a hiker could still identify the route by these cut logs on either side. Their flat, sawn surfaces will remain far longer than any trace of the trail, and they are usually easy to see. Of course this won't help in meadows or grasslands where there are few trees, but in forested areas, when the route is in doubt, look for cut logs.

Ahead, a dense mass of young lodgepoles crowds the trail, and I'm obliged to resume talking to myself. This always feels strange at the start of a trip, but the feeling doesn't last.

This time, in addition to the screening trees, the trail is marked with a pile of bear scat. It is fresh enough to suggest the bear may still be in the area. This calls for more noise that carries farther than talking. Perhaps singing. But what? I decide to begin a new tradition of meeting fresh bear scat with musical scat, and I break into my best Al Jarreau: *Skiddly do bop boo, diddly dooo.* If that won't frighten a bear away, I don't know what will.

Halfway between sites 3L3 and 3L4, the midpoint of today's hike, I stop for lunch. The route has veered upslope, high above where the Lamar River flows between Mirror Plateau and the low reaches of the Absarokas. In a shallow canyon, the river winds in sparkling whites and deep blues beneath rocky cliffs. Above the plateau, the sky is also blue. It's an intense blueness that appears only a few days each summer, a mesmerizing color that draws the eye and holds it, causing one to realize how rarely we notice the sky.

Periodically, I comment aloud on the water, cliffs, and sky, in case the bear has returned in my silence. Resuming the hike, I scare up a chipmunk. It scampers down a long log, jumps to another, and takes that to yet another. An old burned forest is a chipmunk thruway.

Upper Lamar River

A stock party approaches, a small group of riders with a large number of pack animals. With all that gear, they must have had quite a stay, or they are outfitters that brought in a sizeable group of clients, perhaps the ones at the stock trailhead this morning. I step a few yards out of the trail to let them pass.

The lead rider is an older man. "Howdy," he says in a cordial tone as he rides past.

"How you doing?" I return.

"Not too bad," he says. "Only about three hours behind schedule."

Several more riders pass, most followed by a single pack animal tethered to their horse. Toward the rear is a middle-aged man whose horse seems more skittish than the others. I speak to it in an attempt to calm it down.

"It's okay," I say slowly, in what is meant to be a soothing tone. "I'm not a bear. I don't even bite."

"We don't bite, either," the man says with a grin. "Much."

Bringing up the rear is the only woman of the group. "Where are you headed?" she asks.

"The Hoodoos," I say.

"Nice!" she says. "We're headed out, unfortunately."

Their noise fades as we travel apart. Past Calfee Creek, I stop at a point overlooking the Calfee Creek Patrol Cabin, which is far below, on a flat near the Lamar River. From all appearances, it's unoccupied.

At Miller Creek, the route leaves the upper Lamar and turns east, heading up a valley that also burned in 1988. Natural reforestation is well underway, with dense stands of lodgepole restricting the view. "Another area with no visibility," I observe aloud. "Don't want to surprise any bears out here, though I am ready to surprise my campsite."

After another mile or so, the trail reaches the sign for 3M1. A steep spur route drops through forest to the valley floor. No prints of hiking shoes are visible on the path, only horseshoes. The horses have churned the trail into loose dirt, making for difficult footing on the way down.

At the base of the ridge is a strip of dense forest beyond which is a short ford of Miller Creek. The water is shallow and clear. Just across is 3M1, a beautiful spot at the edge of a long meadow. I drop the pack at the food area, sit on one of the camp logs looking over the meadow, and drink the rest of the water.

Once I've cooled down from the hiking, my sweaty shirt feels chilly. Exchanged for a dry one, it is left hanging from a branch, where it quickly dries into a stiff, board-like form. Below it, I notice the dirt is marked by rows of parallel lines. The food area has actually been raked. It must have been done by a stock party. You never see backpackers carrying rakes, or needing them, for that matter. But sometimes you find campsites so full of horse droppings that they could use a good raking. Perhaps it was that friendly group I passed earlier. They seemed like caring types, who would take time to do this. Whoever it was, I appreciate their backcountry ethics.

When dinner is finished and the water bottles are filled, it's time to make camp. A quick reconnaissance finds a patch of loose, sandy soil in the meadow to the east. It should be comfortable, relatively speaking. When the tent is up I climb inside to get things situated before darkness comes. My work is interrupted by several biting flies that followed me in. Usually, flies trapped in a tent are only concerned with getting back out. But these are tenacious in their ferocity, making them impossible to ignore. Like a dog chasing wasps, I lunge and flail about the tent until they've all been dispatched or sent hiding under gear.

As the afternoon light softens to early evening, I reemerge to a golden meadow of lengthy shadows. They all point the way to the Absaroka Mountains and the Hoodoo Basin. As evening deepens, the shadows stretch and merge until the meadow turns dusky. The last vestiges of sunlight linger on the peak of Saddle Mountain, shrinking, dimming, and fading. When nighttime comes, the stars are outshone by the light of the moon, waning gibbous, but still close to full.

Perhaps it was a night like this, though six weeks later in the year, in 1869, when Folsom, Cook, and Peterson were camped a few miles from here, near the confluence of the Lamar River and Calfee Creek. For some reason—perhaps they were feeling homesick—they had an anxious night. As Folsom put it, in his poetic language:

The wolf scents us afar and the mournful cadence of his howl adds to our sense of solitude. The roar of the mountain lion awakens the sleeping echoes of the adjacent cliffs and we hear the elk whistling in every direction.

Today, that sounds like a wonderful night. It would be a joy to hear a wolf howl. And though mountain lions are too few to even hope to hear, an echoing roar among cliff walls would surely stir the soul. Tonight, even a whistling elk would be welcome, though it's too early in summer for that. It can wait for a later trip.

Day 2. 3M1 to the Hoodoo Basin, Site 3M6

On day two I'm up early, looking at heavy rain clouds massed over Mirror Plateau, just a few miles to the west. They appear to be headed north. I'm going east, so maybe we'll miss each other.

With the sun still hidden low behind the Absarokas, the air has an invigorating chill. As much as I'd like to hang out and wait for the warming rays, today is a long travel day, a seven-mile hike followed by a climb of twenty-two hundred feet spread over another five miles. Better get moving.

As I start breaking camp, a cow moose ambles out of the forest on the far side of the creek, about fifty yards away. My hiking plans fade to insignificance. The moose disappears behind a stand of conifers, and when she doesn't appear on the opposite side, I walk up the meadow for a closer look. Still no sign. Thinking she has moved away and maybe gone up the ridge, I turn toward camp. Then I notice two long, dark ears twitching above a patch of high grass, where the moose has bedded down. Through binoculars I watch for a few moments, and then it's time to leave her in peace.

As the camp stove heats water for oatmeal, my thoughts return to the moose. It was a lucky sighting, the type nature sometimes gives when we're lost in our thoughts or busy doing other things. Had the moose appeared a few seconds later, I would've been occupied with breaking camp and would likely have missed her. Is there a lesson here? Perhaps that we are more likely to see wildlife when not overly focused on watching. Or maybe we don't spend enough time being quiet and alert. Or perhaps it's that wildlife sightings are simply a matter of luck, provided we put ourselves in the right setting and remain watchful for whatever comes.

Despite the morning coolness, biting flies attest that the season is still summer. As I spray my ankles with DEET, one of the flies gets caught in the blast. This raises the philosophical question of how a fly feels when sprayed with insect repellant. Is it repulsed by itself or only shunned by other flies? Other, more scientific, explanations notwithstanding, this one seems merely distracted. It remains on my sock and washes its hands.

In the lower branches of a nearby conifer, a red-naped sapsucker appears. Its red chin and white sides stand out among the dark green needles. As birds do, it has a knack for lingering just long enough to tempt me to reach for my camera. But when the image becomes composed and focused, the bird flies quickly away.

My attention drawn to birdlife, I notice a Steller's jay overhead. It's apparently a youngster, who hasn't yet mastered its hawk mimic and sounds rather pathetic. From the forest upstream comes the clucking of robins and intermittent calls of a northern flicker. Beautiful sounds and sights. Sometimes it takes a sapsucker, or a moose, or a patch of intensely blue sky, to make us slow down and notice.

Back on the main trail, the route travels the low face of the ridge, maintaining elevation above the valley floor. Where the slope is crossed by dry washes, the trail bends into them before returning to the ridge's open face. With so many blind turns, I talk to myself quite a lot. It's riveting conversation, full of such gems as, "Another blind turn up here. Watch out for Mama Bear."

Forest gaps reveal stretches of Miller Creek and the meadows beyond, a land full of natural beauty. The route descends to the valley floor, crossing a dry meadow with more sage than grass. The path's faintness is not enough to make route-finding a challenge, but a welcome sign of limited use. More dense forest is ahead.

"Another blind turn down by the creek," I say loudly. "Don't want to surprise a thirsty bear." I keep this up despite having seen no sign of bears today. That isn't the issue. The bigger, unknowable, matter is how many bears have seen me. Or heard me talking to myself. That's why we do it.

The trail swings close to the creek, skirting the base of a steep, rocky slope. Both the National Geographic map and the USGS topo show a footbridge somewhere around here, though there isn't one. Perhaps it was washed out during a particularly heavy spring runoff, or burned in a wildfire, or taken out by a trail crew as unnecessary or unsafe. Here on the ground, there's no obvious sign there ever was a bridge, or the need of one.

A short distance upslope, standing precariously, is a large and gnarly petrified tree stump. Its tans and yellows contrast with the surrounding browns. Below it, encased in a mass of rock, is a small petrified limb or trunk from some ancient tree. It's evidence of a quick burial some fifty million years ago, when the Absaroka volcanoes were active. Here, just as on the Sky Rim, lava and ash ran and fell, sometimes joining massive debris flows (lahars!) that coursed down newly erected mountainsides. Many of these preserved stretches of petrified forests across much of northern Yellowstone, from the Absarokas to the Lamar Valley's Specimen Ridge, to the Petrified Tree near Tower, and across to the Gallatins. All evidence of a volcanic past long before the hot spot's arrival.

The rain clouds have now passed to the north, and by midmorning the day turns hot. The feeling is accentuated by the ups and downs of the trail, resulting in a sweaty hike, though the real climbing hasn't even begun. At the next stream crossing I stop to filter more water, chugging the first cup with an electrolyte packet stirred in. Somewhere across the valley a ghost tree crashes to the ground, with a noise like an explosion.

Not far ahead is the Miller Creek Patrol Cabin, which is also unoccupied and locked. It occurs to me I haven't seen another person since the stock party yesterday afternoon, more than nine trail miles ago.

Across the creek from the cabin is the start of the long climb to the Hoodoo Basin. Though I'm not especially hungry, I should stop for a nutrition break, more calories to fuel the twenty-two-hundred-foot climb.

Near the cabin, I sit on the ground against a log and watch an industrious chipmunk darting around and gathering food. To reach the high seedheads of taller grasses, it pulls stalks down and nibbles off their ends. To reach even higher ones, it scampers atop a large log and stretches straight outward, one hind leg locked beneath it to support its weight, the other extended behind, grasping the log for balance. With its body fully extended, the chipmunk reaches out with both forepaws and pulls in more seed clusters. Having gathered all it can reach, it scampers to the log I am sitting against and runs toward my backpack, focused only on its task. I wave a hand to draw its attention and keep it away from my gear. The chipmunk stops abruptly, apparently surprised to see a human way out here. It leaps to the ground and disappears into the cabin's woodpile.

Seed-gathering chipmunk

Before resuming the hike, I take advantage of the convenience of the rangers' outhouse. The luxury of a sit-down toilet out here in the backcountry is hard to pass up. On the wall inside someone has written in pencil, "Flush it twice."

After an easy ford of Miller Creek, the trail begins climbing almost immediately, switchbacking up the base of the steep slope. After a brief stretch of mature forest, the trail emerges to ascend a ridge cleared by the '88 fires. Most of the dead trees have fallen on this steep terrain, leaving a landscape that's open, though significantly tilted. Scattered about are plenty of wildflowers, fireweed, of course, along with clusters of white blossoms of pearly everlasting, and yellow petals of false dandelions. A few shiny bits of red turn out to be ripe wild strawberries, and another one, upon closer inspection, a ladybug.

The next portion of trail is carved in the steep hillside, with tight switchbacks climbing ever higher. Freshly cut logs testify to recent trail maintenance. A few turns higher on the open slope, long views look down the valley of Miller Creek. The ranger cabin, now far below, appears tiny in a broken sea of fallen gray logs and green saplings.

More surprising are the views to the east and south, where heavy rain clouds have amassed above the higher terrain. These are moving in my direction. As the clouds curtain the sun, the temperature drops, and a chilly wind rises to buffet the exposed slope. Another instantaneous change of Yellowstone weather. Time to hurry upward and get off the face of this ridge.

A few flecks of water prick my skin. They're not enough to call rain, but the flecks grow into drops whipped about by strong gusts. I pause to put on raingear, as much to stop wind as water.

In our indoor culture, we've come to regard this kind of weather as bad, inclement, something to be avoided. But it's not necessarily so. With decent raingear, time in such weather can be quite enjoyable. It only requires a slight change in thinking, an easy step toward a harmony with nature, where weather is only part of the land. Had Hamlet been a backpacker, he might—in addition to incessantly questioning his course of travel—have said weather is neither good nor bad, but thinking makes it so.

When the trail reaches the lower crest of the ridge, the slope moderates, and the route follows the ridge's spine as it climbs gently to the east. Out in the high open, the terrain has a top-of-the-world feel, with sky on all sides. The neighboring peaks have fallen below eye level in all but a few places: Pollux Peak to the southeast, and, to the south, the ever-present Saddle Mountain. Its summit is now touched by a single shaft of sunlight, which pierces the gray sky and adorns the forest with a golden-green glow.

The route enters an area of towering trees long since dead and bleached by years of unobstructed sun. Many are still standing but more lie sprawled about in a sea of stony gray. In the midst of this grows a patch of elderberries, the ripe, black fruit shining in the dense light of a gathering storm. Nearby, lounging on a wide log, is an alpine grasshopper, with black Vs marking its hind legs.

The wind continues to grow, rising from the low valleys and howling through the broken treetops. Unconcerned, a nutcracker squawks from above, sounding just as they do on sunny days. Slightly concerned, I hurry onward, keeping an eye on the swaying snags on both sides of the trail.

Above the higher ridge ahead, heavy rain trails from low clouds. So far, at least, there have been no flashes or rumbles. In a stretch of mature forest, screened from the mighty wind, I stop for another nutrition break. As I open the food bag, a gray jay glides silently in, alighting on a nearby branch and cocking its head to check out the fare.

"Sorry, Gray," I say aloud. "Got nothing for you."

Not only is feeding wildlife, including birds, prohibited in the park, it is just a bad idea. Giving food to wild animals diminishes their wildness and turns them into beggars. They can get by fine without handouts, as long as we leave them enough wild habitat.

Soon I'm back on the trail, reenergized by a nutrition bar and another pack of electrolytes. The weather, both ahead and behind, has intensified, and dense, slanting rain shrouds the peaks and screens the valleys.

As the terrain undulates along the ridge crest, the landscape shifts between forest and grassy expanses, some the color of straw. At the edge of a wider meadow, I stop to assess the storm before venturing across the high open. There has still been no lightning or thunder, but I set out in a sprint-hike to minimize my exposure, both to any potential lightning and the whipping winds. Beyond the next forested band is another grassy area. Hurrying across in my direction, headed down, is a backpacking couple. The man walks in front, periodically clapping and yelling, "No bear, no bear," as they approach the trees.

"No bears in here," I call out in greeting.

For a moment he seems embarrassed.

"It looks like a good day to be going down instead of up," I say in a light-hearted tone. The woman smiles. The man is more serious.

"The worst stuff should be past where you're headed," he says.

From the looks of things, I'm not so sure. But I don't say so. Understandably, they are in a hurry to get down to Miller Creek, and, though gravity is on their side, I don't envy their hike across the exposed face of the ridge. We wish each other luck, and they speed on.

For me, with several miles of high country still to cross, and no sheltered valley to get to, there's no point in rushing, except to get out of exposed areas. Otherwise, it's just a walk in the park. As long as you bring the right gear and the right mindset, there are no bad days in Yellowstone.

A low bank of storm clouds now covers the trail, including directly overhead. Contrary to what the backpacker said, the heaviest stuff looks to be exactly where I'm headed. Still no lightning or thunder, though, just a fierce wind darting flecks of rain straight in from the side.

The shower intensifies, blowing horizontally across the trail. While I don't mind hiking in rain, a blowing, driving, side-flying storm is a different matter. In the lee of a small stand of subalpine firs in an open forest of taller trees, I stop to wait out the heaviest part.

Dropping my pack, I sit downwind of the tree with the densest needles, which block most of the blowing rain. The bear spray sits atop my pack, within easy reach should a grizzly come wandering along to the surprise of us both. The rain is more enjoyable, now that it's not slapping me in the face. As large drops fly horizontally past the screening trees, I dig into the food bag for another snack, an impromptu picnic in a high mountain storm. It's actually a pleasant spot for a break.

After a heavy downpour, the rain subsides for a brief moment, but then resumes, reinvigorated by a new wave of winds. The temperature falls to fifty-one, though the wind and moisture bring a colder feel. During the next lull, I layer a long-sleeved shirt over my t-shirt and add a wool hat, kept dry under the raingear's hood. Quite warm now, comfortable, actually, as I sit on a ridge at ninety-five hundred feet, while winds drive sheets of rain across the land.

Eventually, the wind calms and the rain tapers to a gentle shower, falling straight down like a mild spring rain. Now this is hiking weather. I sling on the pack and set off on a trail that's wet but not especially muddy. Though my clothes have become damp, the raingear and wool cap keep me comfortable. If someone were to ask how I'm feeling right now, I'd say I'm wet, a little chilly, a little tired, but I absolutely love it.

Approaching Parker Peak, the route descends to cross a shallow basin with an expanse of grass. It looks as though there ought to be a herd of elk here. Or bison. There are neither now, but that may change at dusk and dawn. No humans will be around then to see, with no campsites in the area. But that's as it should be. Some places should be left to wild species.

On the many patches of wildflowers, lingering moisture accents foliage more than blossoms, giving the land the lush, green look of spring. Intermittent spots of bare ground are dotted with fragments of petrified wood. With their appearance brightened and softened by rainwater, they resemble fresh wood chips. To differentiate, I adopt the very unscientific method of smacking a few with the bottom of my hiking stick. The ones that go *thud*, I conclude, are fresh wood, while the ones that go *clack* are petrified. Most of these go *clack*.

In another open area, the ground sparkles with shiny black chips of obsidian. They glisten in the dim, overcast light. Archaeologists believe at least some of these fragments are detritus of a worksite used by Native Americans, who made arrowheads and scrapers out of the volcanic glass. As before, I am not tempted to take even the tiniest bit. It would be a crime against nature, as well as history. These pieces belong here.

The sky has lightened from dark gray to a misty, foggy-white. All that remains of the rain is a chilly drizzle that dots small puddles on the trail. It has been a good shower, especially for August. The grasses and wildflowers are getting the moisture they need as they grow and build foliage, flowers, and seeds for next year. Their abundance will feed insects, birds, and other wild species as the water moves from sky to ground and through the web of life. There's poetry in that, of a type only nature can compose.

The route plunges again into forest, but this time it's a dense stretch where the trail travels a narrow corridor of trees. Time for more bear noise. Being so far from the trailhead, socked in by low clouds, and filled with the joy of being in the backcountry, I lose all self-consciousness and break into song. It's a favorite snippet from Mozart:

Non piu andrai farfallone amoroso.

Whew! Singing is more difficult when hiking with a heavy pack in the thin air at nearly ten thousand feet. Better stick with talking for now.

Approaching the shoulder of Parker Peak, the route climbs another open grassy expanse under a sky clearing to soft powdery blue. Parker Peak fills the southern horizon. A permanent snowfield covers much of its northern face, and at its base is a small pond fed by the trickling runoff.

From the edge of the grassy saddle the terrain falls away into the high Hoodoo Basin. The expansive view is quite beautiful, but from this high vantage I see signs of neither hoos nor doos. Runaway expectations again—I had imagined the Hoodoo Basin as a basin filled with hoodoos. They are around here somewhere. I've seen photos. Though their location is not shown on the map, this only adds to the adventure, a search to find them out. I'm glad I added more days to look around.

Looking over the Hoodoo Basin from the shoulder of Parker Peak

As the trail drops into the high basin, 3M6 soon appears. It's a beautiful site, set in a wildflower meadow beneath cliffs leading up to Parker Peak. Tiny streams flow across the gently sloped terrain, joining together at various spots on their long journey down to the upper Lamar River. Eventually, some of these waters will flow through the wide Lamar Valley, where my trip began, and continue on to the Yellowstone. What a wonderful journey.

As more rain clouds drift over, it's time to hang the food and make camp. As I uncoil my rope, I notice a pile of bear scat sitting under the food pole. Fortunately, it is old. It's also small enough to have been left by a black bear. At least that's what I tell myself. I poke it with a stick, knocking a hole through the brittle exterior, confirming it has been here quite a long time. On the opposite side, I notice where someone has poked a similar hole.

When the food is up, I survey the site but see no ideal places for a tent. The most level terrain is near the creek, where a tent could frighten wildlife away from a needed drink. On the higher ground beyond, is a good spot. It's more than a hundred yards from the bear pole, probably closer to one-fifty, but a good tent site is worth the walk. The ground is hard here, but not so sloped, and not too near the water. It will do.

When the tent is up, I head to the largest of the small creeks to stock up on water. The stream flows clear, even after the rain, but quite shallow so high in the basin. After the bottles are filled, I barely make it back to the tent before the rain returns, an intense shower with more whipping winds. As thunder bounces in rumbling echoes between Parker and Hoodoo Peaks, I lie back and listen. The tent is comfortable, except for a slight chill. This is assuaged by the addition of heavy wool socks, the key to warm nights in camp at any time of year.

As darkness falls, the temperature falls with it, and the damp night air has a piercing chill. I bundle up in layers, even wearing my wool hat to bed. As I drift off to sleep, the only dry item left in my clothes bag is a pair of socks. Everything else is either wet or I am wearing it. It's a reminder I'll need to pack more cold-weather gear on my later trips, especially the one to the Bechler, which will last into late September.

For now, it's still midsummer, only a chilly, damp night in the high country. But it's Yellowstone, and I love it.

Day 3. 3M6 to the Park Boundary, Site 3M7

Morning arrives warm and sunny in the Hoodoo Basin. Or I have to assume it did. I missed its actual arrival, having slept in after yesterday's long hike. I emerge from the tent to a meadow of golden light and wildflowers under a sunny sky. Standing in a high meadow twenty-three miles and one significant climb from the trailhead, one feels the essence of remote wilderness. A raptor soars overhead, following the walls of the cliffs. It's a perfect moment.

After breaking camp, I begin the easy hike of only a mile and a half to the next campsite. The initial route descends through more sunny meadows. All are blanketed with wildflowers, seas of yellows and pale purples set abuzz with the hum of bees and flies.

The route switchbacks down to ford a stream only slightly wider than those back at camp. The water flows over solid rock, in contrast to the pebbly, muddy bottoms in lower areas. Three gray jays forage along the trail beyond, floating between trees and ground with their graceful flight. One of them catches a flying insect and carries it to a lichen-covered branch.

From the creek, the trail begins a long climb. With the gained elevation the mountains south and east dip to reveal more blue sky. Into the ascent, my pace becomes slow and trudging, falling into a rhythmic pattern of *shuck, shuck, shuck*. After the last switchback, the terrain levels onto an open grassy expanse lined with mixed conifers. Among them is a surprising number of healthy whitebark pines. As in other places the largest ones are dead, but a few mature ones are green and vibrant-looking, offering some measure of hope.

The sky holds more gray than before, though not due to rain clouds, judging by the faint aroma of woodsmoke. Perhaps one of the recent storms ignited a new blaze. Or maybe the smoke has blown in from distant forests. Peak fire season is fast approaching, and though the park had lifted campfire restrictions at the start of this trip, that will likely change soon, if it hasn't already. Still early in the day, the smoke stays settled low in the valleys outside the park. Overhead, the sky remains clear. Occasional cumulus clouds drift across the face of the sun, wafting shadows along the grassy ridge.

The terrain of this high expanse slopes gently up to the north, where, not far away, according to the map, is the head of a high valley. Leaving the trail, I cover the short distance and reach the edge of a cliff. Across and below are the hoodoos.

They rise in a natural expanse of weirdly eroded rock columns, pinnacles, and spires. Their rough textures are multicolored, mainly tans, browns, and reds. The wondrous setting fills one with a childlike desire to run down to the base of the contorted rock forms and try to see them all.

Restraining myself, I return to the trail, which descends into the eroded valley. From the lower vantage the hoodoos are even more striking, set against a sky of intense blue. From their base, more strange formations are evident, boulders balanced atop thin pedestals, kinked rock columns, and windows through stone. Towering above it all is a high column topped with a huge triangular rock on a thin neck. From below it resembles the head of a giant, petrified praying mantis.

In the presence of these wonderful natural formations, one can only walk slowly along their base, repeatedly stopping and staring, and trying to take it all in. Time becomes meaningless, both in the sense we can never comprehend the eons that sculpted these stony shapes, and because, regardless of how long one may stand and stare, it will never be enough. It's impossible to see and appreciate all the intricate, improbable, and graceful forms, which are changing even now through erosion. A flake here, a grain of sand there, the landscape is still being sculpted.

After some untold time, I come back to myself. Looking around, I see the rest of the high valley is beautiful in its own right. On the south wall are two snowfields, slowly melting in trickling rills across a sandy wildflower meadow. They coalesce in a stream along the hoodoos' base. The shining waters and wildflowers and the expansive blue sky, now softened with white cumulus, frame the improbable shapes of the rocks. It's a scene both rugged and delicate, ancient and new.

The hoodoos

After another long period of timelessness, I remember I need to make camp. While the sun still shines its midday warmth, I want to hang up my damp clothes to dry.

Across the head of the valley the trail climbs again through forest to reach a high grassy meadow. Site 3M7 is on the western edge, along a thin line of subalpine firs and whitebark pines. At the bear pole, I hang my food and explore the site, hoping to find a spot with views beyond the thin band of trees, where the land falls away into a high grassy ravine. Across the open expanse and a hundred feet below, is a bird's-eye view of the hoodoos. It's a wonderful campsite.

Near the meadow's south end, I set up camp near a wide forest opening. Because of the trees and the need to set the tent back from the slope, it's not possible to see the valley floor directly from the tent site, but the views are only a few yards away. Once camp is made and my wet clothes hung from bare branches in the sun, I return to the trees and sit in a shaded spot on a soft cushion of forest duff, studying the rocky formations from above.

Over the course of the afternoon, changes in sunlight, brought about by shifting clouds and the passage of time, cast the rocky shapes in differing colors. With the sun's movement, their shadows stretch and bend, revealing different forms and textures. The effects are mesmerizing.

Oddly enough, "hoodoo" is an official geologic term, one you can find in real geology books. It refers to varying columns carved by erosion. In volcanic terrain like this, vertical fractures in the rock cause it to erode into irregular pillars, and where harder rock is deposited over softer, the upper layers act as protective caps, redirecting eroding forces from ice and rainwater into strange patterns below. As the softer rock wears away faster than the protective caps, they erode into myriad formations of windowed walls, flying buttresses, and thin columns topped with large boulders. These are real hoodoos, unlike the more well-known but misnamed rocks along the Grand Loop south of Mammoth. Those are a jumble of travertine boulders that tumbled down from Terrace Mountain. Beautiful and interesting they are, but they are not hoodoos.

The water source at 3M7, set near the rim of the high basin, could scarcely be called a creek. Below the food area, a short distance down the grassy slope, it trickles through a high valley, descending toward the streams that flow past the hoodoos. Among the many wildflowers along the watercourse is an unusual one (to me), with blossoms in clustered cones of pink spikes, set atop short, succulent stems. They are called queen's crown.

Back at the tent my clothes have dried, and I put them away before setting off to explore the ridges above camp. It's a short hike up a gently sloping meadow to reach the wide ridge crest. The park boundary is here, marked by a small pyramid of rocks holding a weathered post. Attached to it is a white boundary sign, so familiar from the Sky Rim trek. Widely spaced in an undulating line that stretches along the rolling grassy ridges, are more white markers. In the green distance they shrink to tiny white specks.

To the east, just outside the boundary, is the source of Hoodoo Creek, another snowfield in a protected area beneath the ridge's crest. From here it drips, trickles, and eventually flows to the northeast, down a high, wild valley toward the Clarks Fork of the Yellowstone River.

If one were to stand on this crest during a heavy rain, the waters that fell on your eastern side would drain toward Hoodoo Creek and the Clarks Fork, while the showers to the west would run toward the Lamar River and the Yellowstone. In theory, some of that rainwater, which fell only inches apart on this ridge, would eventually meet up again near Laurel, Montana, about eighty miles northeast of here, where the Clarks Fork joins the Yellowstone.

From the grassy saddle, Hoodoo Peak fills the northern horizon, but views in all other directions abound. From Parker Peak a vast panorama of rolling, grassy ridges stretches to the south, swinging eastward to encompass the high basin and beyond. To the immediate south is a low, grassy hill, the highest point in the area, short of Hoodoo Peak. From atop its summit at ninety-nine hundred feet, the views are more expansive.

View toward Parker Peak, from the hill above 3M7

I remain on the grassy summit a long while, sitting motionless, lost in the grand scenery. When a small, sleek animal bounds across the slope below, its bushy tail flowing behind it, my unfocused mind assumes it's a red squirrel. Nearly too late, I realize the body is too long for a squirrel and lighter in color, and the travel more graceful, a series of flowing bounds instead of shorter hops. Looking more intently, I see, just before the animal disappears into the forest below, the black tip at the end of its tail. It's a long-tailed weasel, one I almost missed.

Back at camp in early evening, a light dinner of trail mix and a multigrain bar is observed at the base of a surprisingly healthy whitebark pine. The faint sound of human voices drifts across the valley. It seems so out of place that I get up and look through the forest toward the opposite ridge, doubting my hearing.

Two people, tiny with distance, stand on the grassy ledge across the high valley. It's the place I stopped today for my first look. In the dimming light of approaching dusk, they remain in place without venturing down for a closer view of the hoodoos. But they've had a long day. Because I was at 3M6 last night, they must have camped down on Miller Creek and made the long hike up here today. And they still have to walk back to 3M6. As the sun sinks lower, they turn and disappear.

In contrast to the damp chills of last night, this evening is comfortably warm, a more typical end of a midsummer day. The low-angle sun strikes the backs of the hoodoos, setting their outlines aglow. The altered light reveals new forms, most prominent among them the shape of a giant petrified hawk perched on a rocky column.

A smoky haze on the horizon catches the last of the sunlight and casts it in a pink-orange glow. One can almost feel the heat emanating across the high basin. Or perhaps it's a stirring of the spirit of the wilderness.

Before darkness sets in, I take my cell phone out of its waterproof bag and turn it on in hopes of calling Mari. No bars. Maybe it'll do better on the hill east of camp. Heading straight up through the trees this time, I check again. Two bars. Good enough. I call Mari and let her know everything is fine so she doesn't worry. She says the recent storms have touched off several new fires in and around the park. That explains the smoke.

Summer in Yellowstone.

Day 4. Impromptu Layover Day at 3M7

Dawn is cool at ninety-seven hundred feet, even in midsummer. A few minutes before seven, the temperature hovers at forty-four. When the sun peeks over the ridge behind camp, it alights the hoodoos in a soft russet glow. Unlike the harsher tints of afternoon, this brings out warm pinks, siennas, and umbers in the eroded stone. It almost seems a different landscape.

A nice, cheery campfire soon dances in the fire ring, not so much for warmth as ambience. Its gentle crackling makes for good company. The sky remains clear, and as the sun rises higher it warms the morning air. Another perfect, peaceful moment in the wild.

I sit and stare across the mountains, feeling the rightness of nature and the depth of its meaning. It's a feeling I've learned to accept without question. If one were to try and analyze why the wild holds such meaning—whether it's a matter of being out of the constricting city, or being close to our natural roots, or perhaps something deeper, a spiritual renewal—the sensation would likely disappear. Such matters of spirit, poetry, and soul rarely hold up to cold, clinical analysis. Like wild animals, when you stare at them too long they can be frightened away. But if you allow them space and acceptance, and try to peacefully coexist, they may linger.

From the forested hillside above camp comes a nasally, whistley shriek, the trip's first real sign of elk, other than old tracks. Clearly they are here, as in other high places, having followed greening vegetation up to this basin. After breakfast I'll walk up the hill and scan the grassy ridges for grazing elk. After that, it'll be time to break camp for the short hike back to 3M6.

It will be difficult to leave this wonderful site, though in retrospect, I'm fortunate to be here at all. My original plan had just two nights in this basin, both at 3M6. That left only a day to hike over for a too-brief encounter with the hoodoos before heading back. I would have missed out on the time here at 3M7 and on the ridges along the park boundary, and missed seeing the hoodoos change with the sun's movement.

Now I've talked myself into wanting to stay here another night. I wonder if anyone has this site reserved. A larger question is whether I can reach the Central Backcountry Office to ask. One would think their phone number would be on the permit, but no. Perhaps it's on the National Geographic map, among the information on regulations and guidelines about hiking in Yellowstone. Sure enough, there it is, under Information and Reservations.

Back on the hilltop, I punch in the digits with a mixture of hope and doubt. A man named Brandon answers. After introducing myself, I ask if it's possible to change my permit for tonight, from 3M6 to 3M7.

"Are you up there now?" he asks.

"Yes," I say. "On the ridge above it."

"I'm always amazed at where people get cell coverage out there," he says.

Turns out the site is available. All Brandon needs is my permit number, which I read to him. He calls up my itinerary and enters 3M7 for tonight, and just like that, everything is set. I thank him profusely and say goodbye.

This is perfect. No need to break camp now. I'll return to 3M6 tomorrow. It's a better place to begin the long hike down to Miller Creek on the following day.

Without much of a plan, I wander north across the open saddle toward Hoodoo Peak. At the base of the mountain I began climbing along the park boundary, with no idea of how high I'll get. This is not the route for a full ascent. It's too steep. But that's not my goal. If it were, it would be best to return to 3M6 after all, and follow the shoulder of Parker Peak to a more moderate flank of Hoodoo. Today, I'm just out for a look-see.

The ascent passes another group of hoodoos, not as striking as those near camp, across on a section of cliffs. I continue up the steep slope, picking my way between boulders and past stunted whitebark pines twisted by wind into *krummholz*. Much farther up, beyond where I should already have turned and headed down, I notice a grassy bench above. It apparently extends to a gentler slope on the mountain's eastern flank, a potential route to the summit. Despite knowing better, I decide to go for it, climbing the precipitous slope with feet and hands.

Short of the grassy bench, I am stopped by a combination of sheer incline and loose scree. Each upward step slides backward before I can take another. Grabbing at tufts of grass and anchored rocks for support, I try to climb higher, but when one of the rocks breaks loose, I realize how foolish I'm being. So high on the steep side of a mountain, even a slight loss of balance could turn into a bouncing tumble. And there would be no stopping until the bottom, hundreds of feet below.

Sobered by my foolhardy predicament, I begin carefully making my way down the mountain, trying not to create and become part of a rockslide. At the start of the descent—the steepest and least stable terrain—I butt-scoot to keep a low center of gravity. A short, but unnerving, distance beyond, the footing is solid enough to allow a slow, careful walking, testing each step before transferring my weight. Eventually, I reach the base of the mountain, vowing all the while to make no more foolish ascents.

After dinner, I return to the grassy ridge above camp, staring across the high, open terrain at the sunset. Its oranges and pinks are augmented again by building layers of wildfire smoke. As the rest of the sky darkens, the western horizon glows like burning coals. Fire season is here.

Day 5. 3M7 to 3M6

In the dim predawn, a cow elk calls from the forest above camp. Moments later, a light clatter of hooves moves past the tent, headed toward the call. Peeking out, I see a cow elk walking a short distance away, followed by two growing calves. Having noticed me, the two youngsters pause to look back before hurrying to catch up with mama.

So there are elk up here, but how many? Too many? Not enough? According to whom?

For nearly as long as there has been a Yellowstone, people have been arguing about elk numbers, about how many should be in the park. For some people, the answer comes down to how many were here before trappers, prospectors, and settlers arrived. This approach has two shortcomings. First, there are no reliable records on elk numbers before market hunters began decimating the herds for profit. And second, whatever the number may have been, it is no longer relevant. The ecosystem has been too drastically changed.

In the park's early days, wanton slaughter of wildlife went mostly unchecked until 1886, when the Army arrived. Though no one knew how many elk had been here before, once the killing stopped, a growing consensus held there were too few elk.

In those days, Yellowstone's managers believed tourists expected to see large ungulates—elk, bison, deer, bighorn, moose, and pronghorn—and they saw predators as something like thieves, bad animals that were stealing the good ones. To protect ungulates, park personnel began shooting, trapping, and poisoning predators, especially coyotes, mountain lions, and wolves. At the time, this was considered effective park management. (Though this began with the Army, the National Park Service would continue it with equal or greater zeal when it took over management of Yellowstone.)

As more large predators were killed, elk numbers grew, and the worries shifted from too few elk to too many. Some people believed the increased herds had exceeded the land's carrying capacity. They feared the elk would overgraze the Lamar Valley and permanently damage the vegetation. (Scientists still question whether there really was any overgrazing.)

The claims of too many elk grew louder in years when dry summers—with poor grazing that led to inadequate fat stores— were followed by severe winters. When the snow cleared the following spring, large numbers of winter-killed elk lay scattered across the landscape.

After a public outcry, managers tried different things: winter feeding of hay to reduce die-off, and reducing elk numbers by trapping them and trucking them outside the park to places where overhunting had decimated local populations. But soon those areas were fully stocked, leaving nowhere to send the elk.

In a continued effort to reduce numbers, park rangers began shooting elk with rifles inside the park. They also killed bison and pronghorn in an attempt to control their numbers. In typical bureaucratese, this was called culling, an innocuous-sounding term that avoids saying what was really going on—rangers shooting park animals. It also glosses over the reasoning behind it: the rangers were killing elk because earlier rangers had killed predators because *they* had been killing elk. (It's worth noting how many recent management challenges—such as wolf restoration and non-native fish removal—are directed at correcting earlier management actions that were considered good ideas at the time.)

In the 1960s, Yellowstone rangers gunned down thousands of elk inside the park. They sometimes used helicopters to herd large groups toward sharpshooters, who unselectively took out as many as they could. When footage of the slaughter was aired on national news programs, a huge public outcry arose, and the park abruptly stopped elk culling in the late 1960s. (It's also worth noting how often advances in conservation begin with public outcries.) When the culling stopped, the northern elk herd—the one that winters in the valleys along the Lamar River and the Yellowstone River downstream—had been reduced to fewer than thirty-two hundred animals.

When the elk were no longer shot at inside the park, their numbers predictably increased. At that time, few of Yellowstone's natural predators were left to keep elk numbers in check. Yellowstone's last wolf pack had been gunned down in the 1920s, and grizzly bear numbers had fallen so low that the species was listed as threatened under the Endangered Species Act in 1975. In that largely predator-free environment, elk numbers blossomed. From fewer than thirty-two hundred in 1968, they increased to twelve thousand in the mid-70s, to nineteen thousand in 1994, the year before wolves were brought back.

Outside the park—where elk are seen as commodities that support the lucrative hunting and outfitting businesses—the growing numbers were welcome at first. But then more elk began migrating down to agricultural lands and eating hay intended for cattle. In response, Montana Fish, Wildlife & Parks raised elk limits in hunting districts north of the park. They also issued large numbers of antlerless tags, reasoning that the best way to reduce the population was by killing the elk that would give birth to more elk. Unfortunately, they would leave these aggressive population reductions in place long after wolves returned to the ecosystem.

As the morning sky fills with light, a haze of wildfire smoke tempers its brightness. The smoke has thickened since yesterday. While no plumes attest to any fires nearby, smears of dirty haze line the horizons, filling the air with the smell of burned wood. Over the course of the morning an easterly wind clears much of the smoke, replacing its hazy browns with dense grays from storm clouds.

I break camp and hit the trail at the leisurely time of one o'clock. The dirt path is marked with elk tracks that weren't here two days ago.

At the base of the hoodoos, I take time to linger again and walk along the rock columns, still filled with wonder. Though it's difficult to leave such a beautiful setting, my two days here—all that sitting and staring—have planted this place in my soul. When I go, it will go with me. In a sense, it belongs to me now, and I to it. For that I am richer.

Back at the familiar 3M6, there's no need to search for a tent site, and camp is soon made. Not too soon, it appears, as storm clouds continue to build. After a few light sprinkles, the sun makes a tentative appearance, and the sky overhead looks as likely to clear as to storm. Clark's nutcrackers call from the trees, the sound of high country.

When the next wave of storms crowd in, the temperature goes into freefall. This time the clouds remain, darkening the sky and bouncing thunder forth and back above the high basin. When the rain begins, falling in dense clatters on the tent, lightning flashes brighten the lowered sky, followed by long rolls of thunder. What will this do to the wildfires?

The rain trails off in early evening, and I venture across the meadow for a quick dinner. Though my food bag is far from empty, there's little in there I'm not already sick of. It's mostly the same tiresome fare I carried on the Sky Rim: instant oatmeal, multi-grain bars, and beef jerky. I can barely force myself to eat any more of that stuff. The energy bars, on the other hand, are still palatable, mainly because they are quick and easy to eat and packed with protein, carbs, and antioxidants. My favorite, though, is my homemade trail mix, a combination of toasted corn, rice, and wheat cereal and mixed nuts, low roasted with butter and olive oil and sprinkled with Cajun seasoning. Along with excellent flavor, it has nutrition, sodium, and fiber. It's the one thing among all the items on my backpacking menu that's good enough to eat at home.

Menu fatigue is a problem I've never faced before, having done no more than two long backpacking trips in one summer, and those so spread out that food variety wasn't an issue. It's an issue now, with four long treks, each separated by a week. And the next will be the longest, in both miles and duration. I may need to reconsider the food plan for that one.

The rain seems to have stopped for now, but the sky is tumultuous and thunder bounces across the peaks and ridges of the Hoodoo Basin. As lightning flashes illumine the cloud bottoms in brilliant white-blue, I re-hang the food and return to the tent.

Day 6. 3M6 to Miller Creek, Site 3M2

More rain fell overnight, and the damp air feels colder than its forty-four degrees. In the early light, elk calls ring out from several directions.

Trying to be silent, I slowly unzip the upper tent flap and peek out. A small elk herd grazes an adjacent meadow, visible through narrow gaps in the trees. Only cows are in sight at first, slowly grazing their way across the open ground. Then a young bull appears, his knobby antlers coated in velvet. He looks across at the tent for a moment, then returns to his grazing, stepping slowly ahead as the herd eases across the meadow and into the forest.

Elk seen from 3M6

After a quick breakfast, I am back on the trail under a low sky of roiling dark clouds. On the shoulder of Parker Peak the weather is not yet so ominous to dissuade a quick trip to the summit. It's only a few hundred feet of elevation gain and not especially steep.

Leaving the trail, I drift across the grassy shoulder to a patch of forest. Just beyond is the base of the peak. There is no path across the trickling meltwater, but a faint stretch of wildlife trail begins on the opposite side. It angles upward across the slope toward a grassy flank, which offers the best route to the summit.

A quarter-mile to the west, along the base of the slope, is another, larger, elk herd bedded down in the summer grass. Though my route travels in their general direction, I hope the climb will take me high enough above them so they don't spook. As I angle across the rocky slope, a young cow elk stands near a tree, watching intently as I climb higher above. Soon, more elk are on their feet, their bodies turned west and their heads to the side, looking in my direction. I try to hurry upslope to show I'm not stalking them, but on some signal, they all bolt.

It's a majestic scene, a herd of twenty or thirty elk galloping in a thunderous wave. A lone bull with huge antlers runs near the front. All the others appear to be cows and calves. Plenty of youngsters are mixed in, racing along as fast as the adults, leaping to clear logs and shrubs. A few hundred yards away they stop in a tight line, standing broadside again with heads turned in my direction. Pretending not to see them, I continue upslope.

Across the expanse of rocks, a golden-mantled ground squirrel darts from cover to cover before jumping atop a large stone. Its tail sticks straight up behind it. More movement nearby turns out to be a brownish-gray bird, likely an American pipit, though with such a brief glimpse it's impossible to be sure.

Upon reaching the high grass, it's an easy climb to the summit. Views abound in all directions, somewhat obscured by smoke and clouds. An arm of the peak extends to the southeast, where it holds an oval ring of stones stacked two feet high. It is likely an old Native American site, used either for hunting or vision quests. Though I'm no archaeologist, I prefer to think of it as a vision quest site. This would be a wonderful place to remain for a few days, until one came to know what was truly important.

Back at the base of the peak, a localized rain shower pocks the greenish-brown surface of the pond. It doesn't last. By the time I reach the main trail, the pond's smooth surface shows only the reflection of Parker Peak.

I set out, hiking the densely forested corridor that looks quite bear-y. Tired of talking to myself, and feeling anything but self-conscious after seeing so few people for days, I sing out a different selection from Mozart:

Don Giovaaaaanniiiiiii. A cenar teeeeeeecoooooo.

Okay, enough of that. Though the wrathful song of a vengeful statue should be good for keeping bears away, those sustained notes don't leave much breath for hiking.

Beyond the trees, dark clouds have moved closer and grown heavier, threatening to storm. Thunder rumbles over the valley of Miller Creek. Filtered through clouds, the sunlight casts a dull glow that enriches the greens of conifer and shrub, while fading the yellows of dry grasses. It's a scene of contrasts: sun and cloud; midday and twilight; spring and fall.

The hike reaches the forest of dead trees just as a howling wind rises. It's an intense, sustained blast that sets the skeletal snags all asway. With renewed pace, I hurry past.

Toward the end of the high ridge, the valley of Miller Creek appears far below. Before starting the long descent, I pause to consider whether it's better to push on and try to race the storm, or stop here for lunch and see if it passes.

The wind lulls, but only for a moment, as if to gather strength. Then it comes howling across the slope in blasting, buffeting gusts. After exhausting its power, the air calms. Taking the cue, I set out across the exposed slope and switchback down to the valley floor.

The ford of Miller Creek, which was clear five days ago, is now opaque, clouded from rain and runoff. Though my water bottles are nearly empty, so much silt could clog my filter. I decide to wait. Perhaps one of the side streams, flowing where there's more vegetation, will be running clear.

For lunch, I stop again at the ranger cabin, which is still vacant and locked. Soon I am back on the trail, under a low sky of slate gray. A long peal of thunder rattles up the valley, but the heaviest storms remain in the high country, one westward over Mirror

Plateau, the other south on the upper Lamar. Somehow, both appear to be moving in my direction.

When I'm halfway across an exposed low cliff above the creek, an intense electrical flash lights up the scene. *Woo!* As crashing thunder rattles the valley's walls, I break into a speed-hike to reach the forest beyond. Glad I'm not still up on the ridge. As the sky takes the appearance of dusk, I check the time: 3:39.

The first few raindrops, huge and splatty, fall widely spaced in both time and distance. The rainfall slowly crescendos, building to a drumming shower with a roar to match the thunder's claps and rumbles. In a dry spot between the base of the cliff and several Douglas firs, I stop to put on raingear once again. All this rain in the mountains, while back in the Gallatin Valley the summer has been so dry we've had to water the garden more than usual. Maybe I should rush home and backpack around the vegetables.

Though the shower doesn't last, it is intense enough to saturate the plants and turn the trail into goopy mud. Water, water everywhere, but not a drop in my bottles. Seeing a side channel flowing fast and clear on the far side of Miller Creek, I make a quick ford through the shallow, dirty water—my shoes are wet, anyway—and fill my bags.

Standing in a gentle drizzle as the water filters, I try to recall the last time I've seen another person. There was that couple overlooking the hoodoos on my first night at 3M7, though I barely saw them across the distance. Regardless, that was three days ago. Remote, indeed.

This will soon change, as I approach the mouth of Miller Creek and the Lamar River. Actually, it changes sooner than expected. At site 3M3 a large stock party is busy setting up camp, their horse herd milling about near the trail. As I pass, one of the riders waves a greeting across a span of a hundred yards. It's a high, long-distance wave, which I return in like fashion, almost like passing a torch—the end of my trip and the beginning of theirs.

In late afternoon, the sign for 3M2 appears, though there's no trace of any path to the campsite. Across a wide meadow of rough grass and sage, an orange marker is affixed to a tree. Heading toward it, I find a path in the dense forest beyond.

The route follows the creek for a good distance, headed upstream, before reaching a tight bend that circles the food area.

Across the water the land slopes upward, toward the flanks of Little Saddle and Hague Mountains. Burned in 1988, the slope is mostly bare, except for bleaching logs strewn about at all angles. As I stand watching the flow of the water, a belted kingfisher flies upstream, traveling a few feet above the creek.

It's a beautiful place for a food area, but what about tent sites in this heavy forest? A faint footpath leads farther upstream, and, thinking that is where the tent sites are, I follow it until it stops a very short distance away in a tiny clearing. It is much too close to the bear pole, and worse, the forest all around is full of huge standing dead trees, all leaning in one direction or another. Rectangles of flattened grass show where people have set up tents recently, but each site has at least one large snag leaning toward it. All it would take is a strong gust to send one of these giants crashing down, and this trip has seen more than its share of gusts.

Things are no better farther upstream, so I head back toward the main trail, looking for sites in the forest. Plenty of standing dead are out here, too, so I continue on, all the way to the edge of the grassy meadow. It doesn't offer much in the way of tent sites either, only lumpy terrain covered with tall, coarse grass. And all in plain sight of the trail.

But better conspicuous than crushed. Or sleepless. While there may be only an infinitesimal chance one of those trees will fall tonight, it's a virtual certainty that if I camp near one of them I won't get much sleep. How many falling trees have I heard over the past few weeks? Every *whish* of wind or creaking branch would jolt me awake, imagining splitting trunks and tearing roots.

It takes a lot of walking around in the tall grass to find the least lumpy spot, but soon the tent is up. I crawl inside to assess the comfort. It's not so great, but better than having a tree fall on you.

Back at the cooking area, I find a spot with the longest view of the winding creek to eat dinner. Down here near seven thousand feet, the temperatures are much milder than in the Hoodoo Basin. Though it's after seven o'clock, the air is warm enough to be comfortable in shorts and t-shirt.

Now that camp is made and I've figured out the lay of the land, I realize this is a wonderful campsite. Tents are only for sleeping, or perhaps hiding out from the rain, so it's the cooking area that matters. This one is wonderful. The nearby slope and tight bend of the creek make for an intimate setting, an idyllic spot in the Yellowstone backcountry. Two shorebirds fly close together above the watercourse, returning minutes later to fly back again. Soon afterward, another kingfisher comes clattering down. Or maybe it's the same one as before.

Some people might question why the Park Service doesn't come in here and cut down some of the dead trees to improve safety, but they can't, really. An important part of a national park's mission is to preserve nature. The policy is to leave wild places alone as much as possible. It's a good policy, and one I believe in. We take nature as we find it, on its own terms, without handrails or handholding. A wilderness that's altered to be safe is no longer a wilderness. It's not too much of an inconvenience to camp out in the meadow.

A few rumbles of thunder drift across from the east, reminding me to keep an eye on the sky because the tent is a looooong way off. As the air becomes sharply cooler, and the thunder closer and more frequent, it's time to call it a night.

When I get back to the tent, a large white-tailed buck is standing on the main trail, perhaps fifty yards away. After a few motionless seconds, it fades into the forest with no discernible motion beyond its disappearance. Somewhere high above, a nighthawk makes its raspy, crickety call, the sound of summer evenings. It is followed by the low booming noise male nighthawks make with their wings when they dive. It's the sound responsible for the bird's colloquial name: bullbat.

As I stand near the tent, watching and listening, the thunder grows more insistent. The sky is now fully dark, though it's too early for nightfall. I crawl inside as a heavy rain begins.

It's impossible to get comfortable on lumpy ground covered with bunchgrass. In this uneven terrain, no matter in which end of the tent I lay my head, it feels as though I'm lying downhill. Even so, it's nice to be in a dry tent in the wilderness during a rain storm. As the deluge intensifies, powerful winds buffet the low meadow and shake the tent. I wonder what they're doing to those dead trees in the forest.

Eventually, I drift to a restful sleep. At one-thirty I awaken, feeling quite cold in the damp tent. Time to cocoon myself in the sleeping bag. So much for mild weather down at seven thousand feet.

Day 7. 3M2 to Trail's End

More rain falls at dawn. I remain wrapped in the warmth of the sleeping bag for a while, until I get restless. It's difficult lying here knowing a hike of just twelve miles separates me from the trailhead and the drive home.

Outside, only a few clouds mark the sky, above the southern ridge and moving eastward. On the path to the food area the tall plants, burdened with rainfall, droop across the trail, saturating my shoes and socks. *Squish, squish, squish.* No worries. Clean, dry shoes are waiting in the car.

The creek has risen with the recent rains, and what was yesterday a cloudy, stagnating pool stranded in mud is now part of the flowing creek. Rapids ripple over the walls that once confined it. None of the dead trees fell overnight, but I don't regret my choice. There's no doubt I slept better than I would have back here.

After a quick breakfast I break camp, cramming all the wet gear into the backpack. (There's a tendency to pack more sloppily on the final day, just to get it all loaded and get out on the trail.) When everything is cinched up, I'm homeward bound.

The fresh mud of the trail holds no prints of human, horse, or other large mammal, though sections are variegated with tracks of birds and small animals. Where the route climbs a steep incline, what was once horse-churned dirt has turned to slick mud. Each upward step slides backward as quickly as made, causing me to remain in place despite pumping feet, like someone jogging up a down escalator set on overdrive. Breaking into a labored sprint, I finally top the climb.

On the Lamar River Trail are the first human footprints, more signs of approaching civilization. A mile or so later the tinkling of bear bells titters through the trees, and a large group of backpackers approaches. The teenage boy in front calls to those behind him, "Single backpacker ahead."

I step out of the trail to let the group pass.

"He's off to the right of the trail," the lead hiker declares.

When they reach me, the group, mostly young teenagers, pauses. A small, animated woman in her mid-fifties emerges from their midst.

"We're an adventure group from Missouri," she explains. "All the boys are Boy Scouts, but we also have girls, so we're called an adventure group instead of scouts."

I scan the line of exhausted young faces to the rear of the group, where two men in their late fifties look just as tired and miserable as the kids.

"We're headed to 3M1 tonight," the leader says. "Do you know how far it is?"

Do they not have a map? "It's about three more miles," I say. The kids appear crestfallen at the news.

"Where are you coming from?" the leader asks me.

"Coming back from the hoodoos," I say.

"We may do some of those hoodoos, ourselves," she says.

From the tortured expressions on the faces behind her, this seems unlikely. Now I'm certain they don't have a map.

"It's quite a haul to get there," I say, in a not-too-cautionary tone, "including a climb of more than two thousand feet."

"Well," the leader hesitates, "we may not do that, then. We may just hike down to the creek."

A few miles ahead are the first day hikers, a middle-aged couple, who are quite fit and farther in the backcountry than you'd expect day hikers to be. They offer brief greetings in passing but have no interest in stopping. Clearly not backcountry types.

At the approach to Cache Creek, the trail is blocked by a huge bull bison wallowing in the dust. As I stop a safe distance away, he stands and ambles up the trail in my direction. Not one to contest right-of-way with a bison, I detour off-route, skirting the edge of the forest to give a wide berth. The bison pauses to nibble a bunch of trailside grass, as though giving me time to get out of his way. When I've circled halfway around, he resumes course and moseys up the trail.

More bison are beyond Cache Creek, near the base of Mount Norris. It's a large herd in a widely spaced group that stretches far across the trail. Showing no intention of moving, they graze, rest, or stand around like bison do. The surrounding air has the color, smell, and taste of dust. As I make a long detour to bypass them, a lone bull stands at the edge of the herd, facing outward and watching my progress. He has a right to be wary of humans.

As their population continued to grow, bison began migrating out of the park in winter and spring to reach lower areas where less snow covered the ground vegetation. These low grazing areas are also favored by local ranchers, who harbor a strong dislike for wild bison—they eat grass that could go to domestic cattle, and they've been known to knock down fences.

Once bison leave the park, Yellowstone officials have no jurisdiction over what happens to them. Inside Yellowstone, bison are considered wildlife, but once they cross the line into Montana, they magically become livestock and are treated as a nuisance. In 1995, Montana filed a lawsuit against the Park Service over Yellowstone bison that crossed the park boundary and into the state. The suit was settled in 2000 with a court-mediated agreement that created the Interagency Bison Management Plan.

The IBMP set a target population on Yellowstone bison of three thousand, an arbitrary number with no basis in science. When it exceeded that number, the herd was to be reduced through hunting outside the park and through capturing bison near the boundary and shipping them to slaughter. (There is now a push to quarantine some bison to ensure they don't carry disease and then ship them to other areas.) Bison that weren't killed were hazed back into the park each spring, when newborn calves were still on shaky legs. They were sometimes chased for long distances by government employees on horses and ATVs and in helicopters. Not all of them made it.

The purported purpose of the IBMP is to reduce the risk of bison transmitting a disease known as brucellosis to domestic cattle. The disease, which can cause pregnant cows to abort their calves, is not native to the Yellowstone region. It was, ironically, introduced by domestic cattle brought by early settlers. Since its arrival in the Yellowstone region, brucellosis has been eradicated from the most of the rest of the country. But here it has spread to wild bison and elk, so there's no way to eradicate it from Yellowstone. It would require testing every wild elk and bison in the region and killing those that tested positive. As a precaution, cattle near Yellowstone are vaccinated for brucellosis.

Though the supposed basis for the IBMP is to protect cattle from brucellosis, there is no record of a wild bison ever transmitting brucellosis to domestic cattle. On the other hand, there have been multiple cases of domestic cows near Yellowstone getting the disease from elk. Yet no one is pushing for reducing elk numbers or keeping elk inside Yellowstone. This shows the bison controversy is not about brucellosis at all.

In 2015, Yellowstone and the other parties to the IBMP (the U.S. Forest Service; U.S. Department of Agriculture's Animal and Plant Health Inspection Service; Montana Department of Livestock; Montana Fish, Wildlife & Parks; and three Native American tribal organizations) began the long process of revising the fifteen-year-old plan. Since the original IBMP was written, much has been learned about bison and brucellosis, and the Yellowstone bison population has grown to between three thousand and five thousand animals, depending on how many are slaughtered in any given year. Also, the indiscriminate killing of bison to comply with an arbitrary population number has been unpopular with the public.

The new bison management plan is expected to be finished in late 2017, after two more rounds of public comments. As the Park Service has said, the real issue is a lack of tolerance for bison outside Yellowstone. This is true even though much of the fight is about bison being on public lands, not private property. (In 2015, the Montana governor proposed allowing more bison to remain on some public lands in the state, but this has not been finalized, and the governor's political opponents quickly voiced opposition.)

When the new bison management plan is released, it likely won't put an end to the bison controversy. It will always be open to criticism because the process has not been based upon science or equity, but on politics.

Past the bison and back on the trail, I head into the beautiful, expansive Lamar Valley. My footsteps scare up more swarms of grasshoppers, which scatter and fly in all directions. A sudden gust catches some of them and casts them backward, bouncing them off my arms, face, and chest.

The parking area is crowded, as before, but with more people than when I left. Many are just standing and staring across the valley. You can't fault them for this—in Yellowstone, staring at landscapes is a valid activity.

At my vehicle I shed my backpack and change my sweaty t-shirt for a clean one stashed in the back seat. I also change into clean shoes. In no time at all, I am on the road, headed home.

After a week of traveling by foot, driving forty-five miles per hour feels extremely fast. I look out the window, focusing on the sage and grass at the edge of the roadway. It all seems to be flying by.

The summer also seems to be flying by. After so much anticipation, two trips are already done and the third begins in a week. But the next one's to the Thorofare. It's the longest trip of the summer and the one I've looked forward to the most.

Trip Locator
(More detailed map on following pages)

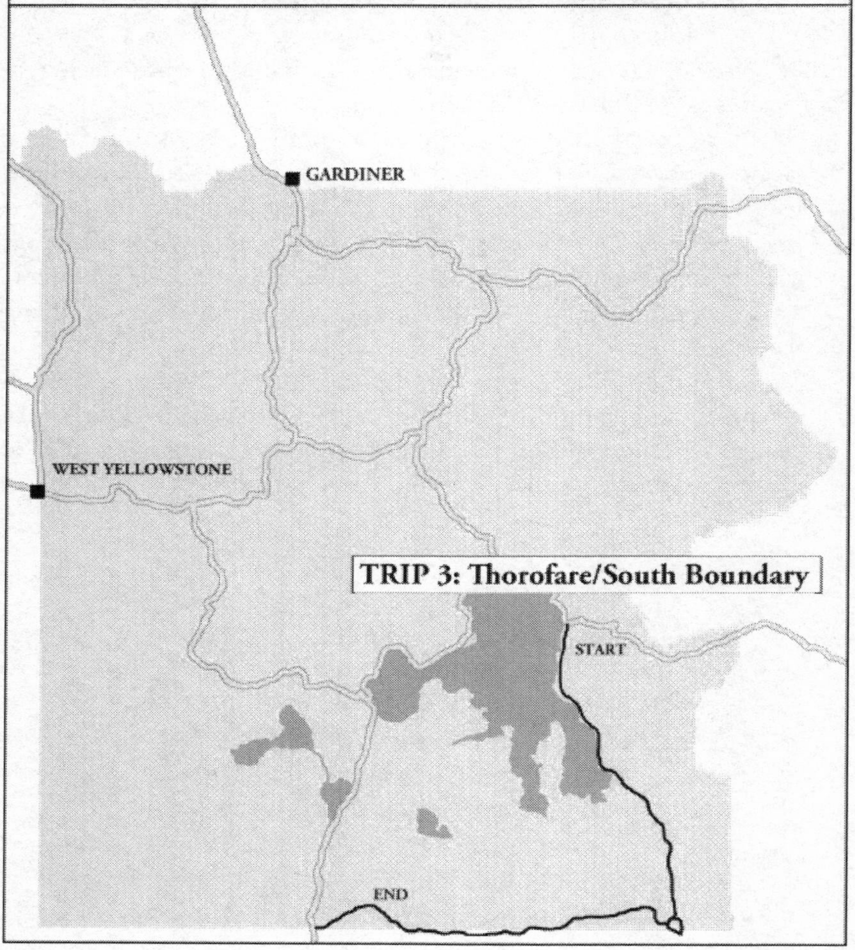

GARDINER

WEST YELLOWSTONE

TRIP 3: Thorofare/South Boundary

START

END

Trip 3
Thorofare—South Boundary
August 19-29, 2012

Trip Overview

- START: Nine Mile Trailhead on the East Entrance Road, east of Yellowstone Lake
- South through the Thorofare to the park's southern boundary
- West onto Two Ocean Plateau to Mariposa Lake
- West over Big Game Ridge
- END: Picnic area just north of the South Entrance Ranger Station

Duration: Eighty miles in eleven days.

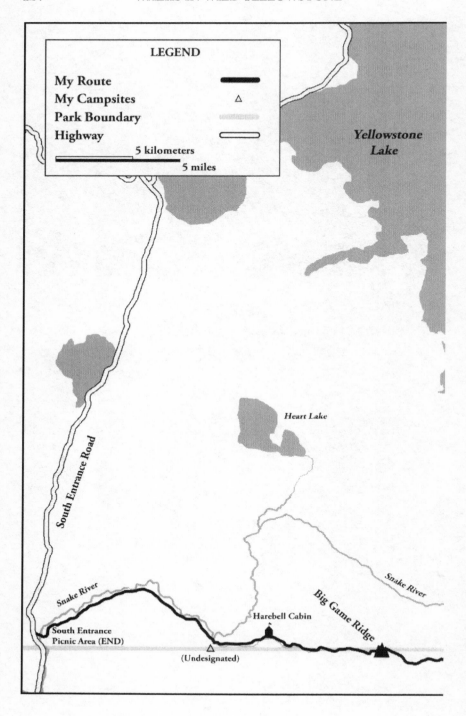

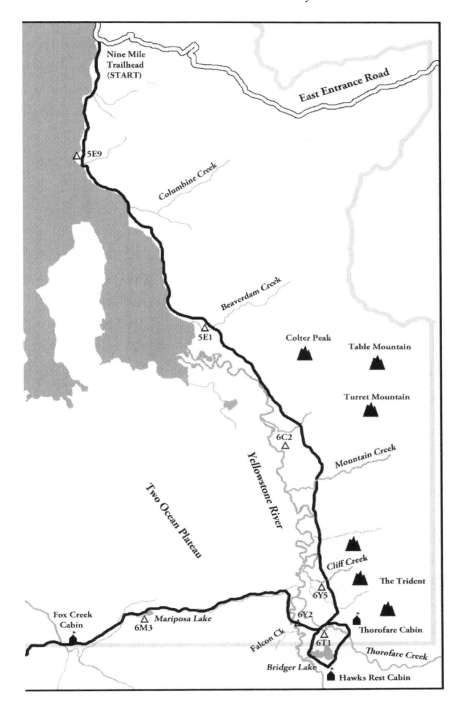

Preparation

As much as I've looked forward to all of the treks this summer, the Thorofare trip has always stood out. The Thorofare is deep wilderness, nearly thirty miles from the closest road. It's also near the headwaters of two iconic rivers: the Yellowstone, far above where it crashes over the Upper and Lower Falls, and the Snake, many miles upstream from where it slides past the park's south entrance. I imagine fording those rivers so near their headwaters will be like traveling back through time and meeting two heroes when they were children, not yet aware of the forces they would one day become.

The day before the hiking starts, Mari and I set out in two cars. We'll leave mine at trail's end at the park's south entrance, and Mari will drop me off at the starting point near the northeast shore of Yellowstone Lake. Because of the distances involved, we'll be staying in the park tonight, at one of the Lake Lodge cabins. To be certain of getting a room, I booked it in early April, just after receiving my campsite reservations.

For the long drive in, my musical selection is a homemade compilation I've titled Thoreau Music. It's a collection of get-away-from-it-all songs, such as Keb Mo's *City Boy*; James Taylor's *Country Road*; Guy Clark's *L.A. Freeway*; and John Denver's *Rocky Mountain High*.

At the backcountry office in West Yellowstone, a ranger who's a bit beyond retirement age is manning the desk. "It's a busy day for permits," he says. "For the whole park combined, we've already issued forty just today." While forty may not seem so large in relation to the size of the Yellowstone backcountry, it's in addition to all the permits issued in recent days for people already out on the trail. August is prime backpacking season.

I hand the ranger my reservation and he looks it over. "E's, Y's, and T's," he says, referring to the campsite designations. "Must be the Thorofare."

"It is," I say. "The Thorofare–South Boundary route."

"I always wanted to make that trip," he says. "But now I've gotten to the age where I'd have to hire somebody with a horse to take me."

When he hands me the freshly printed permit, I scan the comments for anything about dangerous fords or difficulties getting water. Next to site 6M3, the one at Mariposa Lake, is printed: "Strong map and compass skills recommended."

That's a new one. My map and compass skills are solid, but I wonder aloud why they felt the need for such a note at this campsite. The ranger hasn't heard anything about it. Together we conclude the site must be away from the trail, with no path to it, though that's not out of the ordinary in the Yellowstone backcountry.

A few miles past the park's west entrance is the first wildlife jam. Gaggles of cars fill the road's edges, disgorging hordes of tourists who rush toward the Madison River. I skirt a wide cluster of vehicles parked at all angles in and out of the roadway, many with doors left ajar. Beyond it, I check my rearview to see if Mari has made it through.

A car that recently pulled out in front of her now stops abruptly. The driver throws open his door and jumps out. As he takes a few hurried steps toward the crowd by the river, his car—which he forgot to shift into park—lurches forward and almost runs him over.

We make it to Lake Lodge without any other close calls, and though we are prepared for the worst in this peak season, the lodge is pleasantly uncrowded. The young woman working the desk has a nametag indicating she's from Louisiana.

"What part of Louisiana are you from?" Mari asks.

"A little town called Gonzales," she says. "It's between Baton Rouge and New Orleans, on the Mississippi River."

"Just a bit downstream," I say, referring to how the Yellowstone River, after flowing out of Yellowstone Lake—which is just outside the window here—eventually joins the Missouri River and, many miles later, the Mississippi.

After a brief pause, a smile creeps across the young woman's face. "Just a bit downstream," she affirms.

The cabins are set in rows behind the lodge. Ours is a wooden box that's a case study in the efficient use of limited space. A double bed is set in the room's center, within arm's reach of the water heater in the corner, and in the bathroom, the door clears the toilet by less than an inch. Still, we have no complaints. You don't come to Yellowstone to hang out in your room.

In late afternoon we head to the lodge, in hopes of finding portable food for a picnic on the lake. The cafeteria has a sign advertising boxed meals, but the selection is limited.

Despite being compatible in almost all other areas, Mari and I have differing philosophies when it comes to food. My culinary tastes are pretty much meat and potatoes, or cereal or trail mix, but Mari is a foodie, and she likes a little more variety. As a result, while I'm in the cafeteria just looking for something to eat, she's hoping for a nice dinner.

We peruse the bulletin board menu, which offers exactly one kind of boxed dinner: chicken marsala. Mari is happy with this, but I am leery. Whatever chicken marsala may be, it sounds too fancy for a last dinner before the start of a long backpacking trek. I wander across the cafeteria to see what else is available, ending up at a cooler full of prefabricated sandwiches. Mari appears, looking dejected.

"You should get the chicken marsala," she says. "You'll like it."

"What *is* chicken marsala?" I ask.

"Normally it's a lightly breaded chicken breast, sautéed in red wine sauce with mushrooms and onions. But this is just fried chicken strips with some tomato sauce on the side."

In a reversal of culinary outlooks, I'm now pleased with the menu while Mari is disappointed. But she is able to rise above it, and we get two chicken-fried marsalas and head for the lake. On the way there, we swing by the general store for a bottle of wine, always a good consolation for a disappointed foodie.

The lake's surface is calm and smooth, and we spread a blanket on the pebbly sand near the water's edge. Far across to the southeast is the inlet of the lake's southeast arm, framed by the Absaroka Mountains. That's where the Thorofare begins, over there along the base of those peaks. In just a few days . . .

At dusk, glowing pastels of purple, pink, and orange light the surrounding horizons. The hazy sky darkens as the sun sinks deeper behind Central Plateau. A bat appears low overhead, its flight both graceful and erratic. As the daylight dims further, more bats arrive, flitting about and frequently dipping to the water's surface for a drink.

In the murky darkness, a few stars twinkle through the smoky haze, but there's little chance of seeing the Milky Way reflected in Yellowstone Lake, as we had hoped. Still, we linger in the nearly full darkness, listening to the water lapping lightly against the stony shore. Later, we gather our things and head back to the lodge. Over the course of our meandering stroll, the smoke settles in the windless evening, revealing more stars. By the time we approach the lodge in the softened darkness, the Milky Way shines brightly over the lake, like a fluorescent plume from some cosmic geyser.

Not ready for the night to end, we return to the lodge and get two draft beers from a bar in the corner of the main room. These we take outside to the rustic front porch, where the many rows of chairs are all unoccupied, except for four used by two couples at either end of the long porch.

Toward the center, I move two rocking chairs together. They are of equal height, but one is heavier and wider than the other. It's a good his-and-hers selection for Mari and me.

Mari, her attention focused on the surroundings, promptly sits in the larger chair. I stand looking at the empty narrow seat and then at Mari. "You took the Papa Bear chair," I say. "This one's for Mama Bear."

She laughs and moves to the smaller chair, and we sit and rock in the ambience of a beautiful night that's cool but not cold. Another pleasant summer evening in Yellowstone.

Day 1. Lake Lodge Cabin to Park Point, Site 5E9

Though Mari and I check out of the cabin early, the housekeeping crew is already out. They fan out among the rows of buildings, each pulling a flat, two-wheeled cart loaded with cleaning supplies, fresh towels, and linens. At the front of the group is an eager young man, who runs down the drive, pulling his cart behind him like a rickshaw.

After a quick cafeteria breakfast, we drive south to drop off my car at the ending trailhead. Unable to find a sign for the trailhead parking, I stop at the entrance gate, tell the ranger my plans, and ask the best place to leave my car. She directs me to the picnic area just inside the park, near the Snake River.

"Just park there," she says, "but park in the back, so people wanting to picnic can get the nicer spots by the river."

From there, Mari drives me north again, turning east at Fishing Bridge to the starting trailhead past Yellowstone Lake. The only vehicle in the parking area is a plain white van, likely a rental. All of its doors are open and an array of camping gear is scattered in loose rows on the ground beside it.

"Looks like a prison van threw up," Mari says.

We park near the trailhead and I remove my pack from Mari's car. I remembered to weigh it this time, and was only slightly surprised when it topped sixty-five pounds. On a long trip in late August, with elevations ranging from near eight thousand to ten thousand feet, anything can happen, weather-wise. Still, only a small part of the added weight is from cold-weather gear. Most of it is food. Recalling how disgusted I was with the limited menu last trip, I changed things up and packed more variety for this one. More choices, but also more weight and bulk.

The hike begins in an old burned area, a mass of charred lodgepoles—many still standing—among an expanse of grass, wildflowers, and bleached logs. The landscape is alive, with chipmunks and juncos, and with grasshoppers that fly ahead in spreading, clattering waves of yellow and black. At a tiny stream crossing, a Columbia spotted frog sits half-submerged.

The trail is in good shape, wide and flat, with only occasional bits of fragmented rock breaking the surface. Several dead trees have recently fallen across the route, but a clear trail framed by freshly sawn log ends attests to the diligence of trail crews. Theirs is a hard job, cutting logs that lie blocking the trail, sometimes in precarious tangles, and moving the loose pieces out of the path. Too many hikers take their work for granted.

Farther along is a more recent burn, where the freshly charred trees are still glossy black. This was part of the Point Fire of 2011, just last year. Mari and I were in the park when it was burning. We stopped at a pullout on the lake's western shore and watched as, far across the expansive waters—at the place where I'm now standing—fires sent up curtains of dense, gray smoke.

It's fascinating to see the aftermath only a year later. Regrowth is already well underway, with tender shoots of grass and scattered patches of wildflowers rising from the blackened ground. Lupines, yarrow, and mountain dandelions, some of which have already flowered and gone to seed, add a beautiful contrast: lush green growth topped with bright blossoms, all set against glossy black trunks and ash-gray soil.

It's a living example of how nature is not static but ever changing. In this case fire was the agent of change, converting what was dense forest into a new meadow. The trees will likely return, eventually, but for a span of years until they grow tall enough to shade the ground, this will be a thriving meadow, its soil newly enriched by ashes of the former forest.

As a meadow, this land will provide food and habitat for large numbers of species. The change has already begun, evidenced by numerous butterflies and other insects working the blossoms of new flowers, feeding, pollinating, reproducing. Birds glide from tree to tree looking for insects in the charred wood. Near the trail ahead, a lone doe, a mule deer, grazes a patch of tender new growth. Wary, but unafraid, she lifts her head to watch me pass, then wanders deeper into the charred woods.

From just a short walk over recently burned ground, it's easy to see that, contrary to widely held views, fires don't destroy landscapes. They only change them. Though the trees are dead, the land is full of life. And nothing is wasted. The trees' charred remains will provide habitat and feeding grounds for many species, as the wood slowly decomposes to enrich the soil. It's a beautiful thing to see.

The first real water crossing is a ford of Clear Creek. It's wider than all the other fords of the summer—so far—but only knee deep and not flowing too swiftly. It makes for an easy crossing. In the center I stop and gaze upstream.

Until recently, this creek filled each spring season with Yellowstone cutthroat trout swimming up from the lake to spawning areas upstream. Hungry bears knew to come here then, as well as otters and osprey and other fish-eaters, all to draw sustenance from the masses of trout. This was all part of an old natural cycle in which biomass moved from the lake to the surrounding lands.

Unfortunately, it doesn't work that way anymore, all because of manipulation of the ecosystem by humans.

Back in pre-national-park days, many of Yellowstone's waters were devoid of fish. Early observers attributed this to heated and chemical runoff from hot springs, but then someone realized all the fishless waters were either remote lakes or upper sections of rivers, where high waterfalls acted as barriers that kept fish from swimming upstream. (It's important to keep in mind that devoid of fish doesn't mean devoid of life. Each of those waters was already its own functioning ecosystem.)

In 1889, acting park superintendent Captain F.A. Boutelle, himself an avid angler, began stocking popular sport fish in Yellowstone's lakes and streams. With the willing aid of the U.S. Fish Commission, he even stocked waters that already had native fish species. Worse, the species they added were mostly non-natives: brook and brown trout, Atlantic salmon, black bass, and several others. Fortunately, the salmon and bass didn't take, though most of the non-native trout did.

The numbers were considerable. In the first year alone they

added seventeen thousand brown trout and eight thousand brook trout. They also, ominously, put forty-five thousand lake trout into Shoshone and Lewis Lakes.

As so often happens when humans try to improve upon nature, things went awry. Rainbow trout stocked in the Gibbon River descended Gibbon Falls—waterfalls aren't an absolute barrier to fish migration, only to those swimming upstream—and colonized the Madison River. These were joined by introduced brook trout and brown trout that came down the Firehole.

At the time, the Madison already had a native trout species, the westslope cutthroat, which coexisted with whitefish and grayling. The hordes of foreign trout changed things almost overnight. While some of the new species only competed for food, others tended to eat the native fish. And the introduced rainbows, in addition to competing for food, mated with the native cutthroats, producing hybrid offspring that were less robust and didn't reproduce as well. As a result of all this, westslope cutthroats disappeared from the upper Madison.

In those days no one cared about native trout species as long as the fishing was good. (Some people still think this way). And in the early 1900s, the fishing was so good park managers turned Yellowstone into a hatchery. They gathered trout eggs from Yellowstone Lake and many of its tributaries, and sent them off to stock waters in distant parts of the United States and in Europe.

With such a significant drain on eggs, along with high fishing limits and increasing numbers of park visitors, the fishing ceased to be as good as it had been just a few years before. In reaction to the ensuing complaints, and in an act of incredible denial, park managers blamed decreased trout numbers on fish-eating birds. They overlooked, or ignored, that those birds had been part of this ecosystem for untold centuries.

In the 1920s, park employees boated out to nesting sites on the islands in Yellowstone Lake, where they crushed pelican eggs and killed baby pelicans. This was all in the name of wildlife management. The killing was stopped after a few years, not because managers saw the error of slaughtering the very wildlife the park was supposed to preserve, but because of the outcry that arose when the actions became public.

The park didn't get around to ending its hatchery and fish-stocking operations until the 1950s. But this didn't put a stop to all stocking. Some individuals, likely including a few park employees, and small groups, including some outfitters seeking a business edge, sometimes stocked fish in remote ponds for their own use or for their clients. Other non-natives were introduced by bait fishermen, who dumped minnow buckets in park waters at the end of the day. Largely because of this, bait fishing is no longer allowed in the park.

The most damaging case of private fish stocking likely occurred some time in the 1980s, when some idiot put lake trout, caught from the introduced populations in Lewis or Shoshone Lake, into Yellowstone Lake. Park managers didn't learn of the introduction until 1994, when an angler showed them a lake trout he had caught in Yellowstone Lake. It was a dark day for park biologists.

Lake trout are large predatory fish that feed on smaller fish, like young cutthroats. Park managers knew they would thrive in Yellowstone Lake, with an abundant food supply (the native cutthroats) and a lack of competition. Also, instead of swimming up shallow creeks to spawn, lake trout lay their eggs in deep water, where they are safe from predation by mammals and birds.

If the lake trout weren't challenging enough, cutthroats were also threatened by another non-native organism. This one, a parasite, turned up in Yellowstone Lake in 1998, likely brought in by private fishing boats. The parasite causes whirling disease in cutthroats (but not lake trout), by eating into their cartilage. The resulting deformities cause fish to swim in a whirling pattern, which is a twofold affliction—cutthroats unable to swim properly have a hard time catching food, and they are easy targets for predators, including lake trout.

Understandably, cutthroat numbers in Yellowstone Lake have plummeted since the 1990s. Here at Clear Creek, the Park Service has monitored the cutthroats swimming up to spawning areas each year since 1945. Though as many as seventy thousand spawned in this creek in 1978, by 2007 the number dropped to scarcely five hundred. Park scientists attribute the decline to a combination of factors, including lake trout, whirling disease, and the effects of a long-term drought in the late 1990s and early 2000s. The decline of cutthroats has rippled through the ecosystem, as native species that once fed on them have had to move on to other areas or find other sources of food.

Beyond Clear Creek, the trail travels parallel to the lakeshore, though a good distance inland. Through the stubble of charred trunks, the lake is visible under a span of clear sky.

A few miles farther, the trail crosses a brief stretch of unburned forest before it emerges into an area of more blackened trunks, both standing and on the ground. This exemplifies the mosaic pattern often left by wildfires, where monotonous expanses of trees are replaced with more varied terrain—forest with pockets of meadows and meadows with pockets of forest. All those edges are rich habitat for wildlife and birds, used both by meadow species and forest-dwellers.

Beyond the reach of the Point Fire, mature forest returns. No mosaic here, it is all older growth with only a few standing dead trees. In places the forest thins to parkland, with grasses of tans and browns. Along the edges young lodgepoles have sprouted, as the forest grows to fill open areas. It's a trend opposite the one in the burn. Nature is ever in flux, and species move to fill gaps in the ecosystem.

A sign marks the route to site 5E9, which sits on a grassy stretch along the shore of Yellowstone Lake. Another sign down near the water—a large orange diamond—marks the site for campers traveling by boat.

The view is across a broad expanse of Yellowstone Lake, which is ringed with hills. Some of these rise to high mountains, the Absarokas to the south and east, and Red Mountains across to the southwest. Due south are the Promontory and Two Ocean Plateau, not quite as lofty, though they appear mountainous from here. Across to the north is the tiny yellow line of Lake Hotel, and a short distance away, the hazy outline of Lake Lodge.

Overhead, the vast sky is clear of clouds but shrouded in a haze of wildfire smoke. The diffuse brown layer dims the sun's rays from soft warming gold to a faded bronze glare. The metallic light casts thin, gray shadows from the bases of trees.

At the bear pole I hang my sweaty shirt from a broken limb and open my pack to remove the food. For this long trip, all the food wouldn't fit into one bag, so it's divided between two for now. When they are suspended from the pole, I walk north along the shore of Yellowstone Lake.

As usual, it's easy to find the most commonly used tent site, a level piece of ground with flattened grass. Almost as usual, it's beneath a dead tree, in this case, one with a large crack down the trunk. I move on, walking across the meadow toward the lake. In a level spot I drop my pack in the tall grass. It's a decent place for a tent, though it's also home to a horde of grasshoppers. They fly and clatter about as I set up camp. One thuds repeatedly against my hip, hitting again and again in the same spot. I discover it has crawled up the inside of my pants and is now trying to launch itself. I turn it out and shoo it away.

When the tent is up, I look across to see a group of people lounging about in my food area. What the—? I head over to investigate. Noticing my approach, they hurriedly pull on backpacks and hike up the lakeshore. All but one, who remains in place.

When I reach the food area the others are fifty yards away. A lone man, of college-age, stands near my food pole staring into the forest. At my arrival he turns to offer a friendly greeting.

"We're with an adventure company from Texas," he explains, quickly adding he is just an employee. (Don't blame me; I just work here). "The two guys who run things are part of the group that just left."

Their campsite is 5E8, about a quarter-mile south, though that doesn't explain how they ended up in my food area. If the sign marking this site as 5E9 wasn't enough, my two food bags are hanging from the bear pole, and my wet trail shoes are sitting on a log under my drying shirt. What kind of adventure company are they? Adventures in finding the wrong campsite?

"I think we saw you at the trailhead," the young man says. "Was that your girlfriend?"

Oh, the group in the van. "It was," I say. "She didn't look too upset, did she?"

"Nah," he says. "The trail sure was dusty coming in," he adds, still watching the forest. "I was in back of the group and ended up breathing a lot of dust stirred up by the people in front. Since then, I've been coughing and sneezing and my eyes are watering." For all that, he seems in good spirits.

"We're headed to 5E3 tomorrow," he continues, referring to a site seven miles farther, also on the lake. "We have a layover day there to give people a chance to day hike as far as they can get toward the Thorofare. Then we'll take two days to hike back out."

At this point, another man emerges from the forest carrying a roll of toilet paper. Nice. I'm tempted to ask why he didn't do that near his own campsite, but I keep it civil. (The guy just works here.) Their business done, as it were, they hurry off to rejoin their adventure group.

A tour boat speeds across the water two hundred yards from shore, a double-decker with throngs of orange life preservers on top and bottom. This is to be expected on this part of the lake. Tomorrow's hike will take me along the lake's southeast arm, where only hand-propelled craft are permitted.

The boat diminishes as it speeds away, and its growling motor fades in the distance. Silence returns. Two gray jays glide along the forest edge. Still wild and uncorrupted by human feeding, they don't even pause to look at my gear, moving quickly along and scanning the ground and trees for natural forage.

Though I'd hoped the biting flies would have diminished by this time of year, enough remain to get one's attention. They're not as pestilent as the swarm back at Sportsman Lake, but they still encourage long sleeves and DEET.

To the south, the adventure group has gotten their tents set up. One man has stripped to his shorts and waded into the lake for a bath. Not far away, another is fishing. Another boat motors across, cruising quite slowly a hundred yards from shore. Three trolling rods pull lines in the water behind it.

Opposite my campsite, the boat turns and trudges toward shore. It gets a strike on one of it trolling lines, and the driver kills the engine and scrambles back to help an angler land a fish. Clearly a guide. Having found success, they leave the motor off and drift-fish less than a hundred yards from my camp. When their drift carries them farther from shore, the guide fires up the trolling motor and putters back in. They spend the next two hours drifting back and motoring forth in front of my camp. They are the only boat visible on the vast watery expanse. Are there no fish anywhere else?

I put my binoculars on the group, a family of four with a guide. The parents recline idly on cushions while the guide rushes back and forth, piloting the boat and helping the kids with fishing lines. The kids' voices carry across the water, alternating shouts and whines. I might as well be camped at Bridge Bay. At five o'clock the motor fires up in earnest and the group heads toward the marina.

As evening settles, more clouds fill the smoky sky, turning the mountains into gray smudges. Two gulls fly above the water a short distance away.

In the new-settled peace, I take a walk along the lakeshore, looking at rocks smoothed by water and time. The smoke makes for a fiery, peach sunset, an otherworldly glow in a slate-colored sky. Though the smoke and clouds will surely hide the stars tonight, in return we have this living, changing sunset, all aglow with pulses of coral, orange, and violet. It's a fair trade.

In the evening coolness the wind rises to send waves splashing on the rocky shore. The airy gusts and watery crashes raise a chorus of sighs. As the light fades, I return to the tent and sit in the grass staring across the lake. The wind subsides, and the gentled waves take on the sound of a trickling mountain stream, only more rhythmic.

The colors deepen as the sunglow fades, absorbed in the blackness of the smoky horizon. I look overhead for more bats like the ones Mari and I saw on the opposite shore, but there are none. A deep darkness settles under the starless sky, and as the nighttime chill thickens, I climb into the tent.

Some part of the day's diet has set my stomach all agrumble. It must have been breakfast at the lodge, I conclude. Everything else has been my usual backpacking fare. Whatever the cause, over the course of the night, the tent takes on the smell of a thermal feature.

Day 2. 5E9 to Beaverdam Creek, Site 5E1

Emerging from the tent in the early light, I am struck by the appearance of Yellowstone Lake. Not yet fully awake, I've come outside unsuspecting and unprepared for the sight of this expanse of calm water in the morning's soft glow. The view suspends all movement and touches the soul.

Soon the boats are out. One drones across just before 8:30 and stops near the adventurers' camp. As it drifts in my direction I recognize it's the boat from yesterday, with the same guide. The clients are different, of course, and differently dressed, heavily bundled against the morning chill on open water. Clearly, the guide considers this her spot, even though it's quite close to two backcountry campsites. But what's a little rudeness when paying clients expect to catch fish? I'm glad to be moving on, toward the remote, wild expanse of the Thorofare.

The folks at the adventure camp are also packing up. We'll likely see each other on the trail at least once today. More, if we end up leapfrogging each other, as often happens when two parties walk the same route. As I tighten the straps on my pack, the fishing boat's motor roars to life and the group speeds toward the marina. Leaving this early, perhaps the guide can work in three or four groups of clients per day. I'm not hanging around to find out.

The adventure group heads for the trail at the same time I do, so I stop to let them get ahead. Scanning southward across the lake, I notice a boat with a strange profile. Large and boxy, it looks like a commercial fishing boat, perhaps one brought in to trap lake trout.

In another of Yellowstone's growing success stories, the park has undertaken a colossal effort to keep lake trout in check and protect the native cutthroats. Boats pulling large gill nets now work

Yellowstone Lake, snagging lake trout. The fish they catch are killed and dumped back in the water to keep their biomass in the ecosystem.

The program began in 1998, and in its early stages the boats caught ten to fifteen thousand lake trout per year. Even those numbers didn't make much of a difference. So, beginning in 2011, Yellowstone ramped up the efforts substantially, catching three hundred thousand lake trout each year.

For such a large undertaking, the park contracts with a private company, one with experience catching lake trout in the Great Lakes. They use five boats and miles of nets, working all season when the lake isn't frozen. Paralleling this, park researchers are looking at how best to combat lake trout. They've found ways to track them to spawning areas, where they use electricity to kill eggs and live traps to catch hatchlings. The total cost of the netting and research is two million dollars per year. Half comes from the Park Service's budget, the other half from fundraising efforts of the Yellowstone Park Foundation.

All the work and expense are paying off in Yellowstone Lake. Between 2012 and 2015, lake trout numbers declined and cutthroats began to rebound. With current technologies, no one expects lake trout to ever be eliminated from the lake, but the current efforts, while expensive, have allowed the cutthroat population to recover. This benefits not only the cutthroats but also the many native species that prey on them.

At the first meadow the adventure group appears only two hundred yards ahead, strung out in a long line trailing clouds of dust. I pause for a sip of water and decide to use the time to change into shorts and t-shirt in anticipation of a warming day.

Moving south, the route alternates between forest and sagebrush grassland along the shore of Yellowstone Lake. In the trail dust, a few scattered elk tracks are hidden among all the adventurers' shoeprints. At a high open area, I detour toward the lake for an unobstructed view. Not far to the south is the Promontory, the high-ridged peninsula that separates the lake's two southern arms. (Somehow, Yellowstone Lake is a body with three arms and one giant thumb.)

The route continues south through open forest. A dense patch of wild raspberry bushes lines the path, all loaded with full, ripe berries. With so many in one place, I don't feel so guilty about sampling a few, leaving the bulk for wildlife. Just ahead is another patch, even more heavily loaded than the first. I sample a few of these, too. The combination of intense natural sweetness and soft, fruity texture is hard to resist after eating only backpacking food.

Hiking onward, I find a few tiny seeds have gotten stuck in my teeth. Working them loose with my tongue as I walk, I send them flying to either side of the trail. Perhaps some will sprout new raspberry bushes, in affirmation of the age-old relationship between animals and fruiting plants, in which food is exchanged for seed dispersal.

A tiny junco flushes from the trail and flies an erratic arc to a nearby shrub, never rising more than a few feet. Its size and clumsy flight suggest it is newly fledged. A larger junco, likely its mother, repeatedly calls after it from the branches of another shrub. I hurry onward to leave them in peace.

Site 5E6 straddles the trail, its tent sites in the forest and its cooking area down near the lakeshore. Lounging about on the logs at the cooking area is the adventure group, taking a break. Seizing the chance to get past them, I pick up my pace.

Now the soft dust of the trail holds no trace of human passage, only animal prints. The first are of wolves, huge tracks heading to the Thorofare. The largest is almost as wide as my size-thirteen hiking shoe. It's a thrilling sight.

In a dry creek bed, an old washed-out bridge lies sprawled across the gravelly bank like a long-abandoned raft. Barely visible under an old bleached log is an orange sign with the word DETOUR written in black magic marker and a hand-drawn arrow pointing to the right. Beyond it is a shallow crossing of Columbine Creek.

Somewhere near here—out on the southeast arm of the lake—is the line where watercraft are restricted to five miles per hour. You can charter a boat ride from the Bridge Bay marina to drop you off there, if you want to cut out some hiking. While it's not a huge difference, cutting only nine miles, for hikers with limited time, it can be a good head start.

Huge bear prints now mark the sandy trail. At first sight of the large, rounded impressions, my distracted mind, lulled by hiking into blissful complacency, grasps for a familiar category in which to put them. For a brief fraction of a thought, they seem the distorted prints of a barefoot human. But that can't be right—they're cartoonishly exaggerated, tracks that could only be made by the likes of Fred Flintstone. My mind back in the moment, I realize they are bear tracks, and large ones. Fortunately, they are headed north, meaning the bear that made them is already behind me. More alert, I continue on, breaking into soliloquy whenever visibility is even partially limited.

Now the trail holds an assortment of wild tracks—a large bear headed in one direction and wolves in the other. It's an exhilarating sight, these partial stories written in trail dust on a path traveled by more bears and wolves than humans. At least in the past few days. In another mile is the place where the bear came out of the forest to begin travel by trail. Now only wolf tracks remain, still headed toward the wide valley of the Thorofare.

A bit farther is a sign marking the spur route to 5E4. The time is right for a lunch break and a water run, so I take the detour, thinking the adventure group won't stop again so soon. Descending the narrow path through dense forest, I try to look ahead and see if anyone is at the campsite, perhaps on a layover day. It would be rude to crash someone's camp. It turns out to be unoccupied and a bit farther from the trail than I'd thought. A quarter-mile south on the lakeshore, two people sit next to a canoe.

I drop my pack on the loose rocks and set about filtering water. As I rummage in my food bag for an energy bar, a rustling arises from the forest behind me. I reach for my bear spray but quickly let it go when the adventure group appears through the trees.

"Do you mind if we stop here?" one of the leaders asks.

"Not at all," I say. "It's not my site."

"Are you sure you don't mind?" he asks, being friendly.

Appreciating the consideration, I say I'm sure. As the two leaders introduce themselves, the party spreads out along the shore. In addition to the leaders are six clients and one employee, the young guy I met yesterday. He is apparently the lone go-fer. As everyone else lounges on the shore, he hands out food and restocks the group's water.

"Who wants seconds?" he calls, once the water bag is full. A few hands go up. Three people stand and begin a rock-skipping contest on the lake's smooth surface.

I wish them all a good trip and head for the trail. Back on the main route is a forested corridor, where tall, dense shrubs on either side overhang the trail. Not only is visibility restricted to a wall of branches several feet thick, the dirt holds tracks of at least one bear, this one traveling in the same direction I am.

"Look out in here," I say loudly before plunging through the brush. "Don't want to surprise mama griz."

The passage is uneventful. The forest ends at another stretch of grassy sagebrush, where a dark hump in the brush sixty yards away makes me stop and glass the area. It's a large boulder. On a stretch of sand near the lake's southern end is another beached canoe, two people sitting beside it. Two other canoes glide into view on the southeast arm, headed across to the west.

Approaching the south end of Yellowstone Lake

I reach the sign for 5E1 at 4:30. Though the map puts the site east of the trail, the sign's arrow points west. I take the sign's word for it and follow a path that leads to the cooking area. It sits at the edge of a bench overlooking Beaverdam Creek. Stretched far to the south and west is a flat expanse of willows and marsh. Somewhere out there is the upper Yellowstone River, flowing north to the lake.

The trees—both those behind camp and the ones along the base of the bench—are alive with bird activity. A Clark's nutcracker flies out of the upper forest on its way to the creek. When it descends past the edge of the rocky terrace, it appears to be flying two feet above the ground, but it is beyond the bench and flying at the lower treetop level. A few minutes later it returns to perch on my bear pole and survey my gear.

"Sorry, Clark," I say aloud. "Nothing for you here."

The sky has turned overcast, a mix of smoke and clouds backlit by the fiery glow of the afternoon sun. A whipping wind conjures loose cyclones of ash from the fire ring and sends them flying toward the Thorofare. I cast my rope over the pole and hoist the food before setting out to restock the water.

Two routes lead down to Beaverdam Creek: either walk three hundred yards back to the main trail and follow it down, or descend a narrow, rocky path near the food area and cross the bouldered floodplain. The trail route seems best at the moment. Though a longer trip, it won't involve carrying full water bags up a steep and rocky slope.

At the creek, I get as much as my two water bags will hold, slightly more than two gallons. With tomorrow being the first layover day of the trip, I'll need all of it.

More rumbles of thunder to the north, perhaps over Yellowstone Lake. Time to head back and make camp.

The area near the food pole shows several rectangular flat spots where people have put tents. Not very smart. Even if they kept an impeccably clean site, the fire ring is right here, and previous campers may have dumped leftovers into the ashes, which could attract bears. Perhaps, being such a large group, they expected their numbers to frightened bears away. Maybe. But traveling solo, I need to take better precautions.

Beyond the food area the forest is dense, with no chance of a comfortable tent site. The only other option is back toward the trail, where, about a hundred yards from the bear pole, is a passable spot.

It's right on the path into camp, but no one else should be coming in while I'm here.

Camp is made long before sunset, leaving time for a leisurely dinner. Unlike the limited options on earlier trips, the food bag now holds more variety. How this came about was less than scientific. It involved going to a large grocery store, lingering on any aisle that had instant food, on-the-go snacks, or "just add hot water" meals, and grabbing one or two or six of whatever looked worth a try. The result was a mix of toaster pastries, packets of chicken soup, Styrofoam cups of macaroni and cheese, oatmeal cream pies, and a variety of sandwich crackers, all in addition to my standard energy bars and homemade trail mix. It's the most varied food assortment I've taken backpacking, and the largest amount.

Sitting against a log to screen my stove from wind, I boil water for instant macaroni and cheese. It turns out a lot like the boxed stuff I used to eat in the impecunious years after college, but it's passable for camp food. With a second course of cheese crackers, and an oatmeal pie for dessert, it's pure backcountry decadence.

By evening the wind subsides into mild gusts that don't linger. As the air cools, I put on long pants, fleece top, and wool cap and sit against a tree with my empty pack as a backrest. As the light fades, I watch over Beaverdam Creek and the marsh beyond in hopes of seeing a moose among the willows. By nine, the sky is almost fully dark, a nightfall assisted by smoke and dense clouds. In the absence of wind, the sound of flowing water rises through the still night air.

I linger in the deepening twilight, looking over the willows below. Down the ridge, a great horned owl is perched atop a gnarled snag, a dark silhouette against an indigo sky. Its head swivels smoothly as it scans for prey. While I stand transfixed watching the owl, a bat flies out of the trees and toward the creek.

Back in the tent, I lie listening to the sounds of the wilderness. In the dense darkness under a starless sky, the night has a kind of thickness that's almost palpable. The pulsing hoots of the owl push slowly through the air, like sound traveling through water.

Hours later, I'm awakened by the rustle of something walking through the nearby brush. When I shift to get a better listen, it bolts into the forest. Probably a deer, I tell myself, recalling today's trail filled with bear prints.

Day 3. Layover Day at Beaverdam Creek

At dawn, sandhill cranes raise a cacophony of chortles from the marsh, rousing me out to see the new day. A scan of the wide expanse finds nothing but willows. A broader sweep picks up no movement at all, neither mammal nor bird, except a single red squirrel high in a treetop, nipping off cones and letting them fall. The distant hoots of an owl flow softly across the valley.

The temperature hovers at thirty-eight degrees, a chill that will hold till the sun breaks the horizon. Though it's still summer, the equinox is only a month away, and things change quickly at northern latitudes. Shorter days and cooler nights are already upon us, with their thin, dry chills that feel so unlike the thick coolness of midsummer mornings.

Comfort is in clothing layers: three on top, two on bottom, with heavy wool socks, hat, and gloves. The finishing touch is one that warms from the inside—a cup of hot coffee. It's a homemade concoction of instant coffee and sugar, with a liberal addition of instant cappuccino to serve as an amped-up creamer. I think of it as a revised take on a shot in the dark, modified for backcountry mornings—a shot in the light.

The sun appears just after seven. As good fortune would have it, it clears the distant ridge at a small cleft, the lowest spot on the mountain horizon. In the early amber light, the day warms quickly.

Far to the west, a sliver of Yellowstone Lake shines in the early sun. Two crossing canoes glint intermittently. In the middle-distance out over the willows, a golden eagle soars in a clear sky. Closer to camp, a northern harrier clutches the pinnacle of a conifer. It dives in a graceful sweep, gliding low above the tops of the willows.

Before long, the temperature has risen to forty-five. Though I had planned on this first layover day for an off-trail hike up Beaverdam Creek, after carrying a heavy pack over seventeen miles in two days, I feel more inclined to stay in camp. Perhaps the time will be better spent watching for wildlife and absorbing the wild spirit of Yellowstone.

A chorus of coyotes rises in yips and howls from the southeast. A few others join in closer to camp. I walk along the high bench to look for the howlers, but they remain hidden.

Back at the food area, I sit overlooking the marsh. It's a wonderful view. There's no need to hike anywhere today. In the days to come, when I'm stuck back in town, what wouldn't I give to be right back here, with a full day to soak it all in? Time to just be, in the wild backcountry of Yellowstone.

The climbing sun lifts temperatures with it, enough to warrant a change into lighter pants and t-shirt. Afterward, I sit in a shady spot near the base of the bear pole and do a bit of reading, frequently glancing up to scan the terrain.

As ironic as it seems, reading can be an effective way to spot wildlife (in addition to its other merits). Over years of camping and backpacking, I've found many sightings have come when I've been focused on other things, like reading. It's as though the animals sense when we're actively looking for them and when we're not, and they move about, or don't, accordingly.

After becoming engrossed in a book, I glance up. Having gone so deep in the reading, the mental shift is stirring. It's as though I'm seeing Yellowstone again for the first time. The sensation is almost mystical, like seeing everything anew and falling in love with Yellowstone all over again. I sit and stare and wonder.

A flock of twenty white pelicans flies up from the marsh, skirting the camp to the east and headed for the lake. They are beautiful birds, pristine white with a line of jet-black on the trailing edge of their wings. Though one of the largest birds in North America, their flight is improbably graceful.

Their appearance calls to mind the park's discontinued old policy of killing pelicans and their eggs in a misguided attempt to improve fishing for visitors. Though crushing bird eggs is unthinkable today, there are still those who want the ecosystem to be managed for the perceived benefit of humans. A common example is the mistaken policy pushed by many in the hunting industry, who want Yellowstone and its surrounding lands to be managed to increase elk numbers. They would achieve this by reducing natural predators, mainly grizzlies and wolves, in a repetition of the old battles about too few elk versus too many.

In response to criticism over Yellowstone's elk culling, in 1962 the Interior Secretary brought in a group of scientists and wildlife managers for an independent study on management practices. Leading the group was Starker Leopold, ecology professor and oldest son of iconic conservationist Aldo Leopold, author of the excellent and classic *Sand County Almanac*. Though the committee's report was officially titled *Wildlife Management in the National Parks*, it is more widely known as the Leopold Report.

What the Leopold Report recommended was nothing less than a complete overhaul of management practices in national parks. Decisions should be based on science, it said, with a focus on the ecological relationships and natural processes that formed the various ecosystems, before things were drastically altered by settlers and early park managers.

The goal should be to maintain natural relationships (such as between predators and prey) and natural processes (such as wildfires), and to restore those that had been lost or degraded, whenever feasible. The committee recognized this would not always be possible. Too much has been changed and too much lost. But, they noted, "if the goal cannot be fully achieved it can be approached."

The committee envisioned national parks as a "vignette of primitive America," and hoped to restore their original nature. Later scientists realized this was not quite the best approach. It was based on the mistaken belief that nature tends toward a stable equilibrium, what is called the balance of nature. But ecosystems are not static, and they don't maintain steady populations.

By their very nature, ecosystems fluctuate. Sometimes this is because of relationships (herbivore numbers decrease when drought stunts grasses), and sometimes it's due to random events (such as wildfires or harsh winters). Instead of a balance of nature, what occurs is a dynamic equilibrium, with nearly constant fluctuations. These are caused by large numbers of factors, many of which fluctuate, themselves: vegetation growth patterns, competition between species, predation, diseases, the effects of weather, and the many human-caused changes (habitat loss to development and road building, the blocking of historic migration routes, climate change, pollution, and hunting), to name only a few.

In response to the Leopold Report, national park policy shifted to what was known as natural regulation. This tended to be a hands-off policy at first, but managers soon realized that doesn't always work in ecosystems altered by humans. When you stop the alterations, ecosystems don't restore themselves to pre-altered states (as expected by the old balance-of-nature view). Extirpated species don't return on their own—unless a nearby population has an unblocked travel route—and established exotic species, such as lake trout, won't simply go away.

Now the goal is to leave the ecosystem alone as much as possible, while taking action—sometimes drastic action—when necessary to counteract human-caused changes. A successful example of such drastic action is the ongoing effort to keep lake trout in check.

To differentiate the new approach from the old one of natural regulation (with its connotations of hands-off methods), the new policy is known as ecological process management. It's a clumsy name, implying humans are managing ecological processes, when the opposite is more accurate. But it signifies it's the natural processes that are most important.

Whatever it's called, it is the best policy we've had so far, though it's still subject to political interference. We're seeing this in the current battles over bison and the push to enforce artificial population numbers dictated by cattle ranchers and their allies. There are still important lessons to learn.

In midafternoon, a clunking, clacking, clattering ruckus rises east of camp, back where the trail descends to Beaverdam Creek. Occasional human voices ring out above it, unintelligible in the distance.

Moments later, a long train of horse riders and pack animals appears beyond the creek, a quarter-mile away. Dust clouds rise from the many hooves and hang in the air for those behind them to breathe. Through binoculars I watch the riders, many staring at phones held in front of them, as they disappear in a high bank of willows, headed into the Thorofare.

In late afternoon I go for more water, to ensure there's a traveling supply for tomorrow's hike so I won't have to stop on the way out. This time I descend the steep path from camp. Though the route is shorter, it still involves a long walk across the rocky floodplain to reach the creek. The tricky part is climbing back up, walking a steep trail of loose rocks while carrying a load of water.

As the sun settles on Two Ocean Plateau, an evening breeze drifts coolly across the marsh. Where did the day go? Nothing is left but a vague sense of the passage of time, a feeling of having done not much of anything, and the certainty it was a good day, well spent in the wild Yellowstone backcountry. Underlying it all is a subtle feeling of having grown in some indefinable way, of being enriched by the experience. It's hard to imagine a better day.

Daylight fades into smoky twilight as the sun sinks behind the high plateau. Above it, a waxing crescent moon glows pale and yellow through murky clouds. I head for the tent to change into warmer clothes. While I'm inside, a man's voice calls out, quite close to the tent.

"Hello."

Surprised, I scramble out to meet an older man with a large backpack.

"I took a tumble going down to get water," he says. "I think I tore a groin muscle."

"Are you alright?" I ask. Though I have no experience with torn groin muscles, it sounds painful. But he's up and walking and carrying a pack, with no sign of significant pain.

"I think so," he says, "but I'm going to need to cut my trip short. Do you mind if I use your bear pole to hang my food tonight? I'll go back out and camp by the trail."

"Not at all," I say. "You can camp here, if you want."

As we walk toward the food area, I ask where he was headed.

"Down to the Thorofare Cabin," he says. "It was a late-season decision to make this trip, so I didn't have a reservation. And this is a busy year, so it was hard to get good campsites. The ones I could get were all spaced out, making for long hiking days."

To bypass the first nine miles, he chartered a boat out of Bridge Bay to drop him off at Columbine Creek, about eight miles north of here.

"How much do they charge for that?" I ask.

"It's pretty expensive," he says. "Around two hundred dollars."

Even with the boat ride, it would've been a long hike to his first campsite at 6B2, three miles farther south and on the far side of the Yellowstone River, a considerable ford even in daylight. That's a monster first day for an older guy carrying a huge backpack. And he doesn't appear to be in the best of shape.

Though I hate to doubt someone claiming injury, I can't help but wonder if he finally realized his plans were too ambitious. We've all done it, overestimating our capabilities, especially as we get older. But in his case, because of the boat shuttle and the distance he's already hiked, he is nearly seventeen miles from the nearest trailhead. Still, it's better to turn back now than go deeper and really get in a bind.

"I met a couple with a canoe back at Columbine Creek," he says. "They are planning on leaving in three days. I'm going to try to get back there by then and see if I can go out with them."

At the bear pole, he ties a thick climbing rope to his bulging food bag. "Do you need any food?" he asks. "I've got a full load I don't need."

"No, thanks" I say. "I'm at the start of my trip and still have about all I can carry."

He tosses the rope over the pole and raises the bag, securing it to a tree.

"You're welcome to camp here," I say again.

"No," he says, "I'll go camp out by the trail. I saw a good spot out there."

He disappears down the path, walking normally, apparently. If he's really hurt, will he be able to walk all the way back to Columbine Creek? And even if he finds that couple, will their canoe be large enough to carry another person with a heavy pack? What a mess.

Day 4. 5E1 to the Yellowstone River, Site 6C2

In the early light, a red squirrel works the treetops, chattering and dropping cones that fall to the ground with a thud. The coyotes resume their morning chorus.

Before long, my neighbor returns for his food bag. He appears to walk without pain.

"Feeling any better?" I ask.

"It only hurts when I have to step over something," he says. "Part of getting old."

"I know what you mean," I say.

"I'm still going to turn back," he says. "I'll try and make eight miles today, back to the drop-off point at Columbine Creek, and wait for that couple."

I wish him luck as he heads toward the trail. Part of getting old, he says. I remember thinking he looked older at first, but on second thought, he is probably only around fifty—close to my age. This is another part of getting old: overestimating the age of our peers. I suppose the thinking goes something like, "He looks old; I'm not old, so he must be way older."

From the marsh along Beaverdam Creek, a large wading bird rises, squawking frantically. My first thought is sandhill crane, but the slate-gray plumage indicates a great blue heron. Wondering what frightened it, I watch the marsh but see no movement.

Time to get on the trail. Today should be a good travel day, mostly sunny with no wind to speak of, and a hike of less than eight miles to site 6C2.

The ford of Beaverdam Creek is calf-deep and flowing rapidly, but still an easy crossing. Beyond it, the trail travels a wide corridor between walls of dense willows. The path is covered with loose dust, which stirs easily and rises in a brown haze. If I meet a stock party in this, my plan is to move as far to one side as the terrain permits, to avoid being gagged.

The butterflies are different from those on earlier trips. Most are gray comma butterflies, of mottled orange to match the smoky sunsets. With erratically indented wing edges, they resemble tattered monarchs in flight. But their undersides are drab, dappled gray, to blend with soil, rocks, and faded bark. After landing and folding their wings together, they seem to disappear into the background. But when approached, they quickly lift and flutter away, like ragged leaves in breezes only they can feel.

The trail hugs the valley's eastern edge, choosing open forest and meadows over marsh and mud flats. The wide expanses are covered with fading grasses, sage, and in lower areas, masses of willows. Some of the leaves have turned fiery gold, harbingers of fall's impending arrival. Wildflowers remain abundant, though not as lush as a few weeks before. Among them are bellflowers, some sticky geraniums, and a variety of lupine more purple than blue. Nearby is a patch of mahonia, full of powder-blue berries, another sign of fall's approach. Flitting above are two dragonflies, a faded butterfly, and only a few clattering grasshoppers.

The trail climbs the base of a ridge overlooking the valley. At an unmarked junction a wide path descends to the west, where through gaps in the forest, a structure is intermittently visible below. According to the map, it is the Cabin Creek Patrol Cabin, more often called the Cabin Creek Cabin. If this is not redundant enough, just beyond it is a junction with the Trail Creek Trail. I briefly consider heading down to see if a ranger is there, but having passed three locked cabins this summer—two of them twice—there seems little point.

After a long stretch of dense forest, where limited views cue more soliloquies, the route returns to open meadow. To the west is the Yellowstone River, still wide and mighty even above the lake. Along a section of tight bends, huge boulders have trapped a massive logjam. Ever flowing, the river has twisted its course, bending around logs and boulders in a calm channel of vivid aquamarine.

Masses of conglomerate rock rise near the trail. I stop and place a hand on one of the largest, imagining its history back through millions of years. This rock was here when Osborne Russell rode past. And Jim Bridger. Long before, it was here when untold numbers of Sheepeaters, Shoshones, and Crows passed through. Though their recollections are lost in the mists and shrouds of unrecorded history, it is intriguing to imagine sitting by a campfire and listening to tribal elders tell of their times on the Yellowstone.

Going back further, long before the first humans arrived, and now working forward, some bits of these rocks were once layers of muck on a seafloor. After they dried and hardened into stony sheets, they were cast skyward with geological slowness by the collisions of tectonic plates. High and exposed, bits and fragments were set free by erosion in the forces of wind, water, and ice. They blew or trickled or tumbled back downward, only to be cast about again by volcanoes and, later, glaciers, in untold cycles of composition and movement, upward and down.

The story isn't over. Erosion is still at work, dropping newly freed particles toward the river, which flows toward distant oceans, where new sedimentary rock is forming even now. Also, the Yellowstone hot spot remains active. It could change things in an instant, blasting up volumes of ash to bury much of North America.

The trail crosses an old burn, where only a few charred trunks are left standing high on the slopes above. Green masses of young lodgepoles rise also, but they have far yet to grow. Above them is the distinctive summit of Colter Peak.

On their famous expedition, Washburn named what is now Colter Peak for Nathaniel Langford, after Langford and Doane ascended it for a view of the surrounding terrain. But maps back then were crude, and a year later the Hayden Survey attached Langford's name to a less prominent peak farther north. Characteristically, Langford saw this as a slight and complained, but Colter Peak stuck, fortunately. It is more fitting that this prominent mountain in the wild Thorofare be named for a wilderness trekker who crossed the region on foot. As for Langford, it would be more appropriate to assign his name to a noisy steam vent in some highly visible area, a source of hot air constantly calling attention to itself.

The approach to Trapper Creek holds a faded trail marker at the edge of its wide and rocky floodplain. With no corresponding sign on the other side, I make my best guess at where the trail should go and set off.

So late in the season, the creek is low and split into two shallow channels. Beyond the first are some horse tracks, which I follow until they disappear in the gravel. A bit of fresh horse manure provides the next marker, but after that are no more clues.

The lay of the land suggests the trail resumes past the second channel downstream. This crossing is deeper and wider than the first, but no problem. Beyond it, in a patch of sand at creek's edge, is a line of coyote tracks among a mix of smaller prints from rodents and birds. Nearby are the first human footprints I've seen in days. They are easily tracked to the trail.

Less than a mile farther is the spur route to my next campsite at 6C2. My permit says the site is a mile and a half west of the main trail, but the sign says it's only a mile. Either way, it's a short hike. No one is counting steps out here, anyway.

The spur trail follows the edge of a wide meadow. Willow thickets cross it in places, closing across the trail at knee-level. This makes long pants something of a requirement. In other areas, the willows are head-high or taller, dense walls that restrict visibility and require more bear talk. Near the campsite, the route reaches a low, wet meadow crossed by narrow beaver streams. The trail is muddy, and pocked with fresh horse prints, all coming out of the campsite. Along with them is more evidence of recent horse traffic, though more aromatic.

Site 6C2 sits on an outer bend of the Yellowstone River. Long stretches of water are visible both upstream and down, with open views in three directions. The immediate impression is that this is a perfect site. Without thinking to take off my pack, I stand at the river's edge and stare for a long time at the beauty of the upper Yellowstone.

Eventually it becomes time to hang the food and set about finding a tent site. That's when I notice the cooking area is streaked with thick lines of discarded coffee grounds radiating outward, and dotted with cobbles of fresh horse manure. Apparently the previous campers didn't think so much of this site, or didn't care enough to show it some modicum of respect. They were the opposite of the stock party I met on the Hoodoo trip, the ones who had raked the food area clean before leaving.

I can only shake my head as I carry my pack far away in search of a tent site. If they were this careless with the food area, there's no telling what else they spilled or dumped on the ground, attractants to all sorts of wildlife, the *ursus* sort in particular.

I head for a dense stand of lodgepoles away from the river, past numerous sites where people set up tents right at the water's edge. Farther back in the trees is a flat stretch of comfortable ground, padded with pine needles. This will do nicely.

Back at the food area, I put aside my annoyance at the sloppy campers. My mind returns to the moment and thoughts of dinner on the wild banks of the Yellowstone. On the menu tonight is what has become my nutritional secret weapon for long treks: two packets of instant chicken soup. Though it's not what you'd call delicious, and its neon yellow can be off-putting, after a hot, sweaty day of hiking, the protein and sodium are instantly reenergizing.

As the stove heats water, a belted kingfisher flies upstream, traveling low above the river and clattering the entire way. Near the opposite bank, a spotted sandpiper wades in the shallows, examining the river mud and being examined in turn by its reflection in the water's smooth surface.

After dinner I walk downstream, scanning for wildlife, studying rocks, and staring into the hypnotic blue water. When I return to camp, the sun has settled to another fire-season sunset, a beautiful, peach-orange glow. Cool breezes rise from the water.

As darkness descends, I sit against a tree near the river. A blue heron appears, flying downstream with slow grace and following the river's bends.

In daylight's dim remains, two widely spaced *cracks!* ring out across the river. They are the unmistakable sounds of breaking branches—thick branches. In the murky forest two hundred yards away is a dark form that is hard to make out. Because it's not moving there's no way to judge if it's animal, log, or shrub, or even a shadow in the woods. But then, with the ponderous movement of a large animal, it recedes in the darkness and is lost from sight.

What was it? Bear? Elk? Moose? I remain in place, bear spray in hand, watching and waiting. Nothing shows but dark forest, silver river, and blackening sky.

Soon the darkness is complete, except for the light of a waxing crescent moon, nearly at first quarter. By trip's end it will be full, a poetic metaphor. Luminous, growing, fulfilling, enlightening.

I return to the tent and lie drifting toward sleep as the river outside drifts to the lake. Some time later, I'm roused by a series of shrill shrieks.

Not fully awake, my mind grasps about for a possible source. Bird? Coyote? More fully alert, I recognize the calls of an elk, a cow or perhaps a young bull trying to learn how to bugle in advance of the rut.

As the tentative shrieks continue, I settle back to a comfortable sleep, only to be awakened again, this time by a deep chill. Did a cold front blow through, or is it just the changing season? Whichever, my summer practice of sleeping in thermal top and bottoms, covered with an unzipped sleeping bag like a blanket, no longer works. I add a long-sleeved cotton shirt and zip myself in the sleeping bag. It's still not enough, and I rouse once again to pull on my camp pants, fleece top, and hat.

Thus cocooned in the attire of autumn, I lie in the dark, trying to feel the presence of the Yellowstone River. Drifting toward sleep, my mind floats along with the river. The flow is powerful, unstoppable, like the movement of time. Out there in the darkness, it moves and flows, like the progress of years. Or the rising of thoughts from the deep subconscious.

Sleep like a river.

Day 5. 6C2 to Cliff Creek, Site 6Y5

The chill lingers into morning, enticing me to sleep in. Then, lying in the early light, I remember where I am and rush out to see the river. Standing on the bank and watching the water swirl and flow, I realize I should have asked for two nights at this site. Time to stay and contemplate the great river.

My disappointment is lessened by thoughts of things yet to come. Much of the Thorofare lies ahead.

The hike begins at 10:30. With only eight miles to travel today, there's no need to rush. Tomorrow's hike will be even shorter, just two and half miles to Thorofare Creek. After that is a layover day, followed by another short walk to the upper Yellowstone. This is all by design. With so much distance to cover just to reach the Thorofare, once you've traveled here, you should take some time to *be* here.

The sky is smokier this morning, both up-valley and down. Having been on the trail for five days, I have no way of knowing if this means new fires or only a shift in the wind. Perhaps both.

Back on the main trail I turn south, following the old horseshoe prints, which are now overlain with tracks of coyotes, rodents, and birds. It's another wild metaphor: people (and their horses) come and go, but nature remains.

After traversing a long meadow, the route travels a wide corridor through burned forest. A young man approaches, wearing shorts, a green t-shirt, and what looks like a daypack with an axe strapped to it.

"Good morning, sir," he says.

"Good morning," I say, surprised at being called sir, especially way out here. Is he really that polite or do I look so much like an old man to his young eyes?

We both stop. He tells me he is a ranger, which explains the axe. What a job: your office is the Yellowstone backcountry, and the dress code is shorts and t-shirt. He seems genuinely happy.

"I've been at the Thorofare cabin for the last couple of days," he says. "Now I'm headed to the Trail Creek Cabin [on the southeast arm of Yellowstone Lake] to do some work there."

"Is there anyone at the Thorofare cabin?" I ask.

"No," he says. "We're a little understaffed, so the cabin is not staffed full-time anymore, only several nights a week. Usually."

That explains why I've seen so few rangers this summer: they are understaffed. And the people they do have are moving from cabin to cabin. Apparently, they are all roving rangers these days, doing work consistent with their job title.

I mention the backpacker I met at Beaverdam Creek, who said he'd been injured and had to turn back. I wondered how they dealt with such things.

"If it's a serious injury," he says, "we can call in a helicopter, if he wants to pay for it. We don't have a helicopter here because we rarely need it. We have a contract with the Tetons because they have more helicopter rescues up there in the mountains. But if he's close to the trail, we can send someone in to bring him out."

"I'm not sure he was really injured," I say. "He may have just realized his plans were too ambitious."

"Yeah," he laughs. "Sometimes people find they've scheduled more than they can finish."

"But now he's off his schedule," I say. "How do you treat people like that who camp somewhere without a permit?"

"It depends on the situation," he says. "If they camp at a site nobody is using, then that's probably okay. We really like for people to be at their reserved campsites so we can keep track of things, but if they can't finish their trip and are heading out, we try to cut them some slack."

That makes sense. It depends on the situation, and likely on the ranger.

"You see any wildlife on the way in?" he asks.

"Not much," I say. "One muley doe way back near the lake. I heard some elk last night, practicing their bugles."

"Yeah," he says, "they are just trying to get started. I haven't seen much either. I saw four white-tails crossing the trail further in, but that was it."

"Have the fires changed?" I ask, "or is all this smoke due to the wind?"

"They're the same as they have been," he says. "It's the same fires from Idaho. Sometimes the wind shifts and it gets really smoky. It can get so bad you don't even feel like going running that day."

I don't mention I rarely feel like going running anymore. It doesn't take much smoke.

"How is your trip going?" he asks. "Are you going in, out, or across?"

"I'm headed into the Thorofare and then across the South Boundary Trail."

"Are you going out at Heart Lake?"

"No, at the south entrance, at the picnic area there."

"Cool trip!" he says.

"In two weeks I'm headed into Bechler," I say. "Starting out at Pitchstone and going across to Union Falls and up Bechler Canyon toward Old Faithful."

"I've been wanting to do that trip," he says. "This is only my second season here, so I haven't done it yet. This is the right time of year to do it, when the water is down and the mosquitoes are light. Well, I'll let you get on with your trip."

"Thanks for the info," I say.

"Have a good trip."

Continuing on, I wonder why the rangers would be understaffed. Is it due to budget cuts, or because they couldn't find enough good hands, or because few people want to work in the backcountry anymore? This work might not be agreeable to a lot of younger folks, with no cell signal out here for their smartphones and no way to send a text message.

I don't recall hearing you could work as a backcountry ranger when I was younger. This would be a dream job, living and working in the deep backcountry. A few nights at the Thorofare cabin before hiking across to Trail Creek. Do a little trail work, talk to backpackers when you find them, and decide each morning whether you feel like going for a run or not. How did I miss *that* on career day?

Now, in addition to the horse tracks and coyote prints in the trail, are the shoeprints of the ranger. If the route ever falls into question, the shoeprints may be helpful.

Leaving the forest, the trail crosses an expansive grassland that dips toward a marshy area to the west. I pause to glass about for wildlife. Nothing. It seems surprising that all this open land would be unoccupied by larger mammals, though I realize that just because I haven't seen them doesn't mean they're not here. All the tracks and scat on the trail prove they are. Perhaps these animals are more wary than the ones near park roadways, that are accustomed to seeing lots of humans.

At the junction with the Mountain Creek Trail, a sign declares that Eagle Pass, high on the park's eastern boundary, is ten miles away. The Thorofare Ranger Station is now 7.4 miles to the south, and in the other direction, the Nine Mile Trailhead is 24.6 miles back. Being so far from the road is invigorating.

Even after a summer of so much hiking, it's still a pleasure to stop and read trail signs, to assess the distance traveled and see how many miles lie ahead. It's also fun to contemplate other destinations beyond my route. Childlike, I want to see it all, and hate moving on and leaving trails unexplored. What sights are to be seen up this creek? What's over there behind that mountain? Perhaps, I tell myself, as one would tell a child, we'll come back one of these years and hike those other trails. Both my adult self and the inner child know this is unlikely, and even if we do come back, it won't really be the same as it is now. Still, it's fun to dream about places you could go, might go, just possibly. But in the end, like Robert Frost, we are just one traveler, and way leads on to way. At some point you have to choose your road.

Mountain Creek flows in a wide, dry boulder field of a floodplain. A trail marker is visible on the far side. At this time of year the creek is braided, which means several small water crossings. The first is actually a long stranded pool, where a fingerling perhaps four inches long zips under a submerged log. Though the water is two feet deep, this is not a large pool. The young fish will need rain in the near future or it will become an easy meal for bird or beast.

Across the floodplain is the main creek, deepest, as usual, where the trail crosses. A line of tiny riffles downstream indicates a shallower ford. It's barely enough to get my socks wet. The water flows over rocks of brown, gray, and red, and a few mottled pieces of petrified wood, all overlain by trickling rapids, shining silver in the sun.

On the far side is another impounded pool, perhaps twelve feet long, with water a foot and a half deep in the center. There are no fish in this one other than a few shiners. On closer inspection, the pool is not really impounded. A tiny inlet on the upper end trickles through a strip of gravel, and water drains through another rocky bed below. While the shiners can't escape, for now at least, there is an exchange of water and oxygen.

Near the markers for sites 6D2 and 6D3, the trail splits and braids, leaving doubt about which forested path is the real route. The ranger's shoeprints are nowhere to be seen. After a false start on a path that quickly peters out, I locate the official trail, which, for a short stretch follows a muddy creek bed. There are no markers except for bits of fresh horse manure, which are usually as reliable as any trail designation out here. Even more reliable, the ranger's fresh shoeprints appear again, headed in the opposite direction.

Farther on, a sign marks the path to 6Y7, which is set on an oxbow of the Yellowstone River. Getting close, now. My next site is 6Y5. Only two more Y's to go.

An intense crosswind hurtles down from the northern reaches of the Trident, the high, three-pronged plateau that towers above the heart of the Thorofare. Sustained gusts continue, in a bid to either push me off the trail or send me chasing after my sun hat. Cinching the drawstring tight, I trudge onward.

After an easy ford of Cliff Creek, the marker for 6Y5 appears, my home for the night. The campsite is a good distance from the trail, set in a strip of forest on the edge of a vast expanse of willows. The trail to the food area has been rerouted recently, designated by new orange markers in the line of trees. I miss the first of these and follow the old markers, which have been left up for no apparent reason, on an old, worn path. Eventually, I notice two of the bright new markers off to the north. It's clear the two routes travel parallel, both headed to the end of the small strip of forest, so I stay on the old path rather than bushwhacking across to the new one. Almost there now.

About eighty yards shy of the food area, lying across the path, is a freshly gnawed deer leg. Small bits of flesh and cartilage still cling to the joints, and the bones have not been crushed or chewed for the marrow. It's something you'd rather not find in your campsite, more or less a dinner bell for scavengers and opportunistic predators, especially grizzly bears and wolves.

After a campaign of shooting, trapping, and poisoning, the last wolf pack in Yellowstone was killed off in 1926. Unconfirmed reports of wolf sightings trickled in over the following years, but if any of these actually were wolves, they were individuals or pairs just passing through. There were still wolves in the Canadian Rockies, as little as three hundred miles to the northwest, but scientists are certain there was no sustainable wolf population in the park after the 1930s.

The idea of returning wolves to Yellowstone goes back as far as 1944, when Aldo Leopold suggested the few remaining wolves being persecuted in the West should be trapped and released in the park. There was no serious action toward restoring wolves until the 1970s, when the Endangered Species Act (ESA) was passed by Congress with overwhelming numbers and signed into law by President Nixon. Among the first on the endangered list was the subspecies of gray wolf once associated with Yellowstone, a subspecies that's no longer recognized by taxonomists. It was the Rocky Mountain wolf, *Canis lupus irremotus* (a Latin name wolf opponents would later come to love). The endangered list was later revised to include all North American gray wolves.

The ESA, in addition to its protective measures, also contains remedial provisions. These required the government—through U.S. Fish and Wildlife—to restore endangered species, when possible, even species eliminated from only part of their range. Gray wolves once roamed much of North America, but in the 1970s the only gray wolves in the United States were in northern Minnesota. This made them prime candidates for endangered species restoration. Was restoration possible? All it needed was enough wild lands to support the wide-ranging animals. The public lands of the Northern Rockies, not only in Yellowstone, but also in Idaho and northwestern Montana, were perfectly suited.

In 1992, Congress directed U.S. Fish and Wildlife to prepare an environmental impact statement (EIS) on wolf restoration. When the public was asked for comments, one hundred and sixty thousand came in, nearly eighty percent in favor of restoring wolves. As for how to go about it, the government considered several alternatives. Among them were three viable options that would lead to sustainable wolf populations in Yellowstone.

The least difficult was to do nothing and wait for wolves, which had established packs in northwest Montana by then, to make their own way to Yellowstone. This would likely take several decades. In the interim, all the dispersing wolves would have the full protection of ESA, making it difficult to remove any that wandered onto ranches and preyed on livestock. Another option was to transport wolves into Yellowstone under the full protection of the ESA, which also made dealing with problem wolves more difficult.

A third approach would release wolves into Yellowstone, but under a technicality in the ESA. It allowed some reintroduced animals to be classified as experimental populations, which don't get the same level of protection. Under this approach, a rancher seeing a wolf attacking sheep or cattle could harass or even shoot the wolf without running afoul of the ESA. Somewhat surprisingly, some ranchers and their elected officials supported this option. They could see wolves were coming back, either through active reintroduction or recolonization. At least the experimental population approach would give them a little leeway in dealing with wolves when they arrived. Wisely, the government chose this alternative and moved to reintroduce wolves as an experimental population.

The next challenge was where to get wolves that were similar to those that once roamed the park. At the time, the number of gray wolf subspecies was being substantially revised. A hundred years ago, some overzealous taxonomists divided North American gray wolves into twenty-four subspecies, based on geographical range, skull measurements, overall size, and color variations. But wolves travel great distances, and where their ranges overlapped, the subspecies were known to interbreed. The frequent mixing of genes defeated the purpose of recognizing so many subspecies. So, after more scientific analysis with improved methods, the number of subspecies of North American gray wolves was revised downward to only five. (Some biologists support doing away with the subspecies classification for gray wolves, because any recognized subspecies would still be capable of interbreeding.) The five subspecies of gray wolves currently recognized include: the arctic wolf (*Canis lupus arctos*), northwestern wolf (*Canis lupus occidentalis*), great plains wolf (*Canis lupus nubilus*), Mexican wolf (*Canis lupus baileyi*), and the eastern timber wolf (*Canis lupus lycaon*). The former Rocky Mountain wolf, the old *Canis lupus irremotus*, is no longer recognized as a subspecies.

The two subspecies most similar to the wolves that once roamed Yellowstone were the great plains wolf, then found in Minnesota, and the northwestern wolf, which lived mainly in Canada, but was already established in northern Montana and was expected to eventually make its way into Yellowstone. While the northwestern wolves were slightly larger (though not enough to be statistically important, and within the range of natural variation), they were the better option. The Minnesota wolves were unaccustomed to living in mountainous terrain, and they had no experience hunting elk or bison. The scientists made the clear best choice in selecting wolves from a similar mountain ecosystem with the same prey species.

"It's the wrong wolf!" opponents claimed in their comments to the EIS (they're still saying this today). They argued that the only wolves that could be reintroduced in Yellowstone was the old *Canis lupus irremotus*. What they hoped to achieve by insisting on discredited taxonomy, was a conclusion that wolves could never be restored in Yellowstone. If *Canis lupus irremotus* was the only subspecies that could rightfully be brought back, then restoration was impossible because those wolves didn't exist. It was a crafty argument, though less than honest and without scientific merit.

Wolf opponents also seized on the evidence that the northwestern wolves were slightly larger. But they grossly exaggerated their claims, saying the wolves were significantly larger and also more vicious, something akin to super-wolves, which would wipe out all the ungulates, which were unused to dealing with giant wolves. Again, there was no scientific basis to any of this.

When the EIS was finalized in 1994, it addressed the wrong-wolf argument, explaining the changes in wolf taxonomy that recognized far fewer subspecies. It was not what wolf opponents wanted to hear. Even today they continue denouncing the "wrong wolves," using terms like "non-native Canadian wolf," as though nationality means anything to wildlife. Some even use the ESA's definition of experimental population and decry "experimental wolves" dumped on them by the government, as though they are some sort of mutant animals.

In the end, the wrong-wolf claim fails twice: first, in being based on discredited taxonomy; and second, because the wolves brought to Yellowstone were of the same type that were already established in northwestern Montana and were making their way south. Right or wrong, they would've gotten here anyway. Even some wolf opponents have acknowledged this.

After the EIS was finalized, forty-one wolves were released into Yellowstone in the three years from 1995 to 1997. They found a land with artificially high numbers of prey, and species that hadn't encountered wolf packs for seventy years. As wolves reassumed their natural ecological roles, elk and other species had to adapt their behavior. It wasn't long before the old fight over elk numbers revived, having switched again from too many to too few.

When Yellowstone rangers stopped killing elk in the late 1960s, elk numbers climbed from just over three thousand in 1968 to nineteen thousand in 1994. Understandably, this artificially high number began to dip after wolf restoration. "We're seeing fewer elk!" cried the wolf opponents. The obvious response was: Fewer than what? Fewer than the artificially inflated numbers? As the ecosystem adjusted to the return of a natural predator long since extirpated, a reduction in prey numbers was expected, even desired.

But the reductions were not due solely to wolves. There were also the effects of a long-term drought in the late 1990s and early 2000s, starvation in the harsh winter of 1997, and predation on elk calves by increasing numbers of grizzlies, which were recovering after being listed as threatened under the ESA and were dealing with the diminishment of two major food sources: whitebark pine nuts and cutthroat trout. Also during this time, many Yellowstone elk were killed by human hunters.

This is something often left out of the too-few-elk claims: for years after wolf restoration, Montana continued to issue large numbers of antlerless elk tags, the tags they used to directly reduce populations back when people claimed there were too many elk.

From 1995 to 2000, Montana issued nearly twenty-eight hundred antlerless elk tags per year for late season hunts just north of Yellowstone. This removed large numbers of healthy breeding elk from the northern herd. Montana finally got around to addressing the imbalance after 2000, albeit slowly, reducing antlerless tags to fourteen hundred by 2004 and to a hundred in 2006-2009, They finally stopped issuing them in 2010.

As a result of all these factors, the northern elk herd decreased, from nineteen thousand in 1994, to twelve thousand in 1998, and down to sixty-six hundred in 2006. By 2012, the northern herd had dropped to near four thousand elk. This was still more than the number left when park rangers were culling elk in the 1960s.

But as elk numbers continued to decline, so did wolf numbers. As often happens in healthy ecosystems, reduced prey numbers affect predator populations, especially carnivores like wolves (bears are omnivores and can shift their diets toward more plant matter, among other things). Yellowstone's wolf population peaked in 2007, near one hundred and seventy. Since then it has dropped substantially as more wolves have been killed, often by other wolf packs in territorial battles, which are more common when prey is harder to catch, and through the effects of diseases such as canine distemper and mange. A count done in 2013 would find ninety-five wolves in the park, in ten packs.

Concurrently, the northern elk herd would see a rebound. After bottoming out in 2012 at just under four thousand, the number would climb to nearly five thousand in both 2014 and 2015, leading biologists to conclude the northern elk herd had stabilized. The ecosystem was working.

The food area is indeed toward the end of the forested strip. Walled in by trees and a dense undergrowth of shrubs, it's the opposite of many campsites, where cooking areas have the choicest views. This one has no view at all. Yet it's a nice campsite, as good as it can be in a rugged terrain surrounded by a vast sea of willows.

After getting water from the shallow but clear flow of Cliff Creek, I sit on a log and eat an early dinner. While rooting around the bottom of my food bag, I find a flattened oatmeal pie that appears to have been stepped on by a bison. There's also a crushed pack of toaster pastries, its contents loose and crumbly as a packet of oatmeal. If I had milk, I could eat it like cereal. At least the food now fits into one bag, though this may lead to more flattening. For the remainder of the trip, my meal prep will be like rummaging in a grocery store's damaged items cart, hoping to find something good that's marked down but still salvageable.

After dinner, it's time to find a tent site, one far enough away from both the bear pole and that deer leg lying out there. A lengthy reconnaissance turns up only two potential spots, both less than ideal. One is a narrow gap far out in the sea of willows, the other an open burned area on the high ground to the north. Neither looks particularly comfortable.

I head back to the grassy area near the trail, where on the edge of the vast willow expanse is an inviting spot with endless views to the south and west. Although it's in plain sight of the trail, it is a trail less traveled, and this is a wonderful spot. I drop the pack and pace the distance back to the deer leg, just to be sure. It's over a hundred and fifty yards, fortunately. This is it.

Tent site at 6Y5

To the south is a wide view of the Thorofare, rimmed on three sides by higher terrain. The towering ridges of the Trident fill the eastern horizon, and a few miles south is the massive bulk of Hawks Rest. Across to the west is the long profile of Two Ocean

Plateau, which is cleft by the high valley of Lynx Creek, where my route will take me in a few days. Far to the north, Colter Peak remains visible over the shoulder of a low ridge. It looks surprisingly distant, considering how massive it appeared only this morning from my campsite near its base.

There are no signs of wildlife across the flat valley or on the surrounding slopes, and no sounds but the distant squabble of sandhill cranes. With binoculars I scan to the west and south, stopping on any dark spots that could be moose or bears. They all turn out to be bushes or shadowy pockets in willow banks.

At sunset the sky is a blend of smoke, clouds, and the copper light of a hidden sun. Above the western horizon is a mix of blacks, grays, and pulsing reds, an impressionistic image of campfire coals. The eastern sky is dark and cool, vivid slate grays like translucent river stones in clear water. The crescent moon hangs to the south, its lit portion pointed downward, showing the way to a sun now lost behind the distant plateau.

The deepening darkness colors a changing sky. The cleft of Lynx Creek now shines smoky red, as though a giant fire were burning beyond. The southern horizon becomes a failed oil painting, its colors overmixed and muddied to a smoky, purplish smear.

Evening settles still and quiet, except for the chipping of an unseen sparrow and the occasional clucks of robins. From the northeast comes a faint, whispering sigh. Perhaps it's the waterfall on Cliff Creek, which is less than a mile from the trail. I don't recall hearing it earlier, but the winds were blowing then and my mind was occupied with other things. Now the sound is beckoning. With so short a hike to my campsite tomorrow—less than three miles—I may make an early side-trip to see the falls before setting out.

The sky dims imperceptibly toward a complete darkness, the stars blotted out by a blanket of smoke. When it's too dark to see more than a short distance, I return to the tent, lingering outside for a moment. No artificial lights appear in any direction up or down the long valley. This is as it has always been, since uplift, volcanoes, and erosion cast up these mountains and carved this terrain. A sense of the ancient.

Even in the absence of light, the valley's expanse remains palpable. A feeling of largeness. In such a setting, one's spirit, set free of constraints, expands and flows outward to inhabit the land. The soul grows with it.

Drifting toward sleep, my thoughts return to the deer leg. What kind of animal dropped it? Will it still be there in the morning or will something come claim it? Knowing my food is hung out of reach and my tent set far away, I am not worried, only curious. With these thoughts, I fall into a deep, restful sleep.

In the dark hours of predawn, I am lifted to wakefulness by a low rising sound in the distance. It's the deep, sustained howl of a wolf.

Day 6. 6Y5 to South Thorofare, Site 6T1

Before breakfast I set off to find the falls on Cliff Creek. The temperature lingers at thirty-five while the sun remains hidden behind the high Absarokas.

After taking the main trail back to the creek, I set off cross-country on forested ground that's a jumble of downed logs. There's not even a game trail. Though bear encounters are more likely when traveling off-trail, there's little worry in here, as my steps on and over downed wood ring out in the morning silence with cracks and crunches of snapping branches and groaning logs.

In a grass-is-greener moment, I decide travel would be easier on the other side of the creek, where the terrain is steeper but open. Crossing the water and heading for higher ground, I take the most walkable route and end up higher than planned. A Steller's jay flits among the treetops below. Crossing the steep slope of loose rock takes a bit of scrambling as I work my way downward. After traversing another exposed stretch, I round a bend and there in the box canyon below are the falls.

From a cleft in a rocky wall they pour in a narrow stream, plunging in three drops down stony ledges, casting sheets of spray at each. Framing the scene are gray walls, curtained with green mats of moss. Toward the top, a single fir clutches a tentative perch. Beneath it all is a mass of boulders, where the falling waters splash and regroup and drop again. From the base they flow in steep cascades and gather in the creek, where they move more gently toward the Thorofare and the Yellowstone.

I pick my way down to the canyon floor. It's the best vantage to take in the scene. There, one can look upward across the three watery plunges toward the cleft in the wall where a tiny creek turns to a thunderous waterfall. It is a transcendent place.

I take a different route back, staying south of the creek and making my way through brush and over fallen logs. It's a route more suited to mule deer, with their easy four-legged hop that carries them bouncing over obstacles and rugged terrain.

My approach is to walk the tops of logs, traveling down one to reach the next, like a chipmunk, only more slowly and deliberate. A misstep could lead to a fall onto uneven ground covered with logs, boulders, and broken branches. So deep in the backcountry, a sprained ankle or worse injury could be dangerous, especially away from the trail. I step gingerly along, from log to rock to rotting log, and tight-rope down to the next.

Eventually, and without incident, I make it back to the trail. Though the morning air still holds a chill, my shirt is drenched with sweat. I've earned my breakfast this morning, perhaps one of those crumbled toaster pastries, followed by a bison-flattened oatmeal pie.

The sunlight reaches camp before I do, launching the temperature to sixty-six, a swing of thirty-one degrees in an hour and a half. I change out of the sweaty clothes and into shorts. On the way to the food area, the deer leg is still where it was, apparently untouched. Perhaps times are not yet so lean.

By 10:30 I am back on the trail. With only two and half miles to cover, I'll reach the next camp before noon. It's almost a layover day.

The ground holds no new tracks in the soft dust, only the ranger's shoeprints from yesterday and older horse tracks from the group I've been following since Beaverdam Creek. The absence of people in such a beautiful and expansive part of Yellowstone is surprising. Ahead, the trail is marked with fresh bear droppings, full of purple berry skins. More scat.

Diddly skiddly dee bop. Bescoodly boo bop.

Beyond it is a set of smallish bear tracks headed in the same direction I am. In places they cover the ranger's prints, meaning the bear was here in the last twenty-four hours. There's also more scat, but it's older and doesn't inspire song.

At the junction with the South Boundary Trail, a sign says the Thorofare Ranger Station is only seven-tenths of a mile to the east. Beyond it is the park boundary and the Bridger Teton National Forest, at 1.8 miles. The Nine Mile Trailhead, where this trip began, is now 31.3 miles back. My next camp, at 6T1, is only a mile down the South Boundary Trail. While the bear tracks continue toward the ranger cabin, the horse tracks head off on my route. I feel cheated.

This part of the Thorofare is more woodsy than I'd imagined. The trees are fairly young, with some dead logs lying about, but nothing to suggest a recent burn. As I enter a stretch of dense forest, a Steller's jay squawks at me from the trees.

"I know, Stella," I say aloud. (It rolls off the tongue better than Steller.) "I know."

Through a dense corridor of shaded forest, the route approaches a sunny meadow gleaming beyond. Fresh deer and elk tracks mark the dirt, on top of the persistent horseshoes prints. At meadow's edge, I pause to scan in all directions, taking in the vastness of the Thorofare. In all this open space, there's no sign of humans at all, other than the existence of the trail and the aging prints.

Just ahead is Thorofare Creek. It's a little over knee deep at the trail and flowing quickly. A short distance upstream, a line of riffles indicates a shallower ford. I detour toward them, crossing a muddy bank imprinted with hiking shoes. Someone had the same idea. Following the riffles, the crossing is no more than calf deep, on a rocky creek bed underlain with mud. It's sturdy, if a bit spongy. Under the clear, flowing water, is a myriad of stony colors, lots of reds, browns, and tans, with a few grays and off-whites, even spots of green.

Beyond the creek, a large tree holds an orange placard, on which someone has written in magic marker "6T1" with an arrow pointing upstream. There's no path in that direction, so I go cross-country. After charging through a bank of willows like a fullback, I see an opening off to my right, where the horizontal lines of two bear poles signal the location of the food area.

It's a divided area, actually. With few large trees in the open terrain, the bear poles are out near the trail, while the fire ring is down on a lengthy stretch of Thorofare Creek. It's an excellent setup. The views from the fire ring are striking, unobstructed in all directions. Also unobstructed, however, is the fierce, incessant wind. I'm glad no wildfires are burning nearby. On a warm day like today, such strong winds could send them running.

Upstream, the creek bends to the east, toward the southern prong of the Trident. Downstream, it flows northwest until screened from view by forest and willows. Site 6T2 is down there somewhere, across the creek, about a quarter-mile below the ford. You would never know it from here. If anyone is there, they've made a quiet camp.

Fire ring at 6T1

I carry my pack upstream to find a tent site. A little more than a hundred yards from the fire ring is a dense stand of trees that screen most of the whipping wind. In its center, about a hundred and thirty yards from the food area and thirty yards from the water, is a little alcove with plenty of open ground for a tent.

When camp is made, I stand at the creek's edge and gaze into the water. About four feet deep, the creek's flow is a clear aquamarine and moving swiftly. As I stand mesmerized, staring into the current, a submerged waterbird streaks past, traveling two feet underwater. Its orange feet, which appear purple-green through the water, paddle furiously. In an instant it is gone.

What just happened? Stunned by the strange sighting and desperate for another look, I hurry downstream, scanning the creek to see where the bird surfaces. A waterbird pops up much farther away than I'd expected, down near the cooking area. Before I can raise the camera for an identifying photo, the bird dives again and is seen no more.

I return to where the waterfowl first appeared and stare at the water's surface, trying to picture the encounter again and foolishly hoping another swimming bird will pass the same spot. Of course one doesn't. Eventually, I am roused from my reverie by a powerful gust. It whips up a mist from the water's surface and twists it skyward in a miniature waterspout. Small sand storms rise across the creek. I return to the tent to ensure everything is well secured so my house doesn't end up in the next county.

The late afternoon sun sets a russet glow on the walls of the Trident, the rugged cliffs a mix of shadow and sun. Though the name Trident suggests three uniform prongs, they are anything but. The northern rampart bears a rocky turret on its western slope, while the center ridge holds rock columns that resemble hoodoos. The southern prong, from this vantage, is a long cliff face with numerous pocks and holes that appear to be caves. The scene is so varied and intricately detailed that one could stand and stare at it for ages and not take it all in.

Across the low horizon to the south, a bit west of Hawks Rest, is a layer of smoke that wasn't there before. Thin and gray, it drifts in a concentrated mass that's too thick to have blown in from far away. More likely it's from a new fire closer by. Though we've had no electric storms in days, lightning strikes can smolder in dry wood for long periods, until strong winds whip them into a wildfire. These are such winds. The smoke will bear watching.

In the evening I return to the food area and eat dinner on the banks of Thorofare Creek. The new smoke plume to the south has grown into large gray puffs that hover like giant smoke signals. With the cooling of nightfall and a calming wind, the fire shouldn't grow more today. We'll see what the morning brings. Tomorrow is a layover day, with a planned hike that loops out of the park to Bridger Lake and the Hawks Rest Patrol Cabin, before circling back to the Thorofare cabin. The first part will take me toward the fire. Perhaps I'll get a better look.

As daylight dims, I hang the food and sit against a log overlooking the creek. Sitting here in deep wilderness, along a waterway that will soon join the upper Yellowstone on its journey toward lake, canyon, and falls, is to feel in touch with something primordial. In books, the geologic past and deep history can seem merely theoretical. But out here, looking across this immense landscape at a headwater creek and the weathered rocks and caves beyond, the full history feels more immediate. These mountains were formed by volcanoes fifty million years ago? Of course they were; just look at them.

In the wild setting the many meanings of Yellowstone flow together: the geologic and historical, the scientific and mystical. In wild Yellowstone they all coalesce, existing at once: mountains and grizzlies; waterfalls and wolves. Wildfires, elk, petrified trees, along with the human characters who, by good example or bad, helped shape the history of this place. River and meadow, hoodoo and forest, bison and moose. The hot spot of magma under the rocks, geysers . . .

I suddenly realize a flaw in my planning, a shortcoming in the four treks. In all these travels across the Yellowstone backcountry, my route will never approach a large thermal area. Small groups of hot springs will appear occasionally, on the Snake River and in Bechler Canyon. And the final day of my travels will pass Lone Star Geyser. But this now seems terribly inadequate. A summer of backpacking through wild Yellowstone would be incomplete, even inaccurate, without a trip to a geyser basin. It ignores an important part of Yellowstone's character.

What can I do? On the way home from the final trip, which will end only a few miles from the Upper Geyser Basin, I could swing by Old Faithful. But that wouldn't be right, ending a summer of remote backpacking with a trip to the busiest part of the park. It would be culture shock. This summer is about wild Yellowstone, and Old Faithful, with its overpass and endless stretch of concrete parking, is the opposite of wild.

While small thermal areas are scattered across much of the park's backcountry, only two large geyser basins exist away from the roads: at Heart Lake and Shoshone Lake. As good fortune would have it, the route on my final trip will pass within a few miles of Shoshone Lake and the park's largest backcountry geyser basin. If I can add a day at the end of that trip, perhaps at a site on the west end of Shoshone Lake, there would be time to explore the geyser basin.

As darkness falls, I return to the tent and lie listening to the sounds of the Thorofare night. The feeling is again one of largeness, but also of fullness. It is a comforting sensation, a feeling of rightness.

In the early predawn, I am awakened again by the deep howl of a single wolf. As the sustained notes fill the width of the valley, they are punctuated by staccato hoots of an owl. A magical place, indeed.

Day 7. Layover Day at 6T1; Day Hike to Hawks Rest

Floating in the morning's chilly air is a mass of fog and smoke, its center pierced with amber shafts of low-angle sun. Within each broadening ray, gray tendrils swirl and ripple in the breeze. The hovering images of fire, ash, water, dust, and wind are a microcosm of the elements and forces that formed this land. Ends and beginnings. And always a new dawn.

Chortles of sandhill cranes ring out across the wide valley, though the birds remain hidden in the endless sea of willows. A flock of Canada geese flies low above the creek in a loose, honking line. They land on a sandbar downstream.

Still no sights or sounds of humans, though the trail passes almost underneath my bear pole and another campsite sits nearby. This is truly remote country. As the morning warms, the smoky aroma builds, and the sky, though free of clouds, fills with a dirty haze that dims the sun. To the south, the smoke plume has already begun to swell.

Across the creek, the gaggle of geese starts a ruckus of honking and squawking. Alarmed by my appearance at the food area, they stand erect, all facing downstream, honking almost in unison. The sound builds in a rising, clamorous, crescendo until they launch into flight. In a loose, uneven V, they follow the creek toward areas unpeopled and undisturbed.

In midmorning the early stillness gives way to a southerly wind, which pushes more smoke into the Thorofare. In low, wispy masses, it flows along the ground, visibly advancing through forest gaps and creeping and curling above the sage. Everywhere is the strong aroma of woodsmoke.

Still, there's no cause for alarm. Not yet. Though this is the smokiest day of the trip, and of the summer, the fire remains small and miles away. In two days I'll be leaving the Thorofare, climbing westward over Two Ocean Plateau, though smoke also hovers up there, pushed across by the wind like a dust storm.

The drone of an airplane rises from the south, its motor clamorous in the remote setting. The aircraft appears through the dense smoke, turns a broad circle, and disappears again in the gray cloud. Someone is watching the blaze.

At noon my hike begins, heading south toward the park boundary. For a daypack, I'm wearing my backpack, which seems ridiculously empty with only two liters of water, a spare camera battery, toilet paper, and raingear. As always, the binoculars and bear spray are attached to the hip belt. It all feels nearly weightless.

Beginning near the bear pole, my route crosses a dry expanse of sage, grass, and willows. The path holds no horseshoe tracks, only the faint prints of a hiker and a recent coyote. A powerful gust drives more smoke from the south, causing my eyes to water and sting. If I knew more of the lyrics, my new bear song would be *Smoke Gets in Your Eyes*.

The park boundary is marked with an impressive, rustic sign. Its base is three logs planted vertically, and a limb spanning the top holds a hanging placard. To those approaching the park, it says, "Entering Yellowstone National Park. Enjoy the backcountry. Help keep it clean. Hunting prohibited."

A renewed gust drives in more smoke, involuntarily closing my burning, watery eyes. *Woo!* Who would've thought you'd need goggles on a backcountry trip?

Past the boundary the trail turns faint as it approaches a dense forest of young lodgepoles. What appears to have once been a through-route is now covered and blocked by a spread jumble of downed logs. A faint side-path departs to the west, detouring around the thicket. I follow it in hopes it will eventually lead to Bridger Lake. If it doesn't, I can always find my way back here.

The makeshift route turns out to be a good one, skirting the western edge of the forest and curving back to rejoin the old trail. Ahead is an open area that's used, quite apparently, for staging by large stock parties. Log hitching posts are tied across several tree trunks, and the ground has been cleared of nearly all vegetation.

Having hiked national forests across much of the West, I've seen such areas before, but having been so long in Yellowstone, where such private alterations are forbidden, this seems especially ugly and out of place. I hurry past.

Bridger Lake, long and narrow on the near end, comes into view. Among an assortment of brown ducks floating near the shore, are two trumpeter swans, huge by comparison. The swans and I regard each other across the distance. After snapping a few photos, I move on, leaving them in peace.

The lake's outlet channel involves a goodly ford, almost knee deep, though the water is scarcely moving. The bottom is muddy but with a firm foundation. Beyond the ford, dense forest returns, hemming in the view on the winding trail. Having run out of new things to say to myself, I revert to the mundane, "No bear. No bear." There are no bears, at least none visible. A wooden sign attached to a tree declares, "No grazing within ½ mile of the lake."

Just ahead is the site of another large outfitter camp, now vacant. The area looks more like a poorly maintained city park than a wilderness. Toward the center, near a metal food storage box, is a fire ring. It's full of rusted can bottoms, strands of foil, and one unburned plastic lid.

The mess calls to mind the experience Gary Ferguson wrote about in *Hawks Rest, A Season in the Remote Heart of Yellowstone*. The book tells of a summer Ferguson and a friend spent tending the Forest Service cabin where my current route is headed. Though some of the pages describe this majestic valley, its peaks and storms and wildlife, many more recount how Ferguson spent much of his time being lectured by local outfitters, who acted as though they had greater rights to these public lands than everyone else.

The book also tells of the long battle between outfitters and former Yellowstone Ranger Bob Jackson, and how Jackson's strict enforcement of laws against poaching and baiting elk with salt blocks had him stepping on some powerful toes. In the end, it cost him his job. As more prominent feathers came to be ruffled, the Park Service shamefully distanced itself from Jackson's activities, which were never apparently out of line, and hung him out to dry. Ferguson lets us know which side he's on in the book's preface, referring to the local outfitters as "Wanna-be cowboys . . . , each with at least one gun on his hip—angry, hating wolves and the government that reintroduced them."

The trail leaves the forest, emerging on a sprawling grassland. To the south is a wall of dense willows that hide the meanders of the upper Yellowstone. To the front, the blocky mass of Hawks Rest towers over the patrol cabin, which is enclosed by a rustic log fence. Before approaching the building, I make a short detour to the south, onto a long wooden footbridge over the Yellowstone. The river is wide here, but shallow. A single merganser paddles away upstream.

From the bridge is an unobstructed view of the Hawks Rest cabin, a few hundred yards away. A small group of people are out front. One of them walks apart to a spot between two trees and begins swaying in a rhythmic manner, like some kind of bizarre dance. Curious, I raise my binoculars. The dancer is an older man peering through binoculars back at me, while swaying in a half crouch and waving one arm over his head to draw my attention. When he sees I've noticed him, he motions me over with a large, emphatic wave. I return the wave and head toward the gate.

The man introduces himself as Val and says he and his wife are volunteers that staff the cabin during the summer. Standing nearby are three men wearing backpacks. Two of them smile openly through shaggy beards, while the third, who seems impeccably groomed for so deep in the backcountry, is more serious. Val makes introductions all around.

When I ask the backpackers where they're headed, the serious one declares in a deadpan tone, "Canada."

Thru-hikers, then. Why didn't he just say that? I've met plenty of thru-hikers on various parts of the Continental Divide Trail over the years, but never has any of them said they were headed to Canada. Or to Mexico, for that matter. It's a too-clever answer, meant to impress. It's quite out of character for the thru-hikers I've met. They are often the most friendly and likeable folks in the backcountry, always in high spirits and happy to stop and share their stories, which are often quite funny.

I'm a bit taken aback by Mr. Canada, here. Anyone walking this beautiful terrain only to impress people has their priorities badly askew. I decide the best course is to ignore him and talk to his companions. They are more typical thru-hikers, friendly and quick to smile and happy to talk of their trip. It turns out they are from New England. Having already hiked the Appalachian Trail and the Pacific Crest Trail, they are now out to complete the longer CDT.

"We have a reserved campsite in Yellowstone for tonight," one of them says, "but we'll get there by three." His tone indicates this is less than ideal.

Thru-hikers often average between seventeen and twenty-five miles per day, which is necessary to finish a trip of nearly twenty-eight hundred miles before winter sets in, and they prefer not to stop hiking so early. I understand their concern. Today is August 25, and they still have to walk across Yellowstone, then follow the Idaho/Montana border to the south end of the Bitterroot Valley, and then hike a winding route across Montana, past Butte and Helena, across the Bob Marshall Wilderness, and through Glacier National Park. And they'll need to do it all before winter gets serious, and winter can get pretty serious in Glacier quite early.

"You have to send in your reservations in March," the thru-hiker explains, "but on a trip like this it's impossible to know what sites to ask for, because you don't know where you're going to be on a certain day."

It's a fair point. Imagine hiking nearly three thousand miles over six months and having to pinpoint exactly where you'd be on a certain night a month before the end.

"We're planning to swing by the Thorofare cabin this afternoon," he says, "and see if we can get a new permit. We hear the Park Service isn't too friendly with thru-hikers that camp somewhere without one."

I hate to break it to them that the Thorofare cabin is unstaffed at the moment. Their faces turn grim at the revelation. Still, eager to get back on the trail, they say goodbye. Val and I wish them good luck.

Val then gives me a tour of the two-room cabin. One room is the kitchen, though it has a bunk bed to one side, and the other is a tack room, with a sleeping pallet on the floor. There's not an abundance of space and the design is a bit rustic, but it would be a wonderful place to spend a summer.

We return to the small porch and sit in camp chairs overlooking the meadow and the Yellowstone River. On a small table are Val's binoculars and a copy of the *National Geographic Field Guide to the Birds of North America*. As Val offers me a cup of Kool-Aid and some ginger cookies, he tells me he's seventy-three years old. He appears to be in excellent shape. His wife, Cindy, walks up, and Val introduces us.

"Do you guys work for the Forest Service?" I ask.

"No," Val says. "We're just staffing the cabin for the summer."

"We're like campground hosts," Cindy says.

That puts it into perspective. They're volunteers who take care of the place in exchange for the privilege of staying here. It's a good trade.

"Where you headed?" Cindy asks me.

"I'm about to head up to Mariposa Lake and then over Big Game Ridge to the south entrance," I answer.

"I just rode over Big Game Ridge two days ago," she says. "The trail is in good shape."

"Thanks," I say. "On my permit for Mariposa Lake, it says strong map and compass skills are recommended, but I haven't figured out yet what that could mean."

They are as puzzled about it as I am. "There's no way you can miss Mariposa Lake," Val says. "The trail goes right past it."

"That's how it looks on the map," I say.

We agree it must have more to do with where the campsite is located.

"At some of the sites, you can't find a sign," Cindy says, "and there's not always a defined trail to the campsite."

"I always look for the bear pole," I say. "It usually sticks out because it's up high and horizontal and looks unnatural. They're usually easy to see from a distance."

They give understanding nods. "There are a few new fires in the area," Cindy says. "Yesterday was a big day for fires."

I ask her about the new one to the southwest, but she hasn't seen it yet.

"There wasn't any lightning over there yesterday," she says, "but it could've been started by one of the storms a few days ago, and been smoldering all this time."

"Have you made it up to Two Ocean Pass?" Val asks, referring to the crossing on the Continental Divide, about six miles to the southwest. It's where Pacific Creek and Atlantic Creek diverge in a marshy meadow, each bound for a different ocean. It's a storied spot where, theoretically at least, a trout could swim from one watershed to the other.

I tell him I haven't been there but have read about it.

"When I have visitors up here," he says, "I read them the passage out of Osborne Russell's *Journal of a Trapper* that talks about Two Ocean Pass and the parting of the waters. Then the next day I take them up there to see it."

While we are on the topic of books, I make a grave error and ask Val if he's read *Hawks Rest*. Much of it was written right here at this cabin.

He hesitates and his demeanor changes. "I think the guy that wrote that had an agenda when he started writing it," he says.

Uh oh. Anyone who starts out saying someone has an agenda is usually about to tell you of an agenda of their own. While *Hawks Rest* is openly critical of outfitters who treat this land, and the wildlife on it, as though they own it and can do with it what they will, it turns out some of those outfitters are Val's friends. Even so, his response is not to defend the outfitters. It's to blame wolves.

"All the game is gone from this area because of the wolves," Val says. "You used to could drive past the trailhead up on Eagle Creek in the fall and it would be full of trucks with horse trailers. These days it's empty."

It's a type of claims wolf opponents like to make: purported firsthand observations that are impossible to disprove. How can you prove someone didn't see something? More likely it's hearsay that's been exaggerated and embellished through repetition and expanded again by more hearsay. Of course I don't say this to Val. I didn't come here to argue.

He continues: "One of my good friends won best outfitter of the year two years in a row, and his business is now suffering. And it's not just the people who use outfitters. The local hunters aren't coming out here either."

I try to steer the conversation somewhere less contentious. But there's no putting the genie back in the bottle.

"People want to increase game numbers by restricting hunting limits," Val says, "and reducing the number of hunts outfitters can make in a year. That's because all the predators are protected now. The bears, the mountain lions, and now the wolf is protected. Of all the predators, and I admit humans are a predator, the only one we're trying to manage is the human. If you want to protect the wolves, then you gotta kill bears and mountain lions to even things out."

Sheesh. All I did was ask about a book.

He looks across the meadow toward the river. "I've never seen the Yellowstone this low at this time of year," he says. "In the old days the river used to be lined with fisherman catching cutthroats. Now, because of the lake trout, there aren't many cutthroats to swim up here anymore. I had a game warden tell me if you catch two fish in a day in this part of the Yellowstone, then you're lucky. If you catch *one* in Thorofare Creek, you're good. Now the wolves are like the lake trout," he says.

"Except lake trout were never part of this ecosystem," I say, unable to stop myself. "They were introduced. Wolves were a natural part of the ecosystem until they were wiped out."

"Yeah, but this a different wolf," he says.

Okay, here we go. The super-wolf argument. We are beyond the bounds of rational discourse now. I make a show of checking my watch.

What the debate boils down to are values. Val values a land managed to maximize elk numbers for hunting. I value a healthy ecosystem that functions as closely as possible to the one nature put here, even if that means fluctuating wildlife populations and times when animals are harder to see. Because of this, Val and I will never reach any agreement.

"There used to be a wolf pack right here near the cabin," Val continues, "but they had to move on because they'd already eaten all the wildlife."

"I heard a wolf howling last night," I say.

"Well, sometimes you'll have loners passing through," he says, having an answer for everything. "The pack that was here moved on to another drainage further east, out of the park. They went there because game was plentiful there."

"I need to get moving," I say. "I want to swing by the Thorofare cabin on my way back to camp." I thank him and Cindy for the hospitality and shoulder my pack.

"You're welcome to fill up your water bottle from my spring," Val says, pointing toward a small pipe draining a short distance below the trail. "It's the coldest water you'll find, and the best."

"Do you need to treat it?" I ask, only because the pipe is quite close to a trail crossed by humans and horses, and it's inside a fenced enclosure where horses are kept.

"No, you don't need to treat spring water," he says. "I don't treat any of my water and I never get sick. I think all that talk about water treatment is just people trying to sell something."

I thank him again, fill my water bottles from the spring, and leave through the lodgepole gate, closing it behind me. The time is now five o'clock, and camp is more than three miles away. This is going to be a longer day than I'd planned, but I hadn't counted on spending so much time at Hawks Rest. It was an interesting visit, to say the least.

Curious about Val's claims of suffering outfitters and discouraged hunters, I would do some internet searches when I returned home. Specifically, I wanted to see if hunters had really stopped coming to the Thorofare area outside the park. The answer would prove surprising. The searches turned up a large assortment of outfitter ads touting high success rates in recent elk hunts in the area. They were accompanied by arrays of photos of proud clients posing over freshly killed trophies. It became clear that wolf opponents want to have it both ways: "Kill predators, the hunting's terrible!/Hire us, the hunting's great!"

The boundary marker on this trail is not as impressive as the one a few miles west. This one's a single post with a sign saying ENTERING YELLOWSTONE NATIONAL PARK. Beneath it is a smaller wooden sign, faded with age: Thorofare Ranger Station 1; Eagle Pass 17; Yellowstone Lake 17. Though not addressed, the Nine Mile Trailhead is thirty-three miles from here.

Back in the park, I head toward the Thorofare cabin. On the spur route toward it, the inbound prints of the thru-hikers are overlain with fresher prints coming back out. If it's possible for shoe prints to show emotion, these appear rather forlorn.

As expected, the cabin is locked. Beyond it is an old hitching post holding short logs hewn into horse troughs. Nearby is a most meticulous arrangement of firewood, set between three trees, whole rounds on one side and split pieces on the other. All have been cut to the same length. Out back, near the corral, sits another log building. Its door is made of vertical planks and hung with a series of long metal hinges that accent the rusticity. Against the side are propped two old wheelbarrows made completely of metal, standing upright on their noses.

I get back to camp just before 6:30. The new smoke plume looms to the south, taller and wider than yesterday. Fortunately, the wind has shifted, pushing the smoke to the east and clearing the air around camp.

After another dinner on the bank of Thorofare Creek, I watch as the last embers of sunlight glow faintly over Two Ocean Plateau. When the food is hung, I return to sit near the flowing water, watching and listening to the sights and sounds of the Thorofare.

Day 8. 6T1 to the Upper Yellowstone, Site 6Y2

Today's hike will be the shortest of the summer, traveling only a mile before making camp again, on the upper Yellowstone River. As it turned out, this is another stroke of Yellowstone serendipity. My reservation request asked for three nights here at 6T1, but the Central Backcountry Office gave me two, followed by a night at my second choice of 6Y2. Though it seems silly to pick up and move only a mile, this is my last day in the Thorofare. And spending it camped on the banks of the upper Yellowstone River now feels like the better choice.

When the gear is packed, I offer a silent goodbye to Thorofare Creek. Only for now, I tell myself. As beautiful and magical as this place is, I will be back. Even so, it's sad to be leaving such a remote location, one I've dreamt of seeing for so long. But I've spent nearly two days here, have slept near the creek, drunk from its waters, and stood on its banks for long stretches, mesmerized by the timeless flow. This place is now etched in my memory and imprinted on my soul. We travel onward together.

I am back on the trail at 11:00. The wind has shifted yet again, now coming out of the north. It ushers the smoke from the valley, revealing a sky of intense, unfamiliar blue.

The initial route is well defined, though overgrown with barely trodden grasses. In an area that was recently a mire of thick mud, horse hooves have trampled and churned the ground into deep divots and mounds. These have now dried and hardened, leaving rugged, uneven terrain. The hiking is difficult and slow, with a chance of turned ankles.

Beyond, the trail becomes less distinct, then intermittent, then nonexistent. No markers or signs are visible across the willowed terrain. After an unsuccessful search for the true route, I follow a path that appears to have been walked by other hikers. Nope— wildlife trail. Veering toward my original line of travel, I hope to intersect the official trail, if one exists. After a bit of bushwhacking, I cross another faint path. It's headed in the right direction, through thigh-high willows, but it, too, quickly disappears.

Why didn't the Park Service put "strong map and compass skills" on this part of the permit? It raises more questions about the campsite at Mariposa Lake. If they put that note there and not here, what must that be like?

The route-finding turns into a guessing game, searching for gaps in the willows and choosing those most likely to cross the brushy flat to the river. One of these crosses a boggy stream lined with thick mud.

"Ooey, gooey, rich, and chewy," I say aloud, confident no humans are around for miles and miles to overhear me.

Beyond are more fragments of trail that disappear into willows. I stop and scan the line of trees along the river, looking for orange markers. There are none, of course. They'll appear again when the trail is distinct.

Crashing through another brushy gap, I cross what appears to be the official trail. It's the most defined path I've seen in a while. It leads to the river and turns to follow the bank downstream, with nary a trail marker in sight. At least it's free of willows and takes me in the right direction. That is, until it turns and plunges into the river.

The map shows a ford of the Yellowstone on this route, but it's supposed to be beyond the campsite, which I've yet to see. The crossing here is at least four feet deep near the bank, and likely deeper out in the cloudy center, where the bottom is invisible. I keep following the bank downstream, taking a series of fragmented footpaths, or hoofpaths, or pawpaths. Farther down, a more distinct trail appears, this one marked by horseshoe prints. No doubt this is the right route. A short distance ahead is an orange marker and a sign marked 6Y2.

It is a strange campsite, set on a narrow strip of old burned forest, wedged between the trail and the Yellowstone River. Just past it, the river makes a tight bend to encircle the site in a watery hairpin. I check the permit for guidance. Next to the entry for 6Y2 is the following: "No bear pole. Approved camp—" The rest is cut off. Approved what? I wonder. Camping practices? Campsites? Camptown ladies sing this song? It appears I'm on my own.

It's a rustic site, to say the least, quite literally hewn out of a jumble of fallen logs. A few live trees near the river offer good options for a bear hang, but there are no good tent sites, other than too close to the trees.

I decide to hang the food first. A tall tree on the river bank has a straight branch reaching out above the water. Using a rock as a weight, I send the rope over the limb and raise the food bag, making the most scenic bear hang ever—ten feet up and six feet out over the Yellowstone River, with a backdrop featuring the southern two prongs of the Trident.

That done, I explore the area across the trail. Thick swaths of standing dead nullify all options. A short distance west is where the trail fords the Yellowstone, a crossing no more than calf-deep. On the opposite side I turn south, away from the trail, hoping to find better options for tent sites on this side of the river.

Following the bend around to the east, I cross a wide beach of sand and gravel lined with deer tracks and some other prints that could be raccoon. No bear tracks so far, always a comforting sign. No human or horse tracks, either.

Farther upstream is a sandy bench, set back from the river's edge and several feet higher. This is important, in case a heavy rain storm upstream quickly raises the water level. The ground is of soft, deep sand, which is difficult for walking but certainly comfortable for sleeping. Though putting my tent here may not be "Approved camp—," per my permit, with no better options, this is home. The tent is soon up, with my raincoat as a makeshift floor in the sandy vestibule. This should reduce the amount of grit that gets tracked inside.

Standing near the river, I look across at my hanging food bag. I should probably retrieve it and hang it on this side of the river, but, from the looks of things, finding another good tree far enough from the tent will be more trouble than it's worth. The food can stay where it is. I'll just make the ford at dinnertime.

I walk downstream, looking for the best crossing short of the main trail. Near the food tree is a shallow stretch of river, where the ford is a tad over knee deep in the center. It emerges on a muddy bank lined with prints of birds and the webbed tracks of some mammal, either otter or beaver.

Over a late lunch I watch the growing smoke plume, which swells in the afternoon heat. Above it, the sky is a murky smear of rusty brown. Beyond, screened by the ashy haze, is a distant storm cloud, turned muddy red by the smoke. Warped rainbows color its edges.

I hang the food and cross the river again, wandering the bank upstream and exploring like a child. It calls to mind an early memory, when my father took me fishing in his aluminum bass boat. It was in a marshy area in southeast Texas, crossed by a web of narrow channels. Instead of sitting there holding a fishing rod, I always wanted to go explore every waterway, stopping to examine each shell-covered bank for unusual rocks, fossils, or arrowheads. But Dad always wanted to just fish, so I sat there with a line in the water, looking at all those places I wanted to go. The memory hovers in my mind as I walk the bank of the upper Yellowstone, choosing my own destination.

Following a winding river while focused on the ground can throw off your sense of direction. When I finally look up, all the familiar mountains seem to be in the wrong places. To get reoriented, I stop and look again at the river. As I watch its slow, immutable flow ever onward, the surrounding meadows and forest settle into place, and the mountains are where they should be. I know where I am.

In early afternoon, I don long pants and sleeves for a cross-country trek to the south, toward a waterfall on Falcon Creek. Unlike at Cliff Creek, the travel is easy here, across a terrain opened by an old burn, with only small stretches of living trees. A bog of dense willows parallels the route, and the best travel is on the dry ground between it and a strip of forest. In a muddy spot where trees screen the view, a small frog hops from the trail and into the bunch grass.

"I don't want to step on you, Frog," I say aloud, in case any bears are around.

At the mouth of the low valley of Falcon Creek, I turn southwest, slowly picking my way over a lattice of logs in another round of guess-the-best-route. As the terrain grows more rugged, I try to wind along the ridge's contours, hoping to maintain elevation and smooth the ups and downs.

Since the hike began, the smoke has thickened further, blanketing the Thorofare with a dense, dark cloud. The Trident, now far across to the east, is masked by a shroud of black, purple, and red, as though the sky itself were bruised. The smell of burning wood is intense.

At my approach, a golden eagle perched on a snag leaps into flight. The huge bird dips slightly until its powerful, flapping wings give it lift. Rising slowly, it fades into the murky, smoky haze.

Approaching the falls, the slope becomes steeper. I descend toward the creek where travel is easier, until the route crosses an open, nearly vertical stretch with dicey footing. After a quick scramble over loose rock, I reach a solid area where the incline is more moderate.

Moving upslope finds a better view of the falls, now two hundred yards away. They emerge from a rock wall at the head of the canyon, shooting from the cliff's edge. Spanning their base is a huge logjam of long-dead trees, piled in times of greater flow.

I stop at the vast tangle of bleached logs. If there is a route around this jumbled mass, it's not visible from here. And any attempt to walk over it would be arduous and risky, unstable footing with the potential for shifting logs. No need to be foolish. This view is quite enough.

Heading back to camp I take a higher route, bypassing the rocky terrain along the creek. This way has its own challenges, with more downed logs and more stretches of dense forest.

"No bear," I call out before approaching one of these. "I know this is your habitat and not mine. I'm just passing through."

Back at camp, I draw water from the Yellowstone under a still-darkening sky. Low clouds of dense smoke turn the sun to a glowing blood orange. Without the warming rays, the air temperature drops, and what should be the hottest part of the day has turned almost chilly.

I'm inside the tent changing into camp clothes when a light clatter begins on the rain fly. I hurry outside to celebrate a fire-quenching shower, but the noise turns out to be from bits of ash raining down. Fortunately, they've cooled during flight. At the lightest touch, the twisted curls disintegrate into thin black smears. I wonder how close to the fire you'd have to be for burning embers to fall around you and spawn new flames. I hope I don't find out.

More charred bits fall like huge snowflakes. Some drop in the river and float downstream.

From an elevated spot, I study the smoke plume again. Though the fire appears confined in a valley several miles south of the park, it is growing daily. Tomorrow's hike, which turns westward and climbs Two Ocean Plateau, should take me away from it. For the rest of today, I'll take my cue from the birds. They are unconcerned. A chickadee sings in the forest, while a kingfisher rattles upriver. To them, it's just a normal summer day.

As the sun sinks toward the high plateau, the temperature continues to fall. In early evening the wind calms, robbing the fire of some of its energy. The thinning smoke exposes the crest of the Trident, which glows golden in the sun's last rays.

When darkness settles in, I find a high point from which to watch the southern sky. I'm curious to see if the hovering smoke reflects the flames' orange glow. But all is darkness.

From the forest nearby, the raspy hoot of an owl rings across the Yellowstone.

Day 9. 6Y2 to Mariposa Lake, Site 6M3

Morning is cool and sunny under an intensely blue sky. This is at least partly due to a light rain shower that fell overnight. My memory of it is vague, from the dark depths of half-sleep, a dim recollection of patter on the tent. Now, a barely damp ground suggests it wasn't exactly a deluge. (Rain always sounds heavier inside a tent.) And it wouldn't have been enough to extinguish the fire, which is only lying low, like a reptile awaiting the sun's heat.

Time to retrieve the food bag and get packing. *Woo!* Walking into a cold river in early morning will wake you up! Relief is in a hot cup of coffee, with the sun on my face.

After a quick breakfast, the hike begins. Today's destination, eight miles and seventeen hundred feet of elevation gain away, is Mariposa Lake, on the far side of Two Ocean Plateau. This is the day I finally find out if my map and compass skills are strong enough.

The initial route heads north, following the flow of the Yellowstone River. A flock of juvenile mergansers swims ahead, moving in line with the current. Seeing me, they take off, half flying and half running on the water's surface. They don't go far, and I soon catch up, sending them scuttling farther downstream in lines of splashing paths.

On the southern horizon, a low layer of smoke has already formed. It grows with the morning breeze, and a thin haze creeps north to the Thorofare, masking the base of the Absarokas.

The trail up Lynx Creek is in good shape. Among a smattering of horseshoe prints are the tracks of several elk, contrary to claims wolves have eaten them all. After a short ford, the route begins climbing the valley's north side, rising high above the creek.

The smoke is up here, too, having risen from the Thorofare or drained over the ridges of Two Ocean Plateau. The haze thickens with the rising temperature, until what was before a sky of bright blue now appears dingy, as though seen through dirty glass. The air tastes of burned wood. Back to the east, a partial view of the Thorofare is framed by the mouth of the high valley. Beyond the smoky expanse of willow and sage, stands the thin, ghostly outline of the Trident.

A dead tree has fallen across the trail, apparently quite recently. This happens even on well-maintained routes. I step over and resume the aggressive climb, having forgotten the feel of uphill travel after so many days on level terrain. On an especially steep stretch, I sprint-hike upward and pause at the top to breathe. Forget map and compass skills, on this stretch you need strong lung and leg skills.

At elevation, fall colors are more prevalent, faded shades of yellow and red. A goodly number of wildflowers are yet in bloom, paintbrushes and lupines, mainly. But the masses of fireweed among the old, bleached logs have all shed their blossoms, leaving bare stalks of bright magenta. Along the ground and zigzagging across the sprawl of logs, the shadows point northward, growing longer each day.

Leaving the old burn, the trail climbs through mature forest. Somewhere in here is the start of the Two Ocean Bear Management Area, though there is no sign. In this BMA, some off-trail travel is allowed, provided you get a special permit in advance. Because I'm only passing through on this trip, I didn't bother.

Voices signal the approach of a backpacking couple in their twenties. They are friendly folks, filled with the joy of hiking a backcountry trail.

"We're coming from Mariposa Lake," the young man says. "It may have been the prettiest campsite I've ever seen."

It turns out we are traveling the same route in opposite directions. In the four days they've been on the trail, they've seen only one group of backpackers and one horse party.

"You're alone?" the woman asks me.

When I answer yes, they both seem surprised. I mention the thru-hikers I met at Hawks Rest and the lone backpacker at

Beaverdam Creek, the one who decided to turn back on the second day of his trip.

"He said he'd torn a groin muscle," I tell them, "but I wonder if he didn't just realize he'd bitten off more than he could chew."

"I always want to quit on day two," the guy says with laugh. "If I weren't always with someone else, I might tear a groin muscle, too."

We all get a chuckle out of this.

"Is there much smoke back the way you came?" I ask. Their expressions are blank. I tell them about the blaze outside the park that's filling the Thorofare with smoke when the wind is southerly. They are eager to get moving, so we exchange wishes of luck and part.

The trail fords Lynx Creek again and resumes its climb. Above, a red-tailed hawk traces circles in a smokeless sky. I pause for a backward look. The only hint of the fire is to the southeast, where the rounded top of the plume just breaks the high horizon. From here it appears a nondescript billow that could be the puffy top of a cumulous cloud. In all other directions the sky is clear and vivid blue.

At the edge of a meadow, partially screened by a small stand of conifers, three bull elk graze in the afternoon sun. I stand motionless, watching them. After a brief moment, the nearest bull raises his head and looks about with alert eyes. It's as though he has picked up my scent. (No disrespect to the elk's olfactory senses, but this shouldn't be so difficult at the moment.) His head turns in my direction and his eyes lock on me. On some unknown cue, all three bolt into the forest in a rumble of hooves.

The climbing moderates as the slope eases into gently rolling terrain typical of plateau country. Though "plateau" can conjure images of flat and open tableland, in Yellowstone it refers to volcanic land that's only relatively level. In such places, lines dividing watersheds—like the Continental Divide, which crosses near here—can be easy to miss, even if the watersheds are the Yellowstone River and the Snake.

While near the Divide, I turn on my phone to check for a signal. News stations are probably reporting the fire in the most alarmist manner, as usual, so Mari may be worrying. The phone's screen lights up with only the words: "No Service." Perhaps I'll have better luck tomorrow, on the top of Big Game Ridge.

When the trail begins an easy descent, Mariposa Lake is only a mile away. After hearing the other backpacker say it may be the prettiest place he's camped, I'm looking forward to it even more. I forgot to ask if they needed strong map and compass skills to find the campsite.

The shining waters soon appear through gaps in the forest, slightly below and south of the trail. When the route leaves the trees for a grassy meadow, the lake is at the base of a gentle slope, not far away. According to the permit, the campsite is west of the lake. That's where the trail is headed, so I hold off on breaking out the compass just yet.

Across the meadow is a sign for the site. Though no spur trail is visible beyond it, the open terrain holds only one patch of forest, down near the lake's outlet. Clearly visible in the thin stand of trees, is the horizontal line of the bear pole.

I feel cheated. After all my wondering, I didn't need strong map and compass skills after all. I didn't even need weak skills. Of all places to recommend strong navigation skills, they put that here?

I eat my afternoon meal on a log with a wide view of Mariposa Lake. It's a beautiful setting, similar in appearance to High Lake, but with two distinct advantages: it has only one campsite, and it's thirty trail miles from the nearest trailhead.

Lingering over the meal, I try to eat as much as I can from the food bag. It's fuller and heavier than it ought to be so late in the trip. This is further evidenced by my loose pants, which tend to sag and expose the waistband of my underwear. I must look like an odd combination of bearded John Muir and a gangbanger.

When the food bag is up, I walk the site. It's close to the trail, within sight of anyone who may travel past, but the chances of that seem limited. As if to underscore the thought, a small mule deer trots out of the forest, across the trail, and strides through camp. Seeing me, she takes off in that characteristic hop—*boing, boing, boing*—bound for the opposite forest.

The tent goes up beyond the edge of the trees toward the lake. It's not a hundred yards from the bear pole, but it's better than setting up near the water, where thirsty animals come to drink. When camp is made, I sit against a tree at the meadow's edge and stare across at the lake.

The smoke column has grown in the afternoon heat, to reach high above the southern ridge. A portion drifts eastward in the wind, lining the horizon with dappled gray smudges. The plume continues to grow through late afternoon, rising in wide billows of grayish-white, with tints of brown, orange, purple, and blue. It's difficult to guess how far away it may be. Though the plume appears to rise from just past the ridge, wildfires often seem closer when smoke columns fill the sky.

The moon, waxing gibbous and nearly full, hovers above the smoke. It appears pale in the long-lingering light on the high plateau, where the sunset horizon is lower. It's quite a change from my last campsite, where the sun disappeared early behind high rocky walls. Still, the days are getting shorter and summer is fleeting past, as Yellowstone summers do. So full, yet so quick. A week from today will be Labor Day.

In the fading light a large black form appears across the lake, walking the grassy bank with its nose to the ground. The hump on its shoulders is clear, even across the distance. It's a grizzly bear and a large one.

Through binoculars I watch it work the distant shore. As it approaches the southern end, it acts as though it will turn and follow the lake in my direction. This would bring it very near my camp. But the huge grizzly pauses, its nose in the air, and then ambles south, disappearing into the forest.

I remain in place, awash in a mixture of feelings, from exhilaration to relief. Having seen so many tracks and scat piles this summer, evidence of bears, the actual animals had come to seem more removed. That has now changed. They are real, embodied, and they are *here*. The landscape now feels fuller and richer, as do I, having been touched by the spirit of the great bear. I sit and stare across the lake at where the bear passed.

As darkness falls, the moon shines dirty yellow in the smoky haze. Two elk steal out of the dimness, warily approaching the far side of the lake, crossing the path the grizzly walked only an hour before. Near the water they pause and face each other, and without violence, they lower their heads and scrape their antlers together. The rut has not yet begun. One of them soon loses interest in the ritual and wanders away, walking along the lakeshore.

In the trees near camp, a flock of robins clucks and chatters. A single bat darts overhead. As the remaining daylight fades, I can no longer see the elk, even with binoculars and an almost-full moon shining dimly above. Inside the tent I fall asleep to the gentle sounds of night.

I'm awakened at midnight by an intermittent splashing. It's close to the tent, on the near side of the lake. Images of the huge grizzly fill my mind, and I am immediately fully awake, grabbing my bear spray, and listening as hard as I can.

More splashing, out there in the darkness. Whatever it is, it's not moving. Not crossing the water, but standing in place and splashing. Bear spray in hand, I quietly unzip the top of the tent and peer into the night.

The moon, now directly overhead, casts a somber light on the land, but not enough to reveal whatever is in the water. The splashing continues. I try the binoculars, training them on the lower end of the lake, near the mouth of the outlet creek. In the dim light, two forms appear. Bull elk. One is almost up to his belly in the lake. A wave of relief washes over me. No bear.

As my eyes adjust, the elk become clearer in the moonlight. One makes a sneeze of a bugle. It is answered by several short, tentative bugles down the valley. Through the tiny opening, I sit watching and listening. The air is calm and the moonlight glow rests lightly on the land.

Up and down the valley, more bugles ring out, each of differing duration and level of virtuosity. One bull, somewhere above the lake, on the high terrain toward the Divide, seems most prepared for the upcoming rut. He belts out true bugles likely to attract a sizeable harem. Farther down-valley, another bull attempts to answer, managing only a few half-bugles that quickly trail off, as though he has run out of breath. Each of these is followed by a series of low grunts, which—if I'm anthropomorphizing—could be taken to mean something like, "Uh, yeah . . . I meant to do that."

The elk closest to camp, the one standing in the lake's cool water, now ventures his own reply. His first attempts come out as short, frustrated shrieks. But after a long silence, he sends out a single ringing burst that reverberates across the darkness and fills the high valley.

Day 10. 6M3 to Harebell Creek

In the dim inkling of dawn, a low fog rises from Mariposa Lake. Small waterfowl float sluggishly on the surface. A great blue heron, with plumage to match the morning's color, flies up the creek, flapping low above the water. It glides across the lake and out of sight.

The elk have also disappeared. And the wildfire has settled in the overnight calm, leaving a clear sky. Motivated by a temperature of thirty-nine degrees, I head for the food area for coffee. In the trees overhead, two red squirrels chatter and squeal, one chasing the other in an act of courtship, territoriality, or sheer playfulness. They soon turn their attentions to collecting cones.

As the sunlight's first rays emanate from behind the Divide, a single elk bugle rings out far down the valley. This one is more practiced than last night's attempts. Having gotten in the last word, the elk goes silent, leaving no sound but the cawing of a raven.

The morning peace is disturbed by the hoarse roar of a jet not far enough overhead. Though it's not the first of the trip, it is more distracting on so quiet a morning in such a tranquil setting. It passes quickly, and a natural calm flows across the land, an affirmation that in a wilderness this size, so far from the nearest road, the peace is deep and strong enough to absorb a few errant sounds of civilization.

I blow into my gloved hands to warm stiffened fingers, watching as the sun's first rays touch the ridge to the north. The light slowly descends, easing down to reach the meadow, the camp, and the lake. The growing warmth befits its golden glow.

One squirrel remains overhead, though there could be five, judging by the cones raining across the campsite. They impact the ground with dense, percussive thuds. When several land close to me, I look up to ensure I'm not sitting beneath a cone-filled branch. All clear.

Throughout its work, the squirrel maintains a steady stream of high-pitched chatter, intermixed with strings of whistling notes. Having reached some instinctive number of harvested cones, it scampers down and carries them singly in its mouth to middens dug near a fallen tree. When the squirrel climbs again for more cones, I walk over to check its supply. Dug in the soft duff under the log and between its branches, is an array of holes, each large enough to hold ten or twelve small green-tinted cones. Many are already full, though they remain open, exposed to the world and to bears, if any happen by.

A series of throaty grunts rises from the forest above camp. I reflexively reach for my bear spray, memories of last night's grizzly still fresh in my mind. The source of the grunts appears high in a tree across the trail—a mumbling raven. As though to laugh at my skittishness, the squirrel belts out a run of descending chatter. With bears still on my mind, I answer aloud.

"I know, Squirrel," I say. "I know."

The squirrel returns to its harvesting.

"It's a lot of work filling middens up here at nine thousand feet," I call after it. "I know a few squirrels that live at five thousand. They eat a lot of birdseed."

It's nice to have a conversation partner other than myself, now that the bear sighting has turned every noise into an approaching grizzly. I may have gotten lax with my bear awareness and noise-making after so many days of seeing no signs. Fortunately, that bear got my attention.

After breakfast, I change into lighter clothes to match the rising temperature, already at fifty-two. Something in the wind makes me sneeze, and I blow my nose with a loud honk. The sound is almost like one of those unpracticed elk bugles from last night. I hope I didn't issue any challenges.

Back on the trail, my route heads west, moving away from the fire, albeit indirectly. The initial travel is through dense forest that's heavily shaded in the low morning sun. I walk through the elongated shadows calling out, "No griz. No grizzer bear."

A rocky ridge rises to the left, and the nameless stream from Mariposa Lake flows on the right. West of the Continental Divide, this creek is bound for the Snake and Columbia Rivers and the Pacific Ocean. The Yellowstone River, though only eight miles back, now seems far away.

The first real stream crossing holds enough large rocks to cross with dry feet. On a low stone in the creek's center is a large blob of horse manure, an emphatic answer to whether stream water should be treated before drinking. Downstream, the waterway is lined with tall stands of dense willows. The limited visibility, in concert with the gushing stream noise, make this a likely place to surprise a thirsty bear.

"No grizzer bear," I call out, loudly enough to rise above the volume of the water. The precautions are soon vindicated by the appearance of bear tracks. Fortunately, these are days old and dotted by sprinkles from a recent rain shower, likely the one that fell two nights ago. A flock of robins lifts from the nearby ground, flying in fluttering waves from tree to tree.

"Hey, Robin," I call to the nearest one, "you seen any bears?"

Blank stare.

"I saw a big one last night," I add, leaving the reticent robin to its robinizing.

Away from the creek the trail turns dry and dusty. I pick up the pace to stay ahead of the rising cloud from my footsteps. Mixed in with the smell of dust is the aroma of burned wood. That time already? Apparently so. Gaps in the forest hold a thin wash of gray. And in the lower terrain ahead, a diffuse layer of smoke hovers among the treetops. Is it from the same fire or another to the west?

A sign marks the junction where the Two Ocean Plateau Trail takes off to the north. My route continues west toward the Snake River Trail. At least two hikers have passed here recently, judging from the different-sized shoeprints in the dust. Mixed in with these are some older wolf tracks.

Two mule deer bucks with large racks flush from the brush ahead, intermittently running and hopping over the rough terrain. After being so scarce in the Thorofare, large mammals are everywhere up here. People who claim wolves have eaten all the ungulates need to get out more. They are still here. They're just less likely seen from a porch or a truck cruising down a road.

One of the benefits of the wolves' return was that prey species have learned to be wild again. Now, instead of lounging in open meadows, as they did in the artificial conditions when wolves were eradicated, ungulates favor the protection of forests. The hunting may not be as easy as it used to be, but that old kind of hunting was artificial. It was based on inflated numbers of un-wild elk lazing about in the relative absence of natural predators. That wasn't hunting; it was shooting.

With wolves restored, things have become more natural, more wild. As evidenced by all the tracks in the trail and the sightings, the wolves are here, but so are the deer, elk, and bears. In contradiction to the deceitfulness spread by wolf haters, the evidence shows the ecosystem is functioning, and in a way more similar to how it worked for hundreds or even thousands of years before humans came along with guns, traps, and poisons.

Crossing a meadow I am shadowed by two gray jays flying alongside. It is unclear whether they expect me to toss them food or are hoping my footsteps will scare up a few grasshoppers. I continue on, leaving them to their wildness. More wolf tracks mark the trail, these on top of the recent hiking shoe prints. Wildness, indeed.

The next bit of route makes for difficult walking. The hooves of untold numbers of horses and mules have carved the trail into a deep trench. Trying to walk in so narrow a ditch, one's steps tend to bounce off the wall or graze the opposite ankle. I step out and walk beside it, where the shoes of hikers have worn a faint path over time. It's much better for bipeds.

At the ford of Plateau Creek, a streambed of large, orthogonal rocks also challenges one's footing. A good distance beyond, the trail reaches the edge of a large meadow of tall, straw-colored grass. On the far side is the Fox Creek Patrol Cabin. Like all the others, it's unoccupied and locked. Does anyone work out here?

To the south is a marker for the South Boundary Trail, which remains my route. For a brief stretch, my course will correspond with the CDT, though only for a mile or so. Soon the CDT will veer northward to follow the Snake River farther into Yellowstone. My route will continue west, on a trail that weaves in and out of the park on its long crossing of Big Game Ridge.

Ahead is the trip's first ford of the iconic Snake River. Up here near its headwaters, it is still a tiny stream, narrow and scarcely calf-deep. (On a backpacking trip to Heart Lake in 2013, I would meet a thru-hiker who said in a wondrous tone, "I crossed a Snake River right when I entered the park. Is that the same Snake as the big river that flows through Idaho?")

Beyond the river is a tall cairn. Set beneath the top rock is a plastic bag holding a handwritten note, dated August 28, 2012—today:

> SB [southbound] CDT friends. There is a fire going <u>on</u> the trail south of Two-Ocean pass, probably all the way to Nowlin Meadow. (You can see all the smoke rising from the SE, it looks big . . .)

It goes on to describe in intricate detail an alternate route the note's author heard about from a northbound hiker. It ended with:

> I will leave signs and arrows on the trail but of course, without a GPS and/or maps, I won't suggest relying only on these . . . Wish you all good luck, hope to see you in Dubois (or Colorado-Doobie! [the trail handle of another thru-hiker]). Be safe! Tamir [the handle of the thru-hiker who left the note]. P.S. I tried to draw a map of the fire zone and the alternate [route] on the other side of this note.

On the opposite side is a charming and well-drawn map, with a "We Are Here" at the top corner and a large roundish fire zone, complete with enough detail of trails and creeks to be helpful for hikers seeking a detour. At the bottom is a depiction of the highway to Dubois, Wyoming, with drawings of a car and truck.

I place the note back in its plastic bag and set it under the top rock of the cairn, silently wishing the thru-hikers good luck with a fire that has grown considerably in just a few days. I hate that I missed meeting the note's author, likely by only an hour or so. The care and personality in his writing and the accompanying map are more characteristic with the thru-hikers I've met over the years, so unlike the dapper dude back at Hawks Rest, who declared he was hiking to Canada.

When I got home from this trek, I would do an internet search on CDT thru-hikers in 2012 with the handle Tamir. Only one turned up, appearing briefly in the accounts of other thru-hikers. One of them said Tamir is a former member of the Israel Defense Forces who was hiking the CDT before beginning his university studies.

The sunny bank of the upper Snake River is a nice spot for lunch. According to a nearby sign, the Snake River Ranger Station at the park's south entrance—where this trip will end—is 24.6 miles away. Almost halfway there is the Harebell Cutoff Trail, very near the Harebell Creek Patrol Cabin, at twelve miles.

Over an energy bar I open the map and preview the two-thousand-foot climb over Big Game Ridge. For much of its course, the route stays close to the park's southern boundary, veering out and back several times before returning for good in the opposite valley. There are no designated campsites on this part of the trail, so my permit for tonight is open. This means I'll need to find somewhere to camp outside the park boundary like I did on the Sky Rim.

My plan is to hike all the way over Big Game Ridge and make camp just before the trail reenters the park for the final time. That means another nine miles of hiking from here, on top of the six I've already traveled. It will make for a long day, considering the climb, but it will put me near Harebell Creek, which is likely the next water source. Though the map shows a few streams high on the ridge, they are likely dry at this time of year.

The route begins with a not-too-strenuous ascent up an open slope. A few eroded prints of hiking shoes mark the trail, though not nearly as many as were on the CDT. A short distance south, nearly parallel to my route, is a line of the familiar white boundary markers. Still in the park, for now.

Instead of making switchbacks, the trail travels almost straight up the ridge, becoming sketchy across some of the steeper, rocky parts. Farther up, a faint path takes off to the south. The one heading west is certainly the official route, a conclusion confirmed by old prints of horseshoes and hiking shoes in the trail dust. On top of these is an assortment of deer and elk tracks. Some distance ahead, an orange marker is affixed to a tree trunk. Scanning in all directions, I see a white boundary post standing in a clump of trees down the steep ridge to the north. Outside the park already.

The route continues its long climb, alternating between dense forests and open burns, gentle slopes and vigorous ascents. Approaching nine thousand feet, the air becomes cooler and the wind stronger. A tiny trickle of water, actually more of a seep, crosses the trail.

Higher up, whitebark pines appear among the subalpine firs, including one large whitebark that appears healthy. Another sign of hope. Less encouraging is a tattered saddle pad someone left lying in the trail.

More climbing, and climbing. The eastern horizon falls away to reveal a broad expanse of sky. The view is over the now-lower terrain of Two Ocean Plateau, toward the turrets and tables of the distant Absarokas.

The next tiny stream is larger than the last, but only slightly. Because it's likely the last water on this side of the ridge, I stop to get a few liters as a precaution. The trickling flow fills the bag a quarter-full, and quite slowly. This makes for tedious work.

For a moment I consider hanging around long enough to get a few more liters. This would give me the option of camping high on the ridge tonight. As tempting as that is, it's only midafternoon and I'll reach the top by four o'clock. That feels too early to stop so late in the trip. My energy is high and my legs feel fine. And getting beyond this ridge today will put me in range of reaching the trailhead tomorrow. Though I have site 8C2 reserved for tomorrow night, eleven days on the trail is enough, especially with another long trek coming up in just over a week.

After more climbing, an unobstructed view to the southeast provides an excellent look at the fire. Even from this distance and elevation, it looks huge. Energized by wind and the afternoon heat, the flames cast up walls of colorful smoke across the horizon. I'm glad to be going the other way.

Higher still, the trail shows fresh bear prints, not especially large, but a bear nonetheless, possibly one young enough to still be with mama. Time for more noise. With my brain feeling oxygen-deprived, due to the long climb and the thinner air at nearly ten thousand feet, my first impulse is to sing *The Bear Went Over the Mountain*. But singing something that silly would ensure a group of hikers would appear and hear me. I can live with being caught talking to myself or singing Mozart, but *The Bear Went Over the Mountain* is too much. I opt instead for more conversation.

"What are you doing way up here, bear? I hope you found more water than I did."

Fire burning south of the park (view from Big Game Ridge)

Near a steep ascent on a stretch of solid rock, a golden-mantled ground squirrel appears. It hops gracefully to a low boulder and pauses to watch me pass.

"Hey, Squirrel," I say. "Did you see the bear that made these tracks?"

No answer.

"Okay, then."

The trail levels out, finally, at the top of Big Game Ridge. The views to the south, west, and east are striking, but the northern view is blocked by the rise of a short slope. It can't go far, so high on the ridge's crest, so I make the short detour and reach the edge of a high cliff.

Beyond it the land falls away, dropping more than a thousand feet toward a tributary of the Snake River. Now the views are striking in all directions. To the southwest are the Tetons, and to the south, the Wind River Mountains. The Absarokas stand far to the east, and in the north are Heart Lake and a stretch of

Yellowstone Lake, with the Gallatins looming beyond. Also to the north is another smoke plume rising from the forest near Canyon. This one appears smaller than the one I've been watching, but it is much farther away.

A kestrel launches from a tree near the cliff's edge, and as my eyes follow the arc of its flight, they are drawn away by a golden eagle floating far below, still high above the valley floor. The perspective of altitude.

Up here near the top of the apparent world my phone gets a cell signal, the first since on the shore of Yellowstone Lake. Mari is relieved to hear from me. As expected, news reports on the fires have been high on drama and low on details, making it sound as though all of Yellowstone is ablaze.

Back on the trail, the route follows the crest of the high ridge for a good distance. The feel is a bit like the Sky Rim, only higher and much more remote.

Almost all the trees on the lower ridges are standing dead, running strips of skeletal forests burned in 1988. At this elevation and on such steep, exposed terrain, reforestation is slow. Only a few tiny saplings rise above the low grass.

After a few high dips and rises, the trail begins its long descent toward the distant valley of the Snake River. The westerly course takes me directly toward the late-day sun, which is low enough to shine under my hat brim on this high terrain. I pull the hat down, leaving just enough clearance to see, and apply high-SPF lip balm. From a snag near the trail a mountain bluebird watches me pass.

As the descent steepens, the route begins switchbacking on a dry and dusty trail. The neighboring ridges rise to obscure the Tetons and most of the other mountains. Near the base of Big Game Ridge the slope moderates.

The forest here was also part of the burn. It will make finding a campsite a challenge, with the ground covered by a lattice of logs, with little room for a tent and few trees left standing for a bear hang. I'll figure something out when I reach the last boundary crossing, which should be any time now. According to the map, this is the last section that's outside the park. My plan is to stop at the marker where the trail enters the park and make camp there. That will put me only fourteen miles from the trailhead.

The sun sits low on the horizon from down here in the valley. I pick up my pace. Having hiked fifteen miles today, I'm ready to find that last boundary sign and set up camp. I continue on in the waning light, searching for white posts or metal markers.

But there are no markers and no signs. I get a sinking feeling I've already gone too far and am inside the park, likely far inside by now. Where are the markers? Having seen them in all other parts of the park this summer, I had counted on finding them here.

Now I'm certain I've gone too far, but there's no turning back. With the sun now behind the western ridge, the light is fading quickly. I continue on, hoping I've misjudged and a boundary marker will appear.

Maybe I should stop and make an illegal camp somewhere. But I'd rather not waste time crawling through this sea of logs in hopes of finding an open spot and a decent bear hang. I keep hiking, scanning to each side for a clearing large enough for a tent.

As the light continues to fade, I pause to take my headlamp out of my pack and put it in my shirt pocket. The Harebell Cabin is not far away now. Like all the others I've passed this summer, it is likely unoccupied. There should be room to camp there.

When the cabin comes into view, the sky is not yet completely dark, though it's close. Fortunately, the surrounding forest is unburned, with numerous tall trees for hanging food, and plenty of clear grassy ground for a tent. But, unlike every other cabin I've passed this summer, this one has open windows and a light inside. Not wanting to pop out of the darkness and surprise anyone, I call out a hello as I approach. A young man, not in uniform, saunters outside.

"I was supposed to camp outside the park tonight," I tell him. "But I never saw any boundary markers, so I ended up going too far."

"Yeah, that part of the boundary is not marked," he says. "Because that area was burned, nobody hunts there."

Now you tell me, I think. The boundary markers are only for hunters?

"Where you coming from?" he asks.

"Mariposa Lake."

"You've made some miles today!" he says.

I give a tired nod. I don't want to impose by asking, but I'm hoping he'll say something like, "Just camp here in the meadow somewhere, and hang your food a hundred yards away in the forest."

Instead, he says, "The problem with you camping here is that you'll spook my horses. They're wandering around with hobbles on. If they see someone hunkered down here tonight, they're liable to get scared and run off."

"So what are my options?" I ask.

"You can backtrack three miles to the park boundary," he says, a little too matter-of-factly for my taste, as if it weren't nearly dark already and I hadn't just hiked more than eighteen miles and climbed a high ridge. "Or you can continue on to Wolverine Creek."

According to the trail sign, that creek is only 2.4 miles farther, in the direction I'm going. The map shows a side trail there that travels a short distance to the park boundary.

"I'll head down to Wolverine Creek," I say, "and take that trail out of the park."

"There's no trail there," he says.

This just keeps getting better. I check the map again. It clearly shows a trail.

"There's a trail *sign*," he says, "but no trail. It got so little use that it's no longer maintained. You can still find parts of the trail in places," he adds with a self-satisfied grin, "if you know where to look."

Needless to say, I don't know where to look for an unmaintained trail in the dark, which it will certainly be by the time I hike another two and a half miles. I'm trying hard not to show my irritation, both at the Park Service for not marking the boundary here—and not telling anyone it's not marked—and at this young ranger for being so flip about it.

"Just continue down this trail," he says, "until you reach the ford of Harebell Creek. But don't ford there, because that will take you down the main trail. Turn south and ford the creek upstream and then go about a half-mile before you make camp. That'll put you outside the park. If you're a little inside the boundary, I won't be too concerned about it, as long as your food is hung. I'm heading out tomorrow, so I'll come by and check on you."

Muttering a not-too-sarcastic thanks, I strap on my headlamp and set off down the trail in almost total darkness.

It's widely known that bears are more active at dawn and dusk, and they often use trails for easy travel. All the tracks and scat I've seen this summer back this up. With that in mind, I unholster my bear spray and carry it through the darkness, speaking loudly enough to be heard by any bear within a quarter-mile of the trail. This is easy to do, as aggravated as I am at the entire situation.

"This is bullshit, Bear," I say. "Got me out here walking in the dark. Do you believe this?"

It is now completely dark, and the light of the headlamp doesn't show much of the route ahead. I maintain a fast pace, keeping up the conversation, as much as a way to vent my frustrations as to ward off any bears that may be coming up the trail in the darkness.

"The Park Service can't even be bothered to put up a boundary sign, Bear," I continue. "How hard is it to put up a sign? And now this idiot ranger sends me out to find a trail he knows doesn't exist. In the darkness. Just so I don't spook his horses. Don't you go spooking his horses, Bear."

It turns out you can do a lot of talking over two and half miles, even at a fast pace. My conversation wanders a bit.

"Yellowstone is for the benefit and enjoyment of the people, Bear. That's what it says on the Roosevelt Arch. Are you enjoying the benefits, Bear? I'm enjoying the benefits immensely. I might just enjoy them so much I'll accidentally spook somebody's horses. Spook some horses, Bear! But that might get you run out of here, run right outside the park boundary. If you can find it."

The ranger got one thing right: there is a sign marking the old Wolverine Creek Trail. I reach it at 9:15.

"Here's a sign, Bear," I say loudly. "What do you reckon it says? What do you reckon, Bear? It says Harebell—make that Harebrained—Cabin, 2.4 miles. The Snake River Ranger Station is 10.2 miles to the west, and the Wolverine Creek Trail, which apparently doesn't exist, though I gotta take it anyway, heads south, where it's a half-mile to the park boundary. Oh, boy. I can't wait to bushwhack half a mile in the dark, Bear."

I search about for a trace of the unmaintained trail, but all that's visible in the headlamp's light is a dense wall of willows. The ranger said to turn south here. I don't even bother using map or compass to approximate the old route. It's a clear night, and even with the light of a nearly full moon shining low in the east, the Big Dipper is distinctly visible, pointing the way to the North Star. I get a bearing on it, then head in the opposite direction, following the rocky floodplain to the south before fording the creek where it bends.

In the crossing's center, I pause and turn off the headlamp. Across a long stretch of water upstream, slivers of moonlight dance on the ripples. It's a splash of welcome beauty in an otherwise ugly situation.

On the opposite bank is another wall of dense willows. I peer into it, looking for a path, but there's nothing in there but more willows. Backing up, I scan to both sides for a clear way around. There are only more willows as far as my headlamp reaches. Hell with it, I think, and bull my way through, all the while cursing the Park Service, that stupid ranger, and his skittish horses.

Beyond the willows is a steep, sandy bank, which requires a scramble on all fours to reach level ground. Now all I have to do is walk a half-mile south to get out of the park.

I don't even make it a hundred yards. Quite quickly the terrain begins climbing, and the ascent turns steep, up a slope covered with downed logs. This foolishness has gone on long enough. I'm going back down and setting up camp in the first flat spot I find. It will be well inside the park boundary, no doubt, but just let that ranger come here and try to lecture me about it.

The real challenge is finding a bear hang with only the weak light of a headlamp. After much searching and looking straight up to shine the beam on any large branches, I find a tree with a long limb that's high enough. It takes more searching to turn up a rock to use as a weight to get the rope over. Finally, the rope is set.

After a quick dinner in the chilly moonlit night, I hoist the food bag into the dark sky. Then I pick up my pack, pace exactly one hundred yards along the base of the slope and stop. This is camp.

Fortunately, the ground down here is mostly clear of logs, with plenty of space for a tent. I set up on the south side of a small but wide conifer to screen my illegal site from view. From what that harebrained ranger said, the main trail should only be a few hundred yards away, beyond the official ford of the creek.

When I finally collapse in the tent, it's 10:50 and I've walked something like twenty-one miles, including the two-thousand-foot climb over Big Game Ridge. My feet are a little tender, but nothing serious, certainly nothing that will cause problems.

The good news, if there can be any on this day, is that the trailhead is now only ten miles away. I'll be home tomorrow afternoon. As I drift toward sleep, my anger fades and my thoughts return to the sight of moonlight dancing on the waters of the ford. What a wonderful sight. All else aside, if I had walked twenty-one miles only to see that dancing silver light, it would have been worth it.

Almost.

Day 11. Harebell Creek to Trail's End

At first light—long before sunrise—I am out of the tent, ready to clear out before any hikers happen by and see my squatter's campsite. I'm not especially concerned about that harebrained ranger coming out this early. He'll need time to round up his skittish horses.

Dawn's dim light offers a first look at the terrain I rambled across in the darkness. As luck would have it, the area is open with a few healthy trees. It's a good place for a makeshift campsite, certainly better than any I saw yesterday afternoon. But the route I took crossing the creek was the worst I could have chosen, and what had appeared to be a massive wall of willows turns out to be only a localized patch. Adventures in off-trail night hiking with a headlamp intended for in-camp use. If nothing else, the experience shows I need to get a stronger one.

The gear is packed long before the sun clears the eastern ridge. All that's left to do is stock up on water. Heading toward the creek, I find—just beyond the conifer that was supposed to shield my tent from view—a stretch of well-defined trail. Could this be part of the old route up Wolverine Creek, the one the ranger said you could find in places if you knew where to look? It can't be. It's in too good a shape for an abandoned trail, and it travels in the wrong direction. What trail is this?

In one direction it heads toward the creek, which is where I am going anyway, so I follow it down to see where it goes. The trail is in excellent shape the whole way, bending to travel along the creek bank. Then it turns sharply and enters the water right across from where I left the main trail last night. A nearby tree holds a tell-tale orange marker. This is the main freaking trail. And I camped within ten feet of it.

I recall the ranger saying I shouldn't ford here because that would take me straight down the main trail. But the way the trail turns and follows the creek, it really didn't matter where I crossed. I take out my map. Where the ranger said to turn south, he should have said southeast. That would've put me beyond the ridge of fallen logs and closer to Wolverine Creek. But I did what he said, and here I am.

It all seems funny, now that my gear is packed and all traces of my camp are gone. It was the perfect end to a ridiculous day, to wind up camped ten feet from the main trail. I could have done that without the ranger's help, and many miles back.

With full water bottles, I set off in the early morning chill, shaking my head while passing the small conifer that wouldn't have screened my tent from anyone's view. The initial hike is beautiful, along open stretches of the Snake River. It's much larger than when I saw it last, having gained the flow of the Heart River and numerous creeks. Site 8C2 appears on the far side of a wide meadow. A tent stands on the meadow's edge, about a quarter-mile from the trail. With no signs of movement, it appears the campers are still in bed. I pass silently by, apparently unnoticed.

By midmorning I am miles down the trail, still surprised not to have seen that ranger, who said he was heading out today. On horseback he should be traveling much faster than I am. Perhaps he slept in, too. Or maybe someone happened by and spooked his horses.

"Way to go, Bear!"

Beyond another grassy meadow are the Snake Hot Springs, a small but beautiful thermal area right on the Snake River. Near the trail are several shallow hot pools colored green with algae, and scattered patches of white-encrusted soil. On a large rocky slab, a yellow-bellied marmot warms itself in the morning sun. At my approach it slithers into a narrow crevice and disappears. Two other marmots scamper across the open floodplain toward the river, scurrying over rocks to take cover under a log.

Site 8C1, currently unoccupied, sits right on the trail, on a thin strip of level terrain between the river and a densely forested slope. No privacy here. Beyond it are more hot springs and pools, where curling wisps of steam form question marks in the cool air. The aroma of sulfur lingers. From the direction of the larger springs comes an outlet creek, which slides through a bright channel of turquoise and aquamarine. Anchored to the streambed are strands of emerald-green algae waving rhythmically in the current. The air is alive with dragonflies, some brilliant blue, others fiery orange.

Leaving the hot springs, the trail enters an old, dense forest. Two gray jays call in whistley-squawks from the trees. In the deep shade, two marmots hop onto the path and waddle surprisingly quickly up the trail and out of sight.

The trail remains in deep forest for several miles, with no views of mountains or water. Only forest. Through a narrow gap in the trees, something large and dark moves ponderously, parallel to the trail. It is only intermittently visible as flashes of deep brown among splashes of green. Finally, its head appears—a young bull moose. I crouch and lean, trying to get a more complete view, but from all appearances, the moose has abruptly and silently disappeared. All too quick for a photo, but long enough for a memory.

A mile from the trailhead, the first sounds of road traffic arise. Only motorcycles, at first, rumbling and clattering along the South Entrance Road, they are joined by the hoarse *whishes* of passenger vehicles. It's a rare occasion when traffic noise is welcome on a wilderness trek, but this has been a long outing, though wonderful, and I am ready to be home. Flashes of traffic soon appear through the trees, and all that remains of an eighty-mile trip is a long ford of the Snake River and a short walk to the picnic area where my vehicle waits. With lunchtime fast approaching, the picnic sites are likely full. I wonder if anyone will be surprised to see a grizzled backpacker walk out of the forest and into the river.

The ford of the Snake is wide but no more than calf-deep along a line of riffles. Still, it pushes with the considerable force one would expect of the Snake so far from its headwaters. I reach the ending trailhead at one o'clock.

All the picnic sites are full of busy vacationers, the tables covered with ice chests, bags, and bowls filled with portable food. Labor Day is less than a week away and summer is quickly fading. But the picnickers are in a festive mood, talking, laughing, and sharing. No one looks up as a lone backpacker walks past.

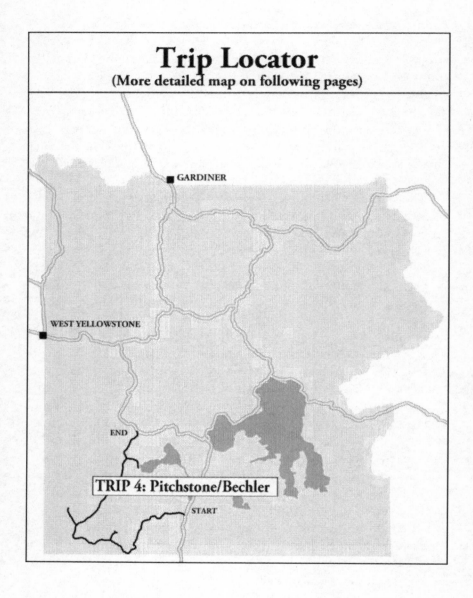

Trip Locator
(More detailed map on following pages)

GARDINER

WEST YELLOWSTONE

END

TRIP 4: Pitchstone/Bechler

START

Trip 4
Pitchstone—Bechler
September 9-18, 2012

Trip Overview

- START: Phantom/Pitchstone Trailhead on the South Entrance Road
- Across Pitchstone Plateau to Union Falls
- Across Bechler Meadows to Dunanda Falls
- Travel up Bechler Canyon
- Climb out of the canyon to cross the high terrain where Madison Plateau and Pitchstone Plateau meet
- Travel to Shoshone Geyser Basin
- Descend along the upper Firehole River past Lone Star Geyser
- END: Lone Star Trailhead near Old Faithful

Duration: Sixty-five miles in ten days.

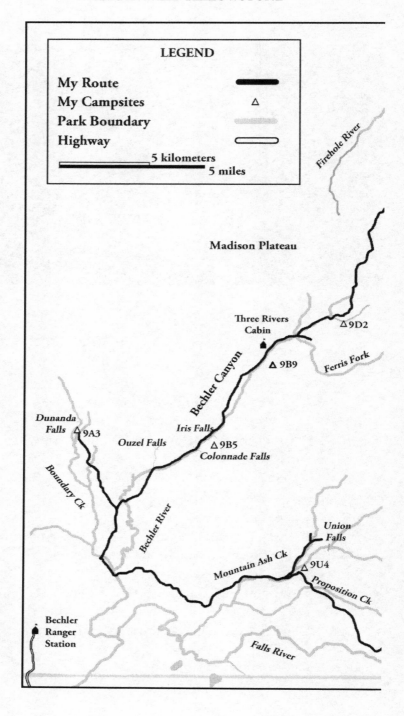

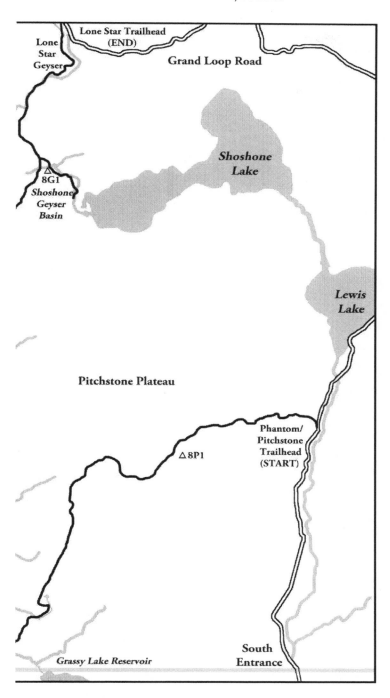

Preparation

Mari and I head for the park to set up the summer's last shuttle. It's Saturday, and we have a reservation at one of the Canyon frontier cabins. Though it would have been closer to both trailheads to stay at Old Faithful or Lake Lodge, we wanted to avoid the crowds at Old Faithful while staying somewhere new.

For this drive in, I have no thematic music, nothing to match the mood of this last trip of a wonderful summer. I considered the obvious, the fall movements of Vivaldi's *Four Seasons*, but they didn't seem right. Though they evoke an autumnal feel, this trek is about more than the end of summer. There is also the nearing completion of a long-held dream and a sense of growing fulfillment.

Also, the coming end is not really an end. It's only a pause. A sleep before a new day. A dormancy of winter awaiting the blossom of spring. If there's music that captures all that, I'd love to hear it. For now it seems best to set out with no music at all, in the silence of the open road, letting thoughts rise as they may.

In the evening, Mari and I walk to Canyon Lodge for dinner. In contrast to the sparse crowds at Lake three weeks ago, this place is abuzz with a resort atmosphere. And this is a week past Labor Day, once considered the unofficial end of a Yellowstone summer.

In my first years of coming to Yellowstone, this was always my favorite time, when summer crowds had gone and roads and campgrounds were not so busy. Now more people arrive each summer, and the crowds spill into what was once the shoulder season. Mari and I saw this firsthand last year (2011) on a late-September trip to the park. We had hoped to camp at the Pebble Creek campground, where I always stayed on my shoulder-season trips. Though we arrived before noon, the "Full" sign was already up. Thinking it might have been left from the previous night, we drove in for a look. Near the site of the campground hosts was another, handwritten, sign: "Yes, we really are full."

At Canyon Lodge we wade through the crowded lounge, a room filled with tables and chairs and groups of people chatting or staring at handheld screens. A party at a large round table is engrossed in a card game. Beyond them, wedged in the opposite corner, is a small wet bar with a crowd three-deep.

The hostess says the wait will be thirty minutes and hands me a large pager. We thread our way back and find two empty chairs near the door and try to converse over the crowd's noise. Though the busy atmosphere is a jolt to my mindset, which has gotten ahead of itself in anticipation of being back in the wild, I remind myself there are different ways to experience Yellowstone, and mine is one of the more unusual. Since the park's early days, people have come to see geysers, wildlife, and waterfalls during the day, and to lounge in comfort and camaraderie at night. There's nothing wrong with that. It's just better for me if I steer clear of these resort-y type places before the start of a wilderness trek.

The pager lights up in a carnival of flashing colors, and Mari and I are soon seated toward the center of the dining room. At a table next to us is a middle-aged couple, who appear to be taking separate vacations together. He is focused intently on an electronic tablet in front of him, while she is engrossed in the pages of a book. Throughout their dinner they never say a word to each other.

After perusing the menu—filled with such entrees as bison burgers and elk jalapeño cheddar bratwursts—I go with the prime rib and Mari gets the pork osso buco. It's not exactly chicken marsala on the shore of Yellowstone Lake, but that experience will always be hard to top.

Day 1. Canyon Cabin to Pitchstone Plateau, Site 8P1

After checking out of the cabin, Mari and I walk to the backcountry office at the Canyon Visitors Center. In addition to getting my permit, I'm hoping to add another night at trip's end, a stay at Shoshone Lake or somewhere within hiking distance of the backcountry geyser basin. Two uniformed rangers are inside, a young man seated at the counter and a woman standing off to the side as though only visiting. I hand my reservation to the young man, and he types the number into his computer.

"When did you first know you wanted to be a ranger?" Mari asks both of them.

"When I was five," the man says without hesitation.

The woman is less committal. "Well … I started out with the Glacier Institute," she says, speaking of a nonprofit that offers classes and outings in and around Glacier National Park. "Then I got a chance to work for the Park Service down here, which was great because I love to ski. But it's hard in the winter because you have to drive so far if you live outside the park. But then I married a permanent ranger, which meant I got full-time housing inside the park. Now I get to ski all winter."

While she is speaking, the young man focuses quietly on his computer. It eventually comes out that, though he very much wants a full-time job with the Park Service, his current position is only seasonal. Now into September, his time here is almost done, and his focus has shifted to getting on with the Peace Corps. On the counter in front of him is a brochure on Armenia.

I ask if there's a chance of adding another day to the end of my trip, perhaps at one of the sites at Shoshone Lake. He checks the computer. "All the sites at Shoshone Lake are taken," he says.

Of course they are. The lake is one of the most popular backcountry areas in all of Yellowstone, even late in the season.

"How about 8G1?" I ask, referring to a site two miles west of the lake, where the route from Bechler Canyon intersects the trail to Shoshone Lake.

"That one's available," he says.

As he types in the change, Mari is telling the other ranger about her first experience in Yellowstone and how it was love at first sight. The ranger stares back with a blank, I-just-work-here expression. Mari's disappointment is unmistakable. Those of us who love Yellowstone expect those who work here, especially the ones wearing the uniform, to love it, too. Sadly, it doesn't always work this way. To some people it's just a job, or what they have to put up with to be able to ski.

The young man prints my revised permit and places it on the counter where I can follow along as he goes over the notes. He points out that 9U4, my site near Union Falls, is listed as a bear frequenting area.

"Have people been seeing a bear around there recently?" I ask, thinking the warning must mean someone reported a grizzly prowling near the campsite in the past week or so.

"I think that has been on there since July," he says.

After the notes, he moves on to a list of backcountry regulations. "There's no collecting of any antlers, artifacts, rocks, or plants in the backcountry," he says, "but we do encourage you to collect any candy wrappers, cigarette butts, or any other trash you might find."

Nice touch.

"If you see a spot with too much trash to collect," he continues, "let us know so we can send someone out to clean it up. Also, we ask you to tell us if you see anything out of the ordinary, like abandoned campsites or scattered fishing gear with no people around so we can go check it out."

This guy sure is thorough. Why don't all backcountry offices do this?

"In the Three Rivers area," he continues, referencing a spot near the head of Bechler Canyon, "there's a hot pot that people like to soak in, called Mr. Bubbles. If you go in there, don't put your head under water. It could contain a dangerous amoeba that you don't want to get in your ears."

His speech finished, he hands me my permit and a card to place in my vehicle while it's parked at the trailhead. Mari and I both thank him and leave.

Traveling south, we turn west at West Thumb. A few miles short of Old Faithful, we stop at the Lone Star Trailhead and leave my car at the rear of the parking area. From here, Mari drives us back to West Thumb before turning toward the park's south entrance.

"Does it still seem strange," I ask her, "dropping my car off in one place and then driving me halfway across the park to start hiking?"

"Every single time," she says.

Two miles south of Lewis Lake we pull off the roadway, but just barely, on the short and narrow turnout that serves as parking for the Pitchstone Trailhead. For the final time of the summer, I pull my pack from Mari's car. We say our goodbye, and, as she always does, Mari stands at the trailhead and watches me depart.

The route begins with a steep climb on a rocky trail, ascending four hundred and fifty feet in less than a mile to reach Pitchstone Plateau. Only sparsely covered with young lodgepoles, the ridge offers views of the Lewis River, its waterway lined with meadows of tan and red. As my elevation increases, the river turns bluer than the sky, which is dimmed by a diffuse white layer of scattered clouds and smoke.

Beyond the river, far to the east, are the Red Mountains. Farther still, though not visible from here, are Two Ocean Plateau and the Thorofare. Now that I've spent time in those places, they feel more connected. And here on this final outing, all the far-flung parts of the Yellowstone backcountry come together in my mind, with a sense of wholeness I never felt before. It's a satisfaction of the old curiosity of wanting to know what's over there, what's beyond those mountains? In some small way, I feel I've begun to know. Thorofare's over there. The hoodoos are waaay over there. And the Sky Rim is up that way. There are still plenty of places I haven't seen, yet, but there will be time for them.

In the dirt of the trail lies a single feather, solid black but for a patch of white near the tip. My best guess is it came from a Clark's nutcracker, judging from the feather's size and coloration and the relative abundance of these birds in the high country. It calls to mind a memory of browsing in a bookstore and finding a field guide to bird feathers—a whole book on just feathers. The concept was intriguing even then, the information contained in a single feather. Though I didn't buy the book, part of me wishes I had it with me now. The rest of me is content with the subtle pleasures of informed speculation. Not every question demands an answer. Some certainly do—the ones that nag and gnaw at you until you search them out—but others, like this one with the feather, feel right with surmises and possibilities. It's akin to the fuzzy boundary between science, with its rigorous proofs, and the unknowability of art. For reasons I can't explain, or don't care to, the story of the feather seems more like art. It just is, itself. I let it fall and watch as it floats to the ground.

A glance up the steep slope finds a patch of sky instead of more trail. At the edge of the plateau the terrain levels out, somewhat, with only a slight incline as it turns westerly, traveling through open forest. The only sounds are clucking robins, chattering red squirrels and chickadees, and a gentle wind whispering in the trees. Now the trip has truly begun.

Most of the older trees in this area burned in 1988, though a few isolated stands survived. As elsewhere, natural reforestation is well underway, raising a green forest of young lodgepoles among a gray mass of dry logs. A robin sits atop an old snag while a noisy flock of more robins passes over its head.

Pitchstone Plateau, as its name suggests, is flattish but gently rolling terrain. Of the many volcanic plateaus in Yellowstone, this is the youngest. Nearly brand new in geologic terms, it's only seventy thousand years old (though it doesn't look a day over forty-nine thousand). It formed when masses of lava flowed out of fissures in the earth, oozing and building upon itself to create a wide plateau that stretches from here clear across to Bechler Canyon, thirteen miles to the west. As the lava flowed, parts of it cooled and hardened, even while the entire mass was still moving. This created the buckles and folds now seen in the gentle ups and downs of the open terrain.

Scattered on bare patches of ground are outcroppings of pitchstone, a dark volcanic rock similar in composition to obsidian but with a coarser texture and duller shine. Obsidian, with its smooth, glassy texture, results when lava cools too quickly for grains to form. Pitchstone results when lava cools slowly. This yields a mottled black rock that resembles clumps of hardened tar, dusted with fragments of dark glass. Set next to burned wood, it also resembles rocks charred in a wildfire, or stones blackened through years of lining a fire ring.

Though the trail remains in full sun, a cool September breeze insists summer has reached its end. The hiking clothes I've worn all season, nylon pants and a long-sleeved sun shirt, feel chilly, especially when I stop walking. As the sun eases toward the southern horizon, nearing its equinox date with the equator, its light, a soft golden glow only a month ago, has now turned hard, silver, metallic. Colder light to match the chilly days.

After a last small climb, perhaps a hundred feet in a quarter-mile, there are no higher ridges ahead, nothing but blue sky and a faded crescent moon hovering low like a wisp of smoke. To the north, the plateau falls away through a high valley to the lowlands on the Lewis River. The valley's mouth frames a partial view of Lewis Lake.

I step off the trail for a nutrition break, and as I dig into my food bag, a lone day hiker approaches from the trailhead. Walking the scarcely traveled trail in the company of his own thoughts, he hasn't noticed me sitting on a log off to the side. I call out a hello, and he stops at the edge of the trail, perhaps ten yards away.

"Where you headed?" he asks.

"Headed across the plateau to the Bechler," I answer. "Then up Bechler Canyon toward Old Faithful."

He knows the route, having traveled much of it himself. As we talk of trails, it comes out that this is the last of my four treks across the Yellowstone backcountry this summer.

"You should write a book," he says.

"That's the plan, actually" I say.

This piques his interest. He leaves the trail and walks closer. As it turns out, he is sixty thousand words into a novel set in Yellowstone.

"It's a combination of genres," he explains, "a bit of supernatural crime and nature writing. It's about an alternative reality where people discover a rare mineral under Yellowstone that can be used to generate power, and they want to destroy the land to mine it out."

"That's not all that alternative," I say.

"I know," he says.

Today he is out for a day hike to Phantom Fumarole and one of the nearby campsites, where a few of his scenes are set. Though he has been there before, he wants to return and verify his descriptions. With several miles yet to go, followed by a six-mile return trip, he needs to move on.

The route crosses alternate bands of forest, tan meadows, and dry washes of black rocks, the eponymous pitchstone. Near Phantom Fumarole, a steam cloud is visible from the trail, though the thermal area itself is a short walk to the north. It is not your typical fumarole—most of which are gurgling holes emitting steam and noise—but a broad area of boiling mud pots and splashing brown puddles. On one side is a hot pool that emits a ghostly steam cloud.

A closer examination is ill-advised, judging by the thin and fragile-looking crust around the bubbling pools. It's the type of surface overzealous hikers sometimes try to walk on, only to break through and burn themselves, sometimes severely, in the boiling waters below. I remain on the perimeter, where the ground is higher and more firm, spellbound by the bubbling waters and steam plume.

A strong gust hurtles across the land, its hoarse whisper vying with the hissing roar of the fumarole. For a moment there's a contest of sounds, of heated air spewing from holes in the earth's surface and cold air driven across it by wind. The two forces merge, whipping a cloud of hot steam directly toward me, covering me in a warm mist that smells of sulfur.

I continue on. Past the thermal area's chalky white ground, the trail crosses a low patch of thick, dried moss. The clumps resemble giant heads of flattened broccoli in shades of faded green, making one wonder how they might appear in early summer, when infused with ample snowmelt.

The writer appears again, his errand complete. We exchange brief greetings before he hurries on, with much hiking and driving to do to reach anywhere from here.

A mile past Phantom Fumarole, site 8P1 sits in a narrow band of forest in a large meadow. The only sounds are a sighing wind and a raucous flock of Clark's nutcrackers flitting from treetop to ground and back again. Pure poetry. Beyond the trees is a spring creek, the grasses and forbs alongside it growing lush and green.

The cooking area is set quite near the trail, though it makes little difference here on this last stop on the long route across the plateau. After hanging the food, I walk the forested strip looking for a tent site. There are few good choices among the trees, which include large leaning snags, but just a bit farther is the meadow's edge, with ample room for a tent. The ground slopes gently downward, away to the south, revealing a striking view of the Tetons, which anchor the southern horizon. Though distant, the peaks are a presence. Over the course of the afternoon their colors shift from cool gray to warm amber.

The Tetons, from 8P1

In the evening I return to the food area. Though campfires are no longer prohibited, I decide not to have one tonight. The moment is perfect as it is, sitting here at the meadow's edge and contemplating the mountains, the land, and the season. There will be plenty of chances for campfires in the upcoming days.

The sun settles low to the southwest, casting a dim copper light on the meadow. Its rays touch a Clark's nutcracker on top of a Douglas fir, turning its light grays to golden umbers. On a nearby snag, a red-breasted nuthatch works the limbs, pausing to pull a worm from the dried and rotting wood.

As evening fades, I return to the tent and sit outside, staring across the meadow. The sun dips behind the low rise of the plateau, leaving the land in shadow. The only traces of sunlight now linger on the western tips of the distant Tetons. As darkness settles, I crawl inside the tent for my last first night in the wild.

I awaken in the wee hours to a dim glow on the rain fly and climb outside to see the waning crescent moon shining in the east. The sliver of reflected light doesn't mask many stars, and at this hour, winter constellations dominate the sky. Orion stands mightily to the southeast. Higher above is Taurus, with Jupiter shining brightly just outside its open V.

Day 2. 8P1 to Mountain Ash Creek, Site 9U4

After a sunny dawn, dark clouds crowd in from the west, sending deep rumbles across the plateau. All this before breakfast is ready. While banks of dense gray shroud the Tetons, back to the east the rising sun shines behind white cumulus, setting its borders aglow and shooting golden rays across at the rain. It is a conflicted sky, both fierce and glorious.

I dally over breakfast, hoping the storms will expend their energy. As the westward clouds thin and break, more thunder rumbles across from the north. I can't wait any longer.

Today's hike will cover seventeen miles, though much of it on level terrain. Given a choice, I wouldn't have scheduled so long a hike on the second day of a trip, when the pack is still heavy with food. But on the route across Pitchstone Plateau there are no other campsites.

Actually, there's one site on the Falls River, eleven miles from here, but it's a mile from two different trailheads on the park's southern border. It seemed wrong to hike such a distance only to camp so close to a road, so I decided to add another six miles to reach 9U4. My reward will be a layover day tomorrow, with nothing planned but a short day hike to Union Falls. You can walk all day if you know a day off is coming.

The threat of rain has moved off to the north, though it's still a windy and blustery morning, chilled by screening cloud cover. The tent fly ripples and pops in the wind, conjuring images of loose gear sent sailing across the meadow as I try to break camp. To avoid this, I climb inside the tent and zip it up before packing the lightest gear first: clothes, sleeping bag, and ground pad. Back outside, instead of removing all the tent stakes, as usual, I pull only the ones on the downwind side. The tent dances and hops in the breeze. When the rain fly comes off, a sustained gust snaps it straight horizontal, where it flutters like a captured, water-repellant ghost. Soon it is scrunched and crammed in the stuff sack, with a water bottle holding it earthbound. The tent, soon released from its tension poles, settles in loose fabric on the ground, a low profile that doesn't draw much turbulence. The rest is easy. Time to move on.

Beyond camp, the trail immediately turns faint and then disappears completely. The route across the expanse of untrodden grass is marked, not with orange tabs, but with a series of short cairns, stacks of small, dark stones three or four high. These are initially spaced closely enough that you can see the next two in line, but not always. Sometimes you have to get quite close to one cairn before another appears somewhere ahead. Adding to the challenge, the low stacks of brown and tan stones blend well with the tall autumn grass.

At least the sky has cleared. Sunlight warms the trail, making a pleasant hiking day. The terrain climbs gently for a stretch and becomes more rocky, with washes and outcroppings of pitchstone. The cairns here are also of pitchstone, making them difficult to pick out among the natural jumbles of black rock. In several places I lose the trail and have to backtrack, retracing my line of travel in a zigzag pattern to find the next cairn.

This continues for several miles, as the route alternates between bare areas of rock and grit, and high, grassy meadows spread wide. Never once does a trace of a trail appear, only low cairns and an occasional metal marker, so old and weathered that the orange paint is gone, leaving a dull metallic gray. These are of little help in the actual route-finding, but passing one—usually lying bent and faded on the ground—gives a little peace of mind, a confirmation the cairns are in the right place.

You get used to it, sort of, falling into a practice of walking directly toward the most distant cairn in sight, while constantly scanning ahead and to either side for the next one. It's more tricky in areas with trees or large rocks, which often hide the markers. When no cairns appear ahead, I keep walking the same line of travel, looking to each side for low rocky stacks hidden behind trees or around bends. It doesn't always work. Several times I walk as much as a hundred yards without seeing another cairn and have to backtrack to the last one and begin a new search.

Across one rocky expanse, there are no cairns at all. Beyond is a line of trees with several openings where a trail might pass, but it's a guessing game which is likeliest. I choose one and head for it, until, a bit closer, a low pile of rocks appears crouched in a different gap.

This type of navigation provides an interesting dynamic. Often, hiking a clear backcountry trail, one tends to fall into a sort of hypnosis, focused only on the path ahead. But out here you're required to keep your eyes up, scanning the landscape for cairns and studying distant trees for gaps or the rare marker. Because this takes all your attention, it keeps you fully in the moment.

Near the highest point of the route, near eighty-eight hundred feet, the exposed terrain is strewn with rocks. Across the high expanse, the cairns are fewer and farther between, and every hundred yards or so I lose the route. Walking a zigzag pattern, I find a small, unobtrusive cairn at the far reach of one swing. Walking toward it, I see another, smaller, one a good distance beyond. Back on track.

Descending from the high part of the plateau, the cairns become more frequent again. The forest grows thicker, too. Surprisingly, two college-aged guys with backpacks appear, walking toward me. I call out a hello, which they return. As with many hiking pairs, one of them does most of the talking.

"We're surprised to see anybody else out here," the talkative one says, echoing my thoughts. They came in at the Grassy Lake Trailhead this morning to do work on a geology project. He shows me their plotted route on a copy of the National Geographic map. The line follows the official trail for another mile or so before veering to the north for two miles, following a line of GPS coordinates. "We have a backcountry site reserved for tonight," he says, "but we may not stay. It's supposed to get really cold."

Before I can ask about the weather forecast, he continues in a more serious tone. "It's pretty dangerous hiking alone."

I tell him this is my fourth solo trip of the summer and that I'm always cautious about making noise to avoid surprising any bears.

"We haven't seen any wildlife up here," he says, "but that's probably because it's so dry." He says this as though the apparent absence of wildlife makes it safer.

"How is the trail behind you?" I ask, hoping to hear it's better than what I've been on.

"Pretty good," he says. "We found a few cairns that had fallen over, but we stacked them back up."

Good citizens.

At this point, the quiet one speaks up. "When you start going down the ridge on the far side of the plateau, the trail is really overgrown," he says. "It could be hard to follow."

I thank him for the information and tell them the trail behind me is sometimes poorly marked. Because they are traveling by GPS, they are unconcerned. We exchange best wishes and part, and I walk on, wondering if the overgrown section will be worse than what I've just been through.

The next bit of route is much like the first, where cairns of two or three brown, flat rocks blend in with the natural terrain. At a spot where the grass is sparse, a short stretch of trail appears, briefly. Fresh shoeprints from the young geologists mark the dust, another navigation aid.

As the terrain continues its gentle descent, more intermittent traces of trail appear. There are no cairns in these areas, where they are unnecessary, but when the trail disappears again, low stacks of rocks rise here and there. When the route enters a forest, the trail is much more distinct. Here, the challenge is the many trees fallen across the route. Most are between ankle to knee high, easy enough to step over, though some are up to waist level. These I walk around when I can and climb over when I must. It's a good workout, but slow travel.

By late afternoon the southwestern edge of the plateau comes into view. The land falls away toward Proposition Creek and the Falls River drainage. From the high vantage, the blue waters of Grassy Lake Reservoir are visible just south of the park boundary, impounded by a rocky dam. Its long, straight line is at odds with the natural setting, a harsh contrast with the wilderness. It screams that, instead of a natural lake behind the false barrier, it is a reservoir. Artificial. And situated just south of the park, the outflow drains northward, flowing artificially into Yellowstone through Grassy Creek, which joins the Falls River.

Just as the quiet geologist cautioned, the descent is hard to find, both due to a nonexistent trail and because shrubs and saplings have grown across the route. The map's contour lines suggest the best descent is on the edge of a finger ridge a hundred yards away. Veering toward it, I ease downward when small clearings allow, eventually reaching the ridge's spine. The brush is dense here, too, but with enough room to zigzag around trees and shrubs to make an easy descent. In places, short sections of a faint footpath and old cut logs—some of which have shifted and scattered downslope—attest this is what's left of the official route.

On the level floodplain, the trail is more evident, though still overgrown. Thankful for long pants, I push through scratchy knee-high brush to the short crossing of Proposition Creek. It's the first flowing water I've seen since leaving camp this morning.

With refilled water bottles, I continue on the overgrown trail toward the Falls River. Just before the river is site 9F2, the only other campsite on today's route. Even after a full day of route-searching and log stepping, I am glad this site—so close to a road and two trailheads—is not my destination. My campsite is only six miles away, and there's plenty of daylight left to get there before dark.

At a trail junction near the Falls River, my route turns northwest. A sign says the Ashton-Flagg Ranch Road is 1.4 miles to the south. It also says Phantom Fumarole is thirteen miles back, though the National Geographic map indicates it is closer to twelve. Such discrepancies between maps and signs are not uncommon.

The trail toward Union Falls is wide and clear. In places the surface is solid rock, a reminder the route was once a wagon road, a rough one, built by settlers in the 1880s to connect Marysville, Idaho, with Jackson Hole. Whatever shape it was in then, today it's overgrown and rocky, with stretches of uneven slabs, often set at an incline. Near one of these, several grouse flush and scamper in a sort of half-flight into the forest.

A mile before reaching the campsite, I find the first wet-feet ford of the trip. It's another crossing of Proposition Creek, now both wider and deeper. Though the water is shaded from the low afternoon sun, a small warming ray touches the upper bank, setting the streamside vegetation alight in beautiful patches of yellow-green.

Beyond the creek, a valley garter snake lies stretched across the trail. Perhaps twenty-eight inches in total, just long enough to cover the width of the path, its color is between black and deep, glossy green, with three yellow stripes down the length of its back and sides. It is a subspecies of the common garter snake, but one that's relatively uncommon in the Yellowstone area. It's found only here in the Falls River drainage and along a short section of the Snake River, as it were, just south of the park boundary. On this cool September evening, it seems in a state of torpor, remaining motionless as I approach within a few feet. To avoid disturbing it, I slowly step over its tail. The snake never moves so much as a twitch. Leaving it in peace, I continue toward camp.

I reach the junction with the Union Falls Trail just after seven. The sun still hovers above the southwestern ridge. Near my campsite, on a trailside tree, is a sign: ATTENTION Bear Frequenting Area. These words are printed in large, red letters over a background of a standing bear with large claws. In smaller print the sign says to make noise, be aware, hang all food, and proceed with caution.

I continue on, saying aloud, "Proceeding with caution. Come on, caution, let's proceed to make camp."

By eight o'clock, the food is up, camp is made, and the bottles are filled. Though the sun has long since fallen behind the distant ridge, a tiny bit of daylight remains.

Day 3. Layover Day, Day Hike to Union Falls

Woo! I awaken to a temperature of twenty-six degrees. In contrast to the mildly cool mornings of the Yellowstone summer, this is a deep, piercing chill that flows through your bone marrow and seizes your joints. And it won't be warming up any time soon, with the sun still hours away from clearing the walls of Pitchstone Plateau.

The good news is today is a layover day, with nothing planned but a short hike to Union Falls. I linger in the tent and read, waiting for the sun to clear the plateau and cast a little warmth. Long before that happens, I get the tent version of cabin fever and decide to get out and see the morning.

One of the hardest parts of cold-weather camping is leaving a warm sleeping bag to put on chilled clothes. It helps if you pull the clothes into the sleeping bag with you to warm them up. Then you throw open the bag and dress as quickly as possible. It's never quickly enough.

Outside, the morning is beautiful, if a bit airish. On the way to the food area, I gather an armload of dead branches from the ground, and soon a nice fire is dancing in the fire ring. Crackle, pop, warmth. After a summer filled with burn bans, it's comforting to reconnect with campfire.

Site 9U4 is a beautiful camp, nestled between the base of Pitchstone Plateau and Mountain Ash Creek. The forest is open and the terrain clear and level. A long stretch of the creek flows on one side.

After breakfast, all that remains of the fire are glowing, flickering coals. I toss two days' worth of trash on top of these, and the pieces shrivel and curl into flames and shrink to the thinnest of ashes. Later, when the fire is out, fully extinguished with cold creek water,

I rake through the soggy ashes and remove the bits that didn't burn, mostly pieces of foil lining from oatmeal packets. Once the ash and dust is shaken off, these go in the trash bag and up the bear pole with the food.

A sign near the food area indicates this site has a pit toilet. I follow the narrow trail to see what type of luxury it offers. It's nothing more than a brown plywood box with an oval hole in the top. Still, it's better than having to make like a bear. At this early hour—and today at this site ten o'clock feels early—the plywood is hard and ice-cold. If you weren't awake before ...

A few minutes before noon, voices drift across from the trail, which passes near my food area before turning to cross Mountain Ash Creek. It is two middle-aged women in day hiking gear, walking toward Union Falls. I decide to delay my hike for a while to let them enjoy the falls by themselves.

An hour later I set out, hiking under a low, overcast sky. Fall colors, from browning maroons to bright aspen-golds, are everywhere. At the trail's edge is the trip's first butterfly, a mourning cloak, its wings of purplish black lined on the outer edge with cream-colored bands.

The route passes a small ranger cabin, a tall, skinny A-frame with a towering radio antenna. It is unoccupied.

The jingle of bear bells precedes the two women returning from the falls. It's clear they don't want to stop hiking, so we exchange friendly greetings in passing.

Ahead, the trail forks, one route heading to Union Falls, the other to Ouzel Pool (known to some hikers as Scout Pool). To one side is an open area with a couple of hitching posts, a food pole, and a sign that says, "No horses beyond this point." Another adds, "All food not within immediate control (at all times) must be appropriately hung at this food pole." Though the notice would seem to be directed at stock users, there's a small food bag hung from the pole and no horses. At least one person is around here somewhere.

Down the route to Union Falls, a distant thundering roar rises, beckoning. After a few climbing switchbacks, where glints of white flash through conifered gaps, the trail ends at a cliff overlooking Mountain Ash Creek. Just upstream are the beautiful, towering falls. No one else is around.

Union Falls is one of the most iconic waterfalls in a region known for its waterfalls. Here in the Bechler, in Yellowstone's southwest corner, nearly eighty inches of precipitation falls each year, much of it as winter snow. And because the area is set at the base of two high plateaus—Pitchstone to the east and Madison to the north—it is a land of cliffs and steep slopes that form waterfalls across the region. In fact, one of the challenges of planning a trek to this area is deciding how many, and which, waterfalls to see, and which ones to try to camp near.

Union Falls, at two hundred and fifty feet, is the second-highest waterfall in the park, behind the lower falls of the Yellowstone (three hundred and eight). Its name refers to the joining of two streams near its brink, though from this vantage there appear to be three, as one of them splits before they all tumble together in intermingled drops, splashes, and cascades down the pyramidal face of a cliff. The thunderous roar from its base fills the small valley.

Union Falls

Out here in the backcountry, there are no platforms or guardrails to protect visitors from their own carelessness or foolhardiness. As a result the area has a wilderness feel, and the falls look much as they have for untold centuries.

Far below, a faint path along the creek travels toward the wide base of the falls, but the only apparent way to get down there is a steep chute of a trail. From the looks of things, the real challenge would be getting back up again, though people have apparently done it. Perhaps there are better routes if one wanted to search around. I am content to gaze at the falls from here.

After some extended time of standing captivated by cascading waters, I come back to myself. It is truly a wonderful spot, one of the many places in Yellowstone where time stands still. I take another long look at the falls, as if to absorb one last bit of their wonder, before heading back.

In the cool light of a cloudy afternoon, chipmunks and red squirrels scamper about, gathering food for the impending winter. They dart across the ground here and run along logs there, as the calls of a northern flicker ring out of the forest. Back at the trail junction, the food bag still hangs from the bear pole, suggesting it belongs to someone who is hanging out at Ouzel Pool.

The trail in that direction is only three-tenths of a mile, along an unnamed tributary of Mountain Ash Creek. It leads to a small waterfall that tumbles into a wider pool, a popular site with hikers seeking a backcountry soak. As attractive as the idea may be on a hot afternoon in mid-August, on this chilly, overcast day in mid-September, it's not so inviting. The mystery of the hanging food bag remains just that, as no one else is around.

Stapled to a nearby tree is a sign that says:

Ouzel Pool Restoration Area
Off-trail travel prohibited
Violators Subject to $50 Fine or Mandatory Appearance

Interesting penalties. While a fifty dollar fine may not be much of a deterrent, a mandatory appearance could put a hurt on someone who lived far away. Imagine the cost and inconvenience to someone living on the East Coast, in having to show up at the Yellowstone Justice Center in Mammoth at some inopportune time not of their choosing. I wonder if it is enforced.

After a peaceful time at Ouzel Pool, I turn toward camp. A wandering garter snake lies in the trail, showing much more yellow than the green valley garter snake from yesterday evening. It also shows more energy in the midafternoon light. Like Emily Dickinson's narrow fellow in the grass, it wrinkles and is gone.

At the hitching area, a lone hiker sits near the empty food pole, repacking his gear. I stop and try to make conversation, but though he is not unfriendly, he is untalkative and avoids eye contact. All I get from him is he came in at Grassy Lake and has been hiking an off-trail loop between Ouzel Pool and Union Falls, the Ouzel Pool Restoration Area notwithstanding.

Back at camp, another campfire warms the evening, extending an autumn day overshortened by high ridges. When darkness and the accompanying chill descend, I douse what's left of the fire and return to the tent.

Day 4. 9U4 to Dunanda Falls, Site 9A3

Another cold morning, with temps in the mid-twenties. After a late breakfast, I am back on the trail, headed toward Bechler Meadows. The sun shines dimly in a faded sky screened by the ubiquitous smoky haze.

The initial route follows the flow of Mountain Ash Creek, its smooth surface undisturbed by rapids, and the clear, bluish water revealing a pebbly bottom. Across to the north is the west-running escarpment of Pitchstone Plateau, with rocks of browns, yellows, and reds, warm colors to match the fall foliage.

Not far ahead, the creek turns south, and the westerly trail makes a knee-deep ford. Beyond, the route splits into a three-track, a horse-dug trench with two footpaths on either side. The forest is open parkland, interspersed with meadows of straw-colored grass. A gray jay glides down from a nearby tree, chasing one of the few remaining grasshoppers.

In a mixed forest of firs growing among masses of lodgepoles, a cow elk grazes thirty yards from the trail. When she sees me, she bolts, setting off a widespread clatter of hooves from an unseen elk herd in flight. In the commotion a large bull bedded down near the trail pops up, and in a blur of immense brown it disappears in the forest with the receding sound of crashing branches and fading hoof beats. Its extensive rack, spreading high and wide, recedes like a flying tree. It's the sort of chance wildlife encounter that lingers long after the animals have departed, fleeting in actual duration, but long-lasting in effect. I stand transfixed, staring into the forest.

The next meadow is tan and dry, and lined with bushes the color of burgundy. In places, bits of low-growing sage creep toward the center, changing the overall color from warm tan to cool gray. Stands of golden-leafed aspens add a shimmering background of intense yellow. Two cow elk graze on the far side. Seeing me, they trot toward the opposite forest, not frantic, just putting space between themselves and me. I hurry past, not wanting to stress them and hinder their feeding. They'll need all the reserves they can muster, to get them through winter.

The Rocky Ford of the Bechler River is indeed rocky. It is also wide. Though the riverbed is solid rock, it is pocked with holes and ridges and dashed with green clumps of moss that undulate in the current. The crossing is knee-deep a short distance downstream, though care is required to avoid slipping on a mossy patch or stepping into a trench. The current, while not especially swift, carries enough force to make one glad it's not deeper.

So wide a crossing takes time, and when I step from the river my feet have taken on a deep chill. No worries, though. It's time for lunch, a chance to take off wet shoes and socks and let them dry as much as possible in the dim sunlight.

Beyond the river is a log, a nice spot for a picnic. After refilling the water bottles, I remove my shoes and peel off my socks, wringing them out before draping them over the log in the sun. The early afternoon air is cool but not cold, quite comfortable where the sunlight falls. A hundred yards away, a flock of brown ducklings swims in a tight line up the Bechler River.

After an extended break, I pull the damp socks and shoes back on. They didn't dry much in the cool air, but the sopping water is mostly gone and my feet don't slosh and squish with each step. They'll warm up once I start hiking.

The route continues along the beautiful Bechler River for a spell, traveling upstream. Then it turns away into denser forest. At site 9C1, several young guys are busy setting up a canvas wall tent. One wears a Park Service uniform, though his shirt is untucked and rumpled and looks slovenly. One of the others calls out a greeting, and we chat briefly across a distance of twenty-five yards. They are a trail crew, out cutting fallen logs and repairing damaged tread.

At the junction with the Bechler River Trail, my route turns north. Near the forest edge, a male blue grouse steps slowly and purposefully into the trail, slightly puffed but not in full display. I pause to let him cross and then continue onward.

Bechler Meadows is such a beautiful and storied place that, when you finally stand at its edge, you have to stop and let it sink in that you're actually here. Beyond the forest edge, spread far to the front is a wide sea of grass, bordered on all sides with dark lines of conifer forest, tiny in the distance. Beyond the trees to the north, the terrain rises steeply to more plateau country, cleft by the mouth of Bechler Canyon. The slopes are dappled with conifers, which appear almost black across the vast expanse.

Near the meadow's edge, the route crosses Boundary Creek via a cable footbridge. A sign says: "Warning—Bridge unsafe for more than one person at a time. No playing on bridge. Violators subject to prosecution." Its floor is a line of thin board-like slats made of plastic, and both sides are fenced with three strands of cable that spread outward from the base in a narrow V. The topmost is at a height to serve as handholds, which prove necessary as the bridge sags and sways through the crossing.

Bridge over Boundary Creek

From here the route sets off across the wide sea of autumn grass. Views abound in all directions, except to the south, where a layer of smoke turns the Tetons a blurry, whitish purple. Another smoke plume rises far to the southeast, apparently from an active fire, perhaps the same one I saw in the Thorofare.

As it crosses the meadow, the trail's surface is covered, not by dirt as in other places, but with flattened, walked-over grass stalks. The appearance is so natural it could be no more than a game trail. A small sparrow stands in the center a short distance ahead, its back toward me and its head turned to the side to watch me with one eye. When I invade its comfort zone, it doesn't fly away, but flutters a short distance down the grassy corridor to stop and watch again as I approach. This continues through several cycles of approach and retreat until we are a hundred yards to the north. Wanting to end the crazy cycle, I pick a section of shorter grass and detour through the knee-high growth to get around the bird. When I return to the trail, the sparrow is behind me, its back toward me and its head turned, watching me with one eye.

As the route moves northward, a line down the western rim of Bechler Canyon stands out as a streak of white amid dark slopes. It is Ouzel Falls, visible from most parts of the meadow, a constant presence, though distant.

Just east of the trail is a water-filled channel not shown on the map. If it's flowing at all, the movement is imperceptible, the water's brown clarity unbroken by even a tiny riffle. Along its course are banks of dense, tall grass, a mix of stalks and seedheads in masses of yellows, browns, and greens. The water between them has sheens of dull silver that match the smoky sky.

As beautiful as these meadows are, there was a time when we came close to losing them. During and after the First World War, a growing agriculture industry, combined with local boosterism hoping to attract more residents, wanted more water—more crops and more green. This led to a wave of dam building across the West. As historian Richard Bartlett put it, "No stream, beaver pond, or lush meadow escaped irrigationists' notice." Even the beautiful Jackson Lake, at the base of the neighboring Tetons, was dammed, in 1916. From there, dam builders moved north, eyeing the flowing waters of Yellowstone National Park, especially the Bechler region, which was scarcely visited in those years.

In 1920, an Idaho congressman named Addison Smith sponsored a bill to allow dams and reservoirs in the Bechler, inside the park boundary. "There is absolutely nothing in the way of unusual scenery or other interesting features in this part of the park," he told Congress. "[T]he entire area contains only the ordinary Western mountain landscape scenes, such as may be seen along the lines of travel for many miles by any tourist approaching the park from any direction."

Had Smith's bill become law, the entire Bechler area might now be a series of reservoirs, connected by ditches and roads, with maintenance buildings and power lines. And at the end of each summer, after all the waters had been drained to flood the fields of a few Idaho farmers, the reservoirs would devolve into mudflats stubbled with trunks of drowned trees.

As outrageous as this seems today, it had widespread support at the time. And there was recent precedent for putting a dam in a national park: the infamous damming of Yosemite's Hetch Hetchy Valley, which was completed in 1923, but had been in motion many years before then. The proposed dams in Yellowstone even had the support of Interior Secretary Franklin Lane, who had also supported damming the Hetch Hetchy.

In 1919, Lane ordered National Park Service Director Stephen Mather and Yellowstone Superintendent Horace Albright to allow a dam survey of the Bechler region. He also told them to follow it up with a favorable report on the proposed dams. In a manner reminiscent of the way the Army made creative use of weak laws to battle poachers, Mather and Albright found creative ways to resist. When the surveyors arrived in Yellowstone in late summer, the horses they needed had already been sent away to winter pasture, and the boats they had asked for had been put into winter storage. Mather and Albright also put off writing their report. They were even prepared to resign if the dams were approved, which they weren't, fortunately. Secretary Lane left office in February of 1920, without saying why.

After a lull of a few years, the dam proponents were back. This time they tried to get in on the push to change Yellowstone's boundaries, the changes that added the Sky Rim and Hoodoo Basin to the park. While the boundaries were being reconfigured, they said, the Bechler should be carved out of the park and returned to the public domain. (This argument is still being used by public lands opponents today. While it may sound like a populist goal to put land back in the public domain, what it dishonestly leaves out is that the once-public lands would then be turned over to commercial interests, who would degrade the natural setting in pursuit of profit.)

More dam proposals came from north of the park. The Montana Irrigation Commission proposed damming Yankee Jim Canyon, just beyond the northern entrance, to store irrigation water for Paradise Valley. Even worse, a U.S. senator from Montana proposed building a dam across the Yellowstone River near the outlet of Yellowstone Lake. This proposal found support in Idaho, where someone came up with the idea of tunneling under the Continental Divide to divert stored water from Yellowstone Lake into Heart Lake, which drains into the Snake River and eventually makes its way into Idaho. The proposals grew from there to suggest dams at Shoshone, Lewis, and Heart Lakes, all of which drain into the Snake River system.

In the end, the waters of Yellowstone were saved through the tireless work of large numbers of conservationists and organizations, led by the National Parks Conservation Association (then known as the National Parks Association). They received helpful support from more conservation-minded Interior secretaries who came after Lane. If not for all their efforts, Yellowstone could have been an entirely different park.

At the next trail junction the route to Bechler Canyon veers to the north. That will be my route in a few days, but today I'm headed west. My camp near Dunanda Falls is only four miles away.

A young backpacking couple approaches, with the hurried pace and grim expressions of hikers pushing to reach a trailhead before it gets late. I step out of the trail to let them pass, and we exchange greetings as they hurry onward.

After a stretch of solid forest, the trail emerges at the junction with the Boundary Creek Trail. A small stock party approaches from the north, so I step out of the trail and uncap a water bottle. They turn out to be three uniformed rangers. The first two are middle-aged, each on horseback. A loaded packhorse is tethered behind the second one. Bringing up the rear is a young ranger on foot. Either he's being punished or there's a shortage of mounts. Or maybe he just likes the exercise.

The ranger on the lead horse is the only one wearing the Smokey Bear hat, and he seems to be in charge. The other two have on green ball caps with the Park Service emblem. The leader returns my hello and continues in a friendly manner, "Do you have you a nice trip going, or are you just out for a few days?"

I give a brief outline of my route: Pitchstone, Union Falls, Dunanda Falls, Bechler Canyon, and out at Lone Star.

"That *is* a nice trip," he says. Then he uses a most amicable way to ask for my credentials: "You got your permit handy?"

It's attached to my pack, as always. The junior ranger steps over to check it, and I present it by doing a half-turn.

"You've got two nights at 9A3," he says, in the overly official tone of young law enforcement officers. "If there's not too much smoke, you'll have a good view of the Tetons from up there. Behind the food area, there's a trail up the ridge. That's where the pit toilet is."

"Is there a sign?" I ask.

"I don't recall if there's one there or not," he says. "I just like to tell people where it is, because sometimes there's not a sign. And even where there is one, people sometimes miss it."

"I've missed one before," I say, referring to my early tune-up trip at the start of the summer. "There was a sign at the campsite, but I never found the pit toilet. A ranger told me later it was way across the meadow."

They chuckle knowingly.

"Are you out working trails or patrolling for poachers?" I ask.

"A little bit of everything," the leader says. "We had to go out and replace a bear pole because an outfitter hung too much stuff from it and tore it down. We're not real happy with him right now."

"I bet not," I say, wondering how much gear it would take to pull a bear pole down. I can't imagine. It brings to mind the rangers back at the beginning of the Sky Rim trip, who weren't sure if the bear pole at High Lake was up. Apparently they do come down.

"Do you have to put those up every year?" I ask.

"We *try* not to," the young ranger says.

"How cold was it at your camp this morning?" the leader asks.

"It was twenty-six where I was," I say. "I may have lingered in the tent for a little while."

He grins and nods. "You seen any people out today?"

I tell them about the trail crew and the couple of backpackers on their way out.

"You picked the perfect time to come," he says. "If you would've come a few weeks ago, it would've been shoulder to shoulder in the swimming hole." I take it he means the many spots where creeks are warmed by thermal outflow, areas called hot pots, where many hikers come for a soak. While it's acceptable to swim or soak in a hot pot, it's illegal, and usually hazardous, to try to get directly into a thermal feature.

"Glad to be here when it's not so crowded," I say.

"How was the trail up on Pitchstone?" he asks.

"Up high, there *wasn't* a trail," I say. "It was all navigation by cairns."

He nods, indicating this is not out of the ordinary.

"In the forested part," I add, "there were a lot of downed trees across the route. And coming down toward the Falls River, the trail was overgrown and disappeared completely. I ended up making my own way down and found the trail again at the bottom."

"About how many downed trees did you see?" he asks.

"About thirty or forty," I say.

His grimace shows this *is* out of the ordinary, and he takes the state of the trails rather personally.

"Well," he says in an almost apologetic tone, "we've needed people down here so much we couldn't afford to send anybody up there."

I can understand that, in these times of budget cuts and unstaffed cabins.

"We'll let you get on your way," he says with a nod and a smile.

I return both, adding, "We appreciate you being out here, taking care of things."

His smile widens. "Well, we appreciate you coming out and seeing Yellowstone."

"Man, I love it out here," I say.

He nods again, and they head toward the Bechler Ranger Station, which, according to the sign, is still six miles away. I continue on toward Dunanda, feeling all official, now that I've had my permit checked.

It was nice meeting real rangers, ones who take pride in the park and in their jobs. They are the opposite of the two sorry specimens I met earlier this summer: the unhelpful ranger back at Harebrained Cabin—the one with the easily spooked horses—and that shiftless ranger at the Canyon backcountry office, who was only biding her time until ski season. It would've been a shame had those two formed my last impression of Yellowstone's rangers.

My shoes have finally dried from the crossing at Rocky Ford, almost five miles back, so of course it's time to make another ford. This one, a small, unnamed tributary of Boundary Creek, is only calf-deep and a few yards wide. A log crosses downstream, but it's long and uneven and sits a few feet above the water. After hiking almost fourteen miles today, it's probably better if I don't try it.

Beyond the ford is site 9A2. A sign says backpackers can camp along the creek, but horse parties must camp three hundred yards away. This is likely where the outfitter tore the bear pole down, though the food area is not visible from the trail.

After a few more stream crossings, each bridged with logs with their tops shaved flat, the trail makes a small ford of a different tributary of Boundary Creek. The water is surprisingly warm, the result of some unseen hot spring upstream. It feels nice on a cool late afternoon, so I pause in the middle of the crossing a few extra seconds. *Ahhh.*

The trail climbs a low rise, where a sign points the way to site 9A3, down the ridge to the west. The cooking area is in open forest, shaded by tall trees and well out of sight of the trail. Just beyond it, a path descends a steep slope to reach Boundary Creek.

Another sign points the way to the pit toilet, which is right where the young ranger said it would be. It has to be one of the nicest backcountry toilets in Yellowstone, a fiberglass fixture with a real toilet seat, and it's set on a low ridge with sweeping views over the forest and the distant Bechler Meadows. Quite a contemplative spot.

The ranger was also right about seeing the Tetons if there's not too much smoke. The faded pink and purple outlines of the high, jagged peaks are just barely visible through the thin gray haze.

Following the ridge crest away from the pit toilet, I find an open spot a good distance from both it and the cooking area. On a bare patch of dirt with excellent views of Bechler Meadows is a clear spot perfect for a tent. As I stand staring over the forest and meadows, I notice a faint whisper coming from the north. It's Dunanda Falls. They are also visible from here, though partially, through gaps in the trees. What a glorious campsite.

It's a site I would've missed, had it not been for a bit of Yellowstone serendipity. On my reservation request for this trip, I asked for two nights near the Bechler River, at either 9B2 or 9M2, which are on the route from Bechler Meadows to the canyon. On the layover day I planned to hike over here to see Dunanda Falls. This site was actually my third choice. But in some mystical orchestration of the Yellowstone universe, this wonderful spot appeared on my reservation for both nights. I couldn't be happier.

Camp is made by seven, when the sun still hovers above the southwestern ridge. Not bad for a fourteen-mile day with a late start. On the way to get water, I stop to pick up a cigarette butt some slob threw down. I put in my pocket for a later addition to the trash.

The trail to the creek descends steeply through dense stands of bracken fern, the colors ranging from deep greens to faded siennas and umbers. Scattered about are tall shrubs of mountain ash, bearing full clusters of red berries.

The creek is in deep shadow, screened by the ridge from the low-angle sun. The waters glint in metallic sheens in the dim light, slate-purple upstream and silver-blue heading down. A few huge boulders have settled in the watercourse. One anchors a tiny island covered with scratchy white flowers.

When I return to camp, the sunlight has receded to the high hilltops. Far up the steep slope to the north stands a lone mature aspen, its whitish bark shining in the fading light. As the sun sinks deeper behind the western ridge, the daylight fades, and the smoky meadows and distant mountains dim to a hazy darkness. The southern horizon is a mix of deep pastels, muted pinks and purples, broken here and there with black silhouettes of single conifers a short distance downslope.

When darkness is complete, I retire to the tent and read for a long while, before climbing out again to see the night sky. The dirty woodsmoke has settled low in the evening coolness, replaced by a vast wisp of phosphorescent smoke—the Milky Way. It is one of those rare skies with too many stars to take in, infinite numbers and space beyond our ability to comprehend.

From the elevated ridge with views to the south, most of Scorpius is visible, all but the lowest bend of its tail, which dips behind the darkened horizon where the Tetons were in the daylight. Sagittarius looms just behind, aglow in a vivid section of Milky Way.

On this cool autumn evening, such bright stars in summer constellations are striking. Foremost among them is fiery Antares, the brightest star in Scorpius. With its fierce red-orange glow, it stands out among the cooler blue-greens around it. It's a raging summer red. Not going gently into winter's cold night.

Day 5. Layover Day at Dunanda Falls

On a low ridge with no higher terrain to the southeast, sunlight reaches camp early. The cold front that blew through two days ago is already fading, and in full sun the tent becomes hot. Time to go out and get breakfast.

Later, back on the ridge, the feeling is one of peace among nature's beauty. A feeling of rightness. I look back over the course of the summer and sense that the earlier treks were all working toward this one, each building upon the last, and flowing into the next, all to reach this wonderful moment. It all brings a sense of connection, a kinship with the Yellowstone landscape, its geology, history, and ecology. For much of the morning, I remain lost in these feelings.

A loose flock of yellow-rumped warblers works the branches overhead. To the north, flashes of silvery white beckon through forest gaps, where Dunanda's falling waters catch rays of midday sun. The falls' distant, gentle roar rises through the valley, melding with birdsong and the gentle breeze, coalescing into the sound of the Bechler.

Though a faint path descends north from camp toward Boundary Creek, the most likely route to the base of Dunanda Falls, that is better saved for later. The brink of the falls should come first, a nod to seeing where a stream comes from before looking where it wants to go.

Back on the main trail, the route passes Silver Scarf Falls. More a steep line of cascades than a straight-down waterfall, these are on a different stream than Dunanda Falls, one of the tributaries my route forded yesterday. The cascades are only partially visible from the trail, prompting a detour down the steep, grassy slope toward a large tree at the creek's edge. From here the full height of the falls are visible, a continuous chute of whitewater, shredded and feathered, bouncing down the rocky path of its streambed.

Back on the trail, the route climbs high above the waters of Boundary Creek, as it must to reach the brink of Dunanda Falls, one hundred and fifty feet from its base. The midday sun lights the opposite slope in rich greens that descend to the low channel. Bits of sunlight touch the waters, in a vivid scene of light and shadow, flashes of whitewater, and shining boulders.

A spur trail leads to the brink, where the waters of Boundary Creek flow over a high cliff, dropping nearly vertically to splash among boulders below. Looking downstream from a short distance above offers an intriguing view. From here the flowing waters seem to disappear into nothingness.

On a nearby shrub, sitting atop a broad leaf, is a spotted tussock caterpillar. It is large and fuzzy, with an orange band around its middle, flanked on either side by black. Both ends sprout tufts of white hair, the eponymous tussocks. Here at the end of its larval stage, it will soon weave a cocoon to overwinter. Then, in spring's rebirth, it will reemerge as a moth of mottled brown and tan, a winged creature on a landscape young and lush.

After exploring farther upstream and returning to watch again as the waters flow past the brink, I return to camp. Down the steep path to the creek, the falls are not immediately visible. They're screened by a bend in the watercourse. Small hot springs dot the opposite bank, muddy seeps streaked green with algae-laden trickles flowing down to the creek. The vegetation is not as dense on that side, so the best route is to cross. Through the ford, the water temperature swings widely, through shifting zones of penetrating cold and comfortable warmth where thermal runoff mixes with the creek's chilly flow.

Before the falls come into view, a thunderous, crashing roar fills the box canyon. Around the bend, the falls appear. One can sense the awesome power of so much water crashing on a stony bed, casting up showers of flying spray and fine clouds that lift and float far downstream. Staring at the tumbling, bouncing waters, one's spirit also rises. Like a light mist, it hovers above, suspended, swirling, rearranging, as time stands still. A rainbow spans the billows.

In late afternoon I begin a slow return, pausing now and again to look more closely at the hot springs. Where larger ones join the creek, people have stacked circles of rocks to hold the warm water in makeshift hot tubs. So late in the season they are all quite shallow, not deep enough to reach the waist of a seated person. A soak seems pointless. To test the temperature, I step into the deepest pool. Though it only reaches my ankles, the sensation is comfortably warm.

Back in camp I return to the ridge for a different kind of soak—soaking in the view of the Bechler. An unseen Steller's jay squawks in the forest below, and a chipmunk works the low branches of a lodgepole overhead. Farther downslope a few red squirrels are busy gathering cones, and a northern flicker flies to one of the taller trees.

In the late-day heat the smoke thickens and shrouds the meadows. The only mountains visible are a few ghostly shapes to the south. When I return to the food area for dinner, faint noises that could be distant shouts intermingle with the roar of the falls. A scan through the trees finds no people. Perhaps I imagined them. I return to my sitting log and eat a cup of chicken soup, listening but hearing only the sound of the falls.

Soon, the dishes (one cup and one spoon) are done and the food is hung. Back on the ridge, I sit watching as warm purple shadows creep over the meadows and forest below. Where has the day gone? I can scarcely account for its passage: breakfast, a bit of staring across the meadows soaking in the view, short hikes to the brink and base of the falls, followed by more staring across meadows, and dinner. Another day flown by. Like time spent with the one we love, moments in Yellowstone slip past too quickly.

Day 6. 9A3 to Colonnade Falls, Site 9B5

With a planned hike of only seven miles on level terrain, breaking camp is a leisurely affair. Soon the gear is packed, and the food bag, lightened by the repast of five days and nights, leaves slack in the pack's fabric. By ten o'clock the morning has warmed, and standing in full sunlight feels like summertime.

Instead of taking the spur route back to the trail, I follow the top of the ridge. A patch of flattened grass under a lodgepole shows where someone camped recently. A single hiking sock sits nearby, a dirty olive-brown that blends in with the shaded grass.

Back on the Boundary Creek Trail, what was two days ago a clear path is now densely patterned with horseshoe prints headed away from the falls. So those *were* shouts I heard yesterday. Judging by the number of tracks and all the long, scattered piles of green manure, it was a large group. In a few places the horse prints are dotted with small canine tracks, a night-passing coyote. They add a touch of wildness to the barnyard appearance of hoof-churned dirt and manure.

The initial hike is generally downhill, traveling under a sky already filling with smoke. The temperature feels more like August than September. Though this is the route I took to get here, the terrain seems unfamiliar, as though I've never seen it before. But when I passed here two days ago, it was at the end of a fourteen-mile hike, when my tired focus was on reaching camp and little else. It's another reminder we tend to see more on shorter hikes. Fortunately, after a restful layover day, and with a leisurely hike today, my outlook is more refreshed and attentive.

The source of the horse tracks soon comes into view, a huge stock party camped at 9A2. It appears to be a guided outing, with plenty of casually dressed guests lounging about while cowboyed-up wranglers tend horses and pack enough gear to stock a flea market. I speed up my pace, hoping to hurry past them, but before I get very far, the chief guides and clients mount up and string out down the trail. The wranglers are left to finish the packing.

After pausing to allow more distance between me and the dust-stirring horses, I continue on. The large camp is spread on both sides of the trail, with piles of gear scattered about. Along the far edge is a line of folding tables loaded with the remains of what must have been an impressive brunch. Passing by, I call out a hello to a packer working near the trail.

He turns out to be a talkative hand, though he never stops working at the considerable task of getting all that gear packed and loaded. He says they're at the end of a six-day trip covering most of the Bechler region, including up the canyon to Three Rivers.

"How was the river in the canyon?" I ask, wondering about the fords. One would expect that, several miles upstream, the river would be shallower than it was back at Rocky Ford. But the river was wide there. Where it's constricted by the canyon it could be more challenging.

"In places, it looked like it was pretty deep," he says, "but it shouldn't be a problem to get across. The trail's in good shape, and the falls are beautiful."

"Great," I say. "Thanks."

"Just so you know," he adds, "I heard a forecast out of West Yellowstone, calling for fifteen degrees with light snow on Sunday night, with a chance of accumulations in the higher elevations."

"Good to know," I say. "Thanks."

Today is Friday, so Sunday's camp will be up near Douglas Knob. That's along the Continental Divide, at nearly eight thousand feet, which qualifies as higher elevation in this part of Yellowstone.

It would be nice to see a light snow out here, a pristine blanket of white spread over the land, crossed only with wildlife tracks. And all against a backdrop of rising steam near thermal areas. It would make a fitting end to a Yellowstone summer, coming out when the snow begins.

Leaving the wrangler to his work, I continue on. The main group is now far enough ahead that dust is no longer an issue. At the Bechler Meadows Cutoff, the horses continue south toward the ranger station, while my route turns east.

After a stretch of dense forest, Bechler Meadows returns. Across a low area, the turf is dry but spongy, with the feel of walking on a thick mat. On their way in yesterday, the stock party added a new odor, one that calls to mind a line from *The Tempest*. Trinculo to Caliban: "Monster, I do smell all horse-piss; at which my nose is in great indignation." Indeed.

Beyond is an area of thick mud, with standing puddles in the horse prints. The ground is spongier here, like walking on a waterbed piled with quilts.

In the warmth of the meadow I stop for a snack break. A quarter-mile away a backpacking couple is hiking out from the canyon, their heads down and focused on the trail in front of them. At the trail junction they pause to study the sign and then continue toward the ranger station. About half a mile behind them is another couple. It seems everyone is headed out on this Friday, but that may be only because I'm traveling farther in, and more apt to see people going the opposite direction.

The Bechler Ford is not wide at all, nothing like the crossing at Rocky Ford, though it's deeper. With no shallow routes visible either up- or downstream, I wade in just below the trail. Halfway across, the stream bed, knee-deep until now, drops into a deep trench carved by the current. With no shallower spots in sight, I plunge ahead through the cold water. At its deepest, it's just over waist high. The footing feels dicey on the muddy bottom, but the trench is narrow, and rises in a short but steep climb out of the river.

As water pours out of my pants pockets, I turn and scan the river, which has tight bends in both directions. Had I known the depth, I might have spent more time looking for a shallower crossing. There's surely one somewhere. No matter. This way was faster, it's a warm day, and I was expecting—even looking forward to—at least one deep ford on this trip. (The following summer I would day hike in from the Bechler Ranger Station and find a much better crossing, scarcely knee-deep, a hundred or so yards upstream. And that was in July.)

The trail follows a bend of the Bechler River, where, just across the water, another stock party has set up camp. Small tents are scattered about in the brush and willows. The camp's two bear poles are fully loaded with an assortment of large and heavy gear:

wooden panniers; full-sized red ice chests; several distended waterproof duffel bags; and a large black saddlebag. Now I see how some of these bear poles come down.

Not much farther is the low-impact site 9B2. It's the site I originally put down as my first choice for the previous two nights. The view is a bit hemmed in, and it's set right on a popular trail. I can't believe my luck in getting my third choice for both of those nights, a stay at the glorious 9A3.

Out in an open meadow, perhaps a hundred yards away, four sandhill cranes make their squawking, rattling, vibratory calls. Wary of my approach, they walk their long legs away from the trail, calling all the while. I stop to give them time and avoid frightening them into flying. They are such huge and beautiful birds. In the interim I remove my shoes and shake out a bit of river grit picked up at the ford.

Next is site 9B3. Its cooking area is only fifteen yards from the trail, which would make you something of a backcountry greeter on this popular route. On the opposite side, a faint path crosses a grassy meadow to some unseen tent sites. Though it's less than ideal, if it were the only spot you could get to camp in the Bechler, you'd be happy to have it.

At the approach of the canyon's mouth, the forest closes in, not dense but tight enough to restrict views and give rise to more bear talk. In places the trail is a trench dug by horse traffic, except where it crosses beds of solid rock, which don't yield to horses' hooves, or much of anything else, except time. Outcroppings of layered rocks and rounded boulders appear high up the slope, masses of grays among the forest greens and yellows.

Farther on, the trees become taller and the forest opens beneath their height. The Bechler River appears to the left, bending toward the trail, as both waterway and path approach the canyon's mouth. Through gaps in the forest, white flashes of Ouzel Falls wink from the southern edge of Madison Plateau.

In the canyon, two groups of hikers appear in quick succession. The first is two men and a woman sitting beside the trail taking a break. I stop to exchange pleasantries, as backpackers do, but they are untalkative. The woman allows that the fall colors in the canyon are beautiful, and one of the men speaks absentmindedly to say the waterfalls were amazing. I continue on.

Next is a group of four, three men and a woman.

"Where you headed?" I ask the first man.

He points to the man behind him. "He's the local."

Apparently, it's another guided trip, though, from the gruff demeanor of the first hiker, perhaps not a pleasant one. The local says they came in at Shoshone Lake and are taking six days to go through the canyon and out at the Bechler Ranger Station. I tell him I'm doing something similar but in the opposite direction.

"How many days you giving yourself?" he asks.

"Ten," I say. "I came in at Pitchstone and crossed over to Union Falls and then Dunanda, and now I'm going up the canyon."

"Wow!" he says. "Alright!"

The walls of the canyon close in, with the high western reaches of Pitchstone Plateau on one side and the southern edge of Madison Plateau on the other. Fall colors abound, vibrant profusions of yellow, orange, and maroon, over a muted canvas of bronze, burgundy, and forest green. It forces one to stop to take it all in.

To the left, just down a short slope, is the Bechler River. The view of the water is mostly open, broken here and there with saplings of Douglas fir and shrubs of mountain ash, flashing sprays of red berries. Where the river tumbles over submerged logs, the water shows tints of glacial aquamarine.

A cow moose appears on the trail ahead, a healthy-looking calf behind her. Seeing me, they bolt across the river, disappearing into a thin line of trees. Creeping along, I scan the opposite forest, but the moose are gone or well hidden. I continue on.

A wandering garter snake crosses the trail, with speed and energy drawn from the full sunlight on this warm afternoon. It disappears in a patch of desiccated thimbleberries. The plants, their raspberry-like fruit long gone, have wide leaves that add large splashes of yellow to the palette of fall colors.

From around the next trail bend, visible through gaps in the trees, a young bull moose approaches. He hasn't yet seen me, and I feel lucky to get a few photos. But it quickly turns into an "uh-oh" moment as the moose continues to move toward me. It's well known that moose can be dangerous, so I quickly scan the terrain for somewhere to retreat. The steep, rocky slope to the right and the river just down to the left leave few options. I could turn around and go back, but there's no way a human can out-hike a long-legged moose.

Though still around the screened trail bend, the moose is uncomfortably close and still unaware that I'm here. A guttural gurgling comes from his throat. I've got to get his attention somehow, or face a close encounter with a surprised and dangerous animal.

"Moose!" I call out. (It's all I can come up with under the circumstances.)

He keeps coming.

I sing out again, louder: "MOOSE!"

He stops and glares at me through a forested gap about twenty yards away. I scan about again for somewhere to go, still without much of an escape plan. If he keeps coming, I'll have to go in the river.

"They went that way," I say to him, pointing across the river, reasoning he must be following the two other moose. It's the first time I've spoken to a moose. I hope he's not offended.

He stares back for a long moment, and slowly turns his head to look uphill. Then he climbs above the trail, only going ten yards, not enough for me to get safely past him.

I take a few tentative steps. He doesn't move.

"A little more, please," I say. He stands his ground, having done his part, apparently. Maybe it's time for me to do mine by taking to the river. But then he moves again, climbing higher before turning across the slope to pass behind a stand of trees. Seizing the opportunity, I speed up the trail.

"Appreciate it," I call out.

After sprint-hiking for fifty yards, I turn for another look. The moose is nowhere in sight, neither on the slope, the trail, or in the river. I continue on, stopping once more to look back. Now the young bull has returned to the trail, walking his original route. He soon disappears into the brush on the downhill side and reappears in the river, close to where the cow and calf crossed. He pauses midstream, forming an iconic image of the Yellowstone backcountry. In an instant he is gone.

It's one of those encounters where the beauty, naturalness, and the wildness of it all coalesce in a moment of unsurpassed richness. The memory is imprinted on the soul as a single image, a bull moose standing broadside in the Bechler River, framed by fall foliage of yellows, greens, and autumn reds. Though fleeting, these moments are indelible. They are the treasure we take with us from Yellowstone.

MOOSE!

With so much beauty and mesmerizing richness, it's impossible to hurry down this trail. Between the majesty of the river, the captivating fall colors, and the appearance of the moose, one almost forgets this canyon is known for its waterfalls. But waterfalls will not stay forgotten. As the trail climbs, approaching the brink of Colonnade Falls, a faint rushing sound grows into a thunderous rumble from below. The source remains hidden by dense forest, but a trailside sign points the way down a spur route to an overlook of the falls.

The trail is muddy from numerous seeps, but it's an easy hike. At the bottom of a three-hundred-foot descent is the oft-photographed view of the double-plunge falls. It is a well-chosen site, a short distance downstream from the lower drop, but high enough to see beyond its sixty-seven-foot height and take in the thirty-five feet of the upper drop a short distance upstream. Flanking the falls on either side are gray, rocky cliffs, marked with vertical lines of columnar basalt. These are thought to be the source of the name Colonnade Falls, though there are no official documents to confirm it.

Back on the trail, just beyond the falls' upper plunge is site 9B5, my home for the night. In the narrow canyon that holds both river and trail, there's not much room for campsites. As a result, 9B5 is wedged onto a thin strip between the riverside trail and the base of the steep and rocky slope of Pitchstone Plateau. The food area is only a few yards from the trail, with little screening vegetation, and the best-looking tent sites are right near the bear pole. From the rectangular patterns of flattened grass, it's clear people have set up right here. More rectangles are scattered farther out, still too close to the bear pole, many along the trail.

The farthest spot from both bear pole and trail is near the base of the rocky slope. It's a spongy, damp area among a web of trickling, seepy springs, but it should offer a cushy, comfortable sleeping surface, as long as water doesn't seep into the tent. With no better options, it will have to do. I just hope my tent floor, after so many nights in the backcountry, hasn't gotten any leaky pokes, punctures, or scrapes.

When the tent is up, I crawl inside. Actually, I more or less dive in onto the ground pad as though it's a raft. After several minutes, all remains dry. This may work, though I'll still try to keep my sleeping bag and clothes from touching the floor.

Other than the slightly cramped conditions, it turns out to be a nice campsite. Situated along the Bechler River, it's within earshot of both the upper plunge of Colonnade Falls and Iris Falls farther upstream. Water is easy to get, just across the trail, in a spot above the upper plunge of Colonnade Falls. As the water filters, one can watch as the flow of the river disappears into space just a short distance downstream.

As with many campsites in the popular Bechler area, this one has a pit toilet. Unfortunately, though, it's situated on the highest ground in the site, with only a line of low shrubs screening your lower half from public view of the trail. Worse, the pit is nearly full from overuse, as it were, both from people that camped here and, likely, many opportunistic passersby. It raises a question of what rangers do when pit toilets become full. There's certainly no way to pump them out like they do in the front country.

The sun disappears early behind the high western walls, casting the land into shadows of untimely dusk by midafternoon. Over the next few hours, the light moves up the eastern wall until the last rays linger on treetops on the plateau's edge. Above the canyon's rim, a raptor traces circles in a sky of intense blue, drifting between sunlight and shadow and back again, from dim cool to brief flashes of brilliance.

Back at the food area for dinner, I sit on a log, lost in thought. A chipmunk behind me emits a sharp squeak of alarm, and I look up to see a small raptor. It's speeding toward me in a low trajectory, its talons open and reaching. With its attention focused on prey, the raptor doesn't notice me until it's nearly upon me. At the last instant, it pulls up sharply, banks toward the river, and flies up the canyon. The chipmunk is nowhere in sight.

As darkness deepens, I consider putting the campsite's fire ring to use, but there's something inharmonious about a campfire so close to a popular trail. After dinner I return to the tent and lie listening to the whisper of the two falls, trying to tease apart their sounds by tone and direction. The upper plunge of Colonnade Falls, just a bit downstream, makes a light whisper-splash that's muffled by the intervening cliffs, while Iris Falls, a middle distance upstream, emits a louder, crashing roar that travels unobstructed from the falls' base.

Day 7. 9B5 to Albright Falls, Site 9B9

Morning, or what passes for it in a shaded canyon, comes slowly. In the early chill, I linger in the sleeping bag, reading. With a hike of only four miles today, there's no need to rush.

Around ten o'clock, I am surprised by a man's voice outside.

"Anybody in the tent?" he says. "Park Ranger."

"Yeah," I say, putting down my e-reader. "Be right out."

It's easier said than done. I'm zipped inside my sleeping bag, wearing only thermal underwear, which may or may not have holes in inopportune places. My sealed clothes bag serves as an extra headrest.

Unzipping the sleeping bag, I kick my legs out and reach for the clothes bag. My camp pants are buried somewhere in the bottom, of course. As I begin yanking out scrunched pieces of clothing, I wonder what the ranger must be thinking about all the rustling going on in here.

"How many people?" he asks in a cautious tone.

"Just one," I say.

When I hurriedly try to pull on the pants, my foot gets hung in the lining, adding to an already lengthy delay. Now it's almost comical. How long does it take to get out of a tent?

"You got any weapons in there?" the ranger asks.

"No," I say.

"No knives, guns, or anything?"

"No," I say. "Unless you count bear spray."

"Well, just leave the bear spray in there when you come out," he says.

Finally, I get the pants on and climb outside. The ranger is positioned at the foot of the tent. His hand is on his holstered pistol. It's not a threatening posture, only cautious, the manner of a well-trained cop who has spent a long time listening to a stranger rustling around in a tent. When he sees I don't intend to cause problems, his hand eases away from his weapon as though it was never there.

As he looks over my permit, I ask if he's heard a recent forecast, repeating what the outfitter told me about a chance of snow tomorrow night.

"It's supposed to be cold," he says, "but only a thirty percent chance of light snow."

"Cool," I say. "I was thinking a big dumping might hide the trail."

"Let's see," he says, studying my permit. "You're headed north. There's only one spot up there where the trail could be hard to find. Up by Douglas Knob there's a big meadow. Just stick to the right if you can't see the trail. For most of it, it's a good little ditch you won't have any problem seeing."

He asks about the rest of my trip, and I tell him my plans to hike to Shoshone Geyser Basin on the way out.

"Be careful around the hot springs there," he says. "Before you get close to any edge, make sure you walk all the way around and look at the rim to make sure it's not undercut."

Then his voice takes a more official tone. "I need you to come back to the cooking area with me."

"Is something wrong?" I ask, knowing the food is hung and my camp is as far from the bear pole as it could be without getting into rocks or brush.

"Nothing serious," he says. "Only I'll need to write you up a warning."

As we walk, I wonder what the warning could possibly be for. I pride myself in keeping a clean camp.

Where the trail narrows between two walls of brush, I pause to let him lead the way. He stops and swings an open hand forward in an after-you gesture. It's another act of a well-trained cop: never let someone you don't know and trust get behind you.

At the fire pit, a hole has been dug in the deep ashes. A full-sized shovel lies nearby. Beside the hole is a pile of foil and other unburnable trash.

"Did you have a fire last night?" the ranger asks me. It's more declaration than question. (Did you have a *fire* last night.)

"No," I say.

He pauses, studying my face. Then his demeanor relaxes. "You know," he says, "I thought maybe this wasn't yours. All the ashes and rocks are cold, but nothing is wet. I don't need to give you a warning, after all."

"Nope," I say. "Not mine. I can show you a baggie of burned foil I dug out of my fire pit back at Union Falls."

"That's fine," he says. "You're good." He picks up the trash and stuffs it into his pants pocket. Then he uses his shovel to dig the ashes out of the fire pit and scatter them around in the surrounding brush.

"Don't you like to have a fire at night?" he asks as he works.

"Sometimes," I say. "Depends on how I'm feeling and how the campsite is situated. This one's right on the trail. I almost decided to have a fire at Dunanda Falls, but it was so far to get water, I decided not to."

He smiles. "I keep waiting for them to make that a non-campfire site."

I'm feeling relieved at not getting that warning. "I thought you were going to say something about my tent location," I say. "It's not quite a hundred yards from the bear pole, but it's as far away as I could get without doing some serious bushwhacking."

He waves off any concern. "You're fine," he says. "We have all these requirements on paper, but in some of these sites, once you get out here, there's no chance of following them all to the letter. The problems are the people that camp right on the river."

As he continues spreading ashes, I try to remember the questions I'd been saving for the next ranger I met.

"I was wondering about the pit toilets," I say. "What do you do when they get full? I can't imagine getting any kind of equipment back in here to clean them out."

"When they get too full we just dig a new one," he says.

"I thought maybe, since they're only used for a couple of months each year, they might take care of themselves and break down over winter and spring."

"They tend to decrease some over the winter," he says. "In the spring, the water table goes way up, and when it falls they settle down a little bit. But they still fill up, and then we just dig a new one. This site is one of the prime candidates for a new one. We just haven't had time to do it yet."

While we're talking about lack of resources, I mention my route across Pitchstone Plateau and all the downed trees.

"Yeah," he says, as though well aware. "There's been a lot going on this summer, so we haven't gotten to all the trail maintenance. We had to fly a couple of people out with injuries. One guy jumped into Ouzel Pool and dislocated his shoulder, and another hurt his back. And there have been a lot of wrecks on the roads, several with fatalities. And over by Heart Lake, we had a law enforcement incident. It has been a crazy summer. Every time we try to send someone over to work on Pitchstone, something else happens."

I recall reading about the law enforcement incident on the online Yellowstone forum, Y-Net. According to the post, a ranger doing routine campsite checks found a man with a shotgun. Because he also had active federal warrants, he was arrested on the spot and flown out by helicopter. (I would later confirm this with another ranger, who made the brilliant observation, "Bad guys go on vacation, too.") It sheds some light on why this ranger was so cautious when I took a long time getting out of the tent.

"I've hiked all over the park this summer," I say, "and haven't seen many rangers until I got to the Bechler."

"Have you seen all the people out here?" he asks. He opens a logbook of the campsites in the area. "Tonight there are no available sites anywhere in the Bechler region, not counting Pitchstone, where nobody goes, and Robinson Creek, where nobody goes."

And I was thinking it wouldn't be as crowded in mid-September.

"I just ticketed one group," the ranger continues. "They walked off from camp and left a fire with flames a foot high. I caught up with them and told them, with five percent humidity and a chance of thirty to forty mile-an-hour winds, you can't be doing stuff like that. Actually, I wrote them several tickets."

He asks where else I've hiked this summer. I mention this is my fourth trip, and I'm hoping to get enough material for a book.

He stops and gives me a scrutinizing look. "You been to Thorofare?" The implication is: Don't even try to write a book about the Yellowstone backcountry if you haven't been to the Thorofare.

"I have," I say. "About two weeks ago."

With a satisfied nod, he says, "That used to be my area. Did you go up Mountain Creek?"

"Is that the one up to Eagle Pass?"

He smiles with remembrance. "Yes. In my opinion that's the prettiest part of the park."

"Really?" I say, surprised.

"Yes," he says, "and I've heard some other people say the same thing." He speaks of climbing Eagle Peak and some of the other high mountains in the area. It's evident he is an avid climber.

"I'm not much of a peak bagger," I tell him. "I'm happy to walk up a mountain, but I don't do any technical climbing. I've heard Eagle Peak is tough and has turned back a lot of experienced climbers."

"It isn't *that* bad," he says. "Going up, there's really only one move you have to make, where there's a large boulder up at the head of a slot."

Now I'm certain he's a climber, talking about moves. The only moves backpackers make are trying to maintain balance while crossing fast-moving streams.

"But you should never climb alone," he adds. "And if you can, take somebody with you that has some medical skills."

That settles it. No mountain moves for me. I try to stay clear of activities where I need to bring my own medic.

He's finished with his shoveling and is ready to go looking for more sloppy campers.

"I could keep you here all day asking questions," I say. "Thanks for all the info."

"I talk to a lot of people out here," he says. "Some aren't that easy to talk to, so this has been enjoyable." Before he sets off, he adds, "You'll pass a spring on your hike today, just before you get to 9B8. It shoots right out of the ground. It's some of the best-tasting water in the park."

"Can you see it from the trail?" I ask.

"Oh, yeah," he says, "but you'll hear it first."

"Thanks," I say. "I'll hold off and refill my water bottles there."

He sets off in the direction of the Three Rivers Patrol Cabin, carrying his shovel.

I set about eating a quick breakfast and breaking camp. As I cinch up the backpack, a group of young people pass on the trail headed downstream. Soon I'm on the trail, too, headed up.

It's a short walk to Iris Falls, where the plunge of forty-five feet makes a crashing roar. The water's impact on the rocks below casts up a fine mist, which catches the sun's rays, building a rainbow bridge over the river. Some of the mist wafts up to the trail, coating the observer with a cold spray. Farther upstream, waterfalls give way to cascades of blue and white.

Bechler River

At the next ford of the Bechler River, a dismounted horse party sits lounging on the near side. As I exchange hellos with several of them, a woman steps forward.

"I think we met you earlier this summer," she says. "At Sportsman Lake."

She's the woman I spoke to when the misguided trail sign sent me into the wrong campsite. "I remember," I say.

She introduces herself and her husband, Erin and Mike. They run an outfitting company out of Gardiner. "You really get around," she says.

I tell them about my four trips around the park, saying that after to Sportsman Lake I went up to Hoodoo Basin and then through the Thorofare.

"When were you at Thorofare?" she asks. "We were just there two weeks ago."

"That's when I was there," I say.

"That sure is beautiful country," Mike adds.

"You guys get around, too," I say.

"Yeah," Erin laughs, "but we're on horses."

Everyone gets a chuckle out of this.

"We'll be in Pelican Valley in a week," she says. "We'll probably see you there." More chuckles.

She goes back to tending her clients while Mike tells me about their trip. They had hoped to start their week-long outing at the Grassy Lake Trailhead, but didn't get the campsite they wanted. So they started at the Bechler Ranger Station, and are now returning from Three Rivers on their way out. Though I'm curious about what this would cost, it would be rude to ask, especially in front of clients. When I get home I'll check their website and find a seven-day trip across the Bechler costs thirty-three hundred dollars per person (in 2012).

As I prepare to move on, Mike says, "The ford is a little deep here. If you cross on the trail, there's a hole on the far side about waist deep."

"Thanks," I say. "I'll look for a shallower spot."

While this is going on, I hear another woman behind me say, "What are you doing, Erin?"

"I'm going to give Cliff one of these cookies," Erin says.

I turn and see her holding out a large granola cookie bulging with M&Ms. "Here you go," she says.

"You're lucky," the other woman says. "Those are all homemade."

"I have no doubt," I say. "Thank you, Erin."

I put the cookie in my shirt pocket and approach the river to survey the crossing. A line of riffles stretches diagonally from the opposite bank, about ten yards below the trail. I head downstream before stepping in and heading for the riffles. The water is just over knee-deep, though there are some deeper holes. My walking stick proves handy at checking depth where the bottom is screened by shadows or rapids.

As I climb out on the far side, a cheer erupts from the horse party, all of whom have been watching my progress. One of them even recorded my crossing on video (I could've taken a dive and gone viral.) I give them a wave and continue on.

A quarter-mile ahead are three women in their fifties, joking and laughing as they hike south. They came in at Lone Star and are planning to go out tomorrow at the Bechler Ranger Station.

"Isn't this the best weather?" one of them asks me.

"It sure is," I say.

"How's the ford?" another asks. She points to the water line on my pants, just above the knee. "Is that all it is?"

"That'll be waist-deep on us," another one says, touching off another round of laughter.

What a fun group.

I continue on, now traveling through denser forest. Soon a rumbling gurgle announces the spring the ranger mentioned. It is about ten yards down a gentle, grassy slope. Just as foretold, the water shoots right out of the ground, emerging from the face of a short but steep slope beneath an overhang of grass. From here it tumbles down a narrow whitewater channel toward the Bechler River. I put an open bottle under the torrent and take a sampling drink, pure-tasting and cold.

The fourth and final ford of the Bechler is only calf deep. Beyond, it's a short distance to my next camp, at 9B9. A trailside sign says it's a minimum impact site, with no wood fires.

The food area is set back a nice distance from the trail. It's at the base of a high, rocky slope, where Albright Falls, which are not named on either the National Geographic map or the USGS topo, tumble down from Pitchstone Plateau. Near their brink, high on the rocky slope, is Batchelder Column, an isolated pillar of stone. It's an interesting juxtaposition, rising rock and falling water.

From the falls' base it's impossible to see the higher terrain beyond the rim of the canyon. Because of this, the falls seem to originate magically at the top of the cliff. A glance at the map finds the plateau rising another thousand feet to the southeast, back in the direction of the trip's first campsite at 8P1.

Though Albright Falls are quite tall, their descent is not a straight-down plunge but a series of steep cascades similar to Silver Scarf Falls. Two-thirds of the way down, they turn sharply north and trickle across the foot of the ridge. At the bottom they regroup in a small stream and turn southward again, flowing around the campsite.

From the food area a faint path leads up a small rise to the pit toilet, which is modestly screened by trees and shrubs. This pit has only recently been dug, so recently, in fact, that it hasn't been used. A circular piece of cut sod lies nearby, presumably on top of the old pit. Scattered about is a loose pile of freshly unearthed rocks, one the size of a human head. That must've taken some digging.

Another trail from the food area leads to the southwest, reaching a long meadow. I make camp on its western edge, in an unscreened spot likely to catch the morning's first warming rays. Back at the food area I have a leisurely lunch while staring up at the peaceful falls. It is a carpe diem moment, brought about by the realization this trip and this summer will soon come to an end. Only three nights in the backcountry remain.

Though I had planned to make a day hike this afternoon, to the thermal area on the Ferris Fork—the site of Mr. Bubbles—it now seems the time would be better spent here in this wild setting. Tomorrow's short hike will go right past the Ferris Fork before climbing out of Bechler Canyon. There's no need to get ahead.

I scan the rocky cliffs for pikas or other signs of wildlife. Only a couple of Clark's nutcrackers are moving about, in a squawking, flapping frolic in the high treetops. In the shallow stream near camp, an American dipper walks a partially submerged log, its thin legs causing tiny V-shaped ripples in the water's flow. After diving under the creek's smooth surface, the bird emerges several feet downstream and stands on a rock, dancing its bobbing dance.

The fall colors lining the stream are already fading, the reds toward browns and the golds and yellows to aged bronze. They dim further with the fading afternoon light, and seem to absorb the day's warmth as a chill settles over the valley.

Just before evening another ranger, younger than the one this morning, appears. After a summer of wondering where they all were, now two in one day. This one is also friendly. When he looks at my food bag suspended from the bear pole, I ask if he wants to see where my tent is. He does, so we walk down the path to the meadow.

"This is good," he says. "No problems here."

As we return to the food area, I mention the freshly dug pit toilet that someone, likely him, recently finished. "There were some big rocks that came out of there," I add.

"I couldn't do it without my rock bar," he says. "It's a pry bar as tall as I am. I try not to carry it unless I'm traveling by horse."

Next I ask about the thermal area up the Ferris Fork.

"You can get in Mr. Bubbles," he says. "There's a trail right to it."

"How is it getting to the falls farther up?" I ask, referring to a series of waterfalls on the Ferris Fork, which have exotic names like Tendoy, Gwinna, Sluiceway, and Wahhi.

"There's a little social trail that goes part of the way up," he says. "Beyond that, it's all off-trail travel. Some of it's pretty rough, going down into little canyons where you can see the falls."

The ranger moves on, under a sky already filling with dark clouds. As evening settles, a light sprinkle begins. Back in the tent, I fall asleep to the sound of a waterfall for the fourth consecutive night. The wonderful voice of the Bechler.

Day 8. 9B9 to the Gregg Fork, Site 9D2

The day starts cold and gray, under a low sky of dense clouds. In the sun's absence, the damp air has a piercing chill. Or maybe it's the blustery wind. Either way, it's a beautiful day in the Yellowstone backcountry. There are no bad days out here.

Approaching the end of this last outing, I've become less ambitious about packing up each morning and moving on. Dragging my feet, in a sense. The days have turned short, both in duration and number, and I want to hold on to the time that remains.

I wander the campsite, staring into the creek or at the falls, or watching the plants, the rocks, the sky. Fresh deer tracks near the bear pole serve as reminders that, though unseen, the wildlife is here. We only pass through this place, but they remain, as the ecosystem lives and breathes, often beyond our notice. There's a certain comfort in that.

By late-morning, the gear is packed, and the short hike begins. Beyond an unnamed creek, the route moves toward the head of Bechler Canyon. The terrain is open forest, filled with autumn colors with a warmth at odds with the conditions. As the route makes a gentle climb toward the canyon's upper end, the walls taper downward, or seem to. Though still high, they are not as towering as before.

Glimpses of the Three Rivers Patrol Cabin appear through the trees, a hundred yards to the west. I wonder if the two rangers are in there, or if they're already out patrolling the canyon, ensuring irresponsible campers don't leave the place littered and burned. They're doing good work. I wish there more of them.

Small thermal areas line the trail on either side with pale white sinter. The color is echoed by lingering blossoms of yarrow, the bleached wood of nearby logs, and rapids in the distant river. All show shades of flattened white on this overcast day.

A trickle of thermal runoff crosses the trail, winding toward a small pond. Thin steam clouds hover above its still surface. Beneath it are submerged mats and spongy masses, of greens and rusty browns, echoing the colors of the terrestrial foliage.

A cold drizzle begins, and I stop to put on raingear. While the pack is off, I linger and look, taking in the high valley. It's a setting that, like much of Yellowstone, is too beautiful to rush through. Not far away is the Three Rivers confluence, where the forks of the Bechler—the Phillips, Gregg, and Ferris—flow together to form the river that gives name to this part of the park.

The trail crosses the Ferris Fork on a shaved-log bridge. Just upstream are the small but beautiful Ragged Falls, where tatters of whitewater cascade down a solid rock bed. A nearby sign says Old Faithful is 15.5 miles in one direction and the Bechler Ranger Station 14.4 miles in the other.

A spur route turns up the Ferris Fork, past a hitching post where horses must be left. After a stretch of open forest, it crosses a long meadow, where numerous hot springs waft steamy clouds into the cold morning air. A side stream crosses the route, its dark, flowing waters striped yellow-orange with long strands of thermophilic growth. They wave hypnotically in the current.

From an unseen hot spring farther upstream comes thick steam clouds, which jump and twist in the wind. Closer, where the hot springs should be in sight, a headwind shoves a wall of dense steam across the land, shrouding all views. As I walk in the heated, dampening mist, a new, swirling gust disperses the cloud, revealing a large hot spring on a bench above the creek's opposite bank.

Its mineral-rich waters flow from a blue central pool. Over the centuries they've built intricate deposits, white basins and shelves, where the heated waters continue to splash and run amid a rainbow of colors. Mats of heat-loving mosses, green, gold, and rust-colored, divide shining white channels. Some of these fall into a delicate basin, a scalloped white fountain that shines through the sprays, then tumble in radiant showers into the creek below.

A bit farther upstream is the famous Mr. Bubbles, a large pool with an effervescent jet of airy water churning near its center. To increase the pool's depth and retain the warm water, people have built a wall of stones between it and the Ferris Fork. The pool is deep enough for a soak, but on this frigid, drizzly morning, it doesn't look inviting.

Above Mr. Bubbles the trail becomes faint. As the ranger said, it's little more than a social trail, which quickly fades in the rugged terrain. Having seen a goodly number of cascades and waterfalls in recent days, I decide to save this route for another day.

Back on the main trail, the climb out of Bechler Canyon begins. Through the first half of the seven-hundred-foot ascent, the trail rises high above the Gregg Fork, which flows at the base of a narrow canyon to the northwest. A short detour takes in Twister Falls, with their curved bed. Above the falls the stream is closer to the trail's elevation. When the high valley bends eastward, a small log bridge crosses the Gregg Fork. Past the bridge is site 9D2, my camp for tonight.

The site's cooking area sits trailside. Though it's almost three o'clock, three college-aged kids, two men and one woman, are lazing about near a large campfire. It appears they are starting to break camp but in no particular hurry. I walk to the fire ring and address one of the men. "Packing up?"

"Uhhhhh . . . yeaaaaahhhh, dude," he says. "We're getting ready to head down to Mr. Bubbles."

"Cool," I say, setting my pack against a log.

"We didn't get to the park until seven last night," he explains. "The office was already closed, and we didn't want to camp in a campground with everyone else, so we just hiked in here with headlamps. Almost thirteen miles. We didn't get here until around two a.m." He points to the woman. "I spent the whole time telling her the story of the Lord of the Rings."

Her expression is inscrutable.

I silently wonder how it might have gone had someone been camped here legally. These kids wouldn't have noticed a tent set up out in the darkness, and everyone would have gotten a surprise this morning.

"This site doesn't have a bear pole," the guy says, "so we just hung up our food across the creek."

A short distance upslope from the fire ring is a bear pole in plain sight. I don't bother to tell him.

"We're about to head down to Mr. Bubbles," the spokesman says again. "We're just gonna stash our stuff back across the creek where we hung everything last night. We'll come back later and head out from here."

"Okay," I say.

He turns to his friends, who are sluggishly gathering their gear. "Hey, guys," he says, thumb pointing at me. "He says he'll watch our stuff while we're gone."

I did? Whatever. I'm just ready for them to get moving. As they finish packing, the woman asks her companions, "Do you have everything you need? Bathing suits?"

The second man, who has been silent until now, speaks up. "Man," he says, "I don't *need* a bathing suit."

They all break into laughter.

As they head noisily down the trail, I hang my food and set about surveying the site. The camp is on a steep-ish slope, with one level area down by the creek, where the cooking area is, and another on a bench uphill. The higher area is obviously where people set their tents—at least the people that get here in daylight—but the place is trashed. Though a sign points the way to a pit toilet across the trail, people have defecated on the open ground in various places and left the results, including toilet paper, lying about.

I walk a long distance away from the trail in hopes of finding an unsullied site. Beyond a stretch of dense forest well over a hundred yards from the bear pole, is a clear spot just wide enough for a tent. It appears untrammeled. A good location, all things considered.

Though the afternoon has warmed some, dense clouds threaten more rain. I set up the tent to be ready for whatever comes, then return to the food area for dinner. At six-thirty, two young guys headed toward the Bechler stop at the creek, only a few yards away. I step over to say hello. It turns out they are headed to site 9B5, my campsite two nights ago.

"We still have a long way to go," one of them says with a German accent. He opens their map, which is nothing more than a page-sized photocopy of the National Geographic trails map. Either it doesn't show trail distances or they don't show up on the faint page.

"Is it about five miles?" he asks.

"Probably closer to six," I say.

"When does it get dark here?" he asks.

"Around seven-forty-five, now," I say, adding the obvious, "but a little earlier every day."

"And a little colder," he says. With renewed urgency they head down the trail, with an hour of daylight remaining and six miles to cover. Soon after they leave, the drizzle resumes.

After hanging the food, I climb back to the tent, arriving just as a real rain comes clattering through the trees. I dive inside without getting too wet, while rumbles of thunder and a strong chilly wind enliven the evening air. Warm and dry in the tent, I while away a pleasant evening with reading.

Later, out in the fading dimness between dusk and night, laughing voices pass on the trail. No doubt it's the squatters returning from Mr. Bubbles. I wonder if they'll hike all the way out tonight or crash in someone else's site. Whatever. I remain in the tent, in dryness and in peace.

Day 9. 9D2 to Shoshone Meadows, Site 8G1

The morning temperature is thirty-three. So much for the forecast of fifteen degrees with snow. Down at the cooking area, under a shining sun, the ground is already dry.

The initial hike climbs the shoulder of Douglas Knob, a forested hill rising a few hundred feet above the plateau. Beyond, the terrain levels onto a wide meadow. This is where Pitchstone and Madison Plateaus flow together. The land has the familiar look of gentle undulations and bands of forest interspersed with wide meadows. Crossing the first meadow, the shadow of a large raptor passes on the ground. I look up to see a circling red-tailed hawk.

To the west, a short distance away, is the Littles Fork. Shallow and marshy in this flat terrain, it meanders in tight bends. As the trail eases toward it, the ground becomes a wet and muddy bog. Though I had thought to be done with fords and was hoping for a dry-feet day, there's no way around the muddy strip. I splash across, sinking up to my ankles.

Back on dry terrain, the trail is solid and dusted with shiny black particles of obsidian sand. Nearby sits a gray comma butterfly, its delicate orange wings pulsing in the midday sun. A tiny bit of summer still holding on.

Past sites 9D3 and 9D4, the route crosses the Continental Divide twice in less than half a mile. The first is into the upper watershed of the Firehole River, which will later flow into the Madison on its way to the Missouri. The second moves into the drainage toward Shoshone Lake and the Snake River. Beyond, the trail begins a long descent through forest that alternates between open and dense.

At the bottom is Shoshone Meadows, a grassy bowl surrounded by open forest, with a creek running through it. At the junction with the Shoshone Lake Trail, a sign says Lone Star Geyser is four miles to the north. And though it's not on the sign, the final trailhead, where my vehicle waits, is less than three miles beyond that. If I were so inclined, I could keep hiking and go out today. That had been my original plan, before I added another stay tonight for a chance to hike the Shoshone Geyser Basin.

The Shoshone Lake Trail is part of the CDT, which I've not seen since the upper reaches of the Snake River, east of Big Game Ridge. The access to my campsite at 8G1 is on that trail, a short distance above the junction. The site is nice and roomy, and though the cooking area is close to the trail, at the site's far end is an open spot set back from the busy route and screened by a low forested ridge.

Before setting off for the geyser basin, I hang my pack from the bear pole, where it won't be chewed by wildlife seeking salt in the sweaty residue. In a sustained gust, one of the larger trees begins to sway. This creates a high-pitched squeak that calls to mind the land of Oz and a tin woodsman seized by rust, murmuring, *Oooiiiiiilllll.*

I start hiking again just before four o'clock, carrying only bear spray, hiking stick, one water bottle, and camera. With a little over two miles to travel each way, I'll have an hour and a half to explore the geyser basin if I want to return in time to eat dinner before dark. My headlamp is in my pocket in case the hot springs make me lose track of time.

The trail follows the flow of Shoshone Creek through a low valley of rocks and conifers, crossing the stream several times. Near Shoshone Lake, the route turns south to cross a wide meadow. On the far side, all across the landscape, columns of steam rise straight in the tranquil air.

The geyser basin is expansive, and it immediately becomes clear that an hour and a half is not nearly enough. Spread far and wide is an array of thermal pools and hot springs, deep holes in the rocky ground like windows into the earth. The transparent waters show shades of blue, green, orange, and brown. Some appear quite deep. They have a mystical, magnetic power that pulls you in to try to see into the depths. I heed the ranger's advice and walk around each pool before approaching, to ensure the land has not been undercut. But mostly I observe from a safer distance.

No people are anywhere in sight across the wide, open basin. Neither are there any boardwalks, handrails, or warning signs to protect careless visitors from their own foolishness. The unencumbered setting makes for a deeper experience. It's easy to imagine this place looks much as it has for thousands of years.

Toward the basin's southern end is the distinctive triple cone of Union Geyser, one wide, tall cone in the center, with a shorter one on either side, one set slightly farther apart. A low rumble gurgles from the dark depths, though the geyser's last known eruption was in the 1970s. Nearby, a western garter snake zips through the grass.

From here I circle back along the creek, past an assortment of multi-colored hot pools and roaring fumaroles. The fading daylight reminds me I'm still two miles from camp. I cross the basin to reach the trail and make it back to 8G1 with barely enough light to eat dinner without a headlamp.

As dusk fades to night, I sit staring across the darkening meadow, contemplating my last night in the wilderness. Out in the forest, a large tree falls. It begins with a loud, resounding *crack!*, followed by the creaking of strained wood and an extended crumbling of branches. All these culminate in a booming impact that reverberates through the ground.

It's good that we still have places where trees are left to fall when they're ready, or when nature is. Left alone, these ecosystems move in their own cycles: from seedling to tree to rotting log, and back to seedling again, or some other living thing. Each cycle grows from the last, and each feeds into the next.

The fallen tree takes me back to the first night of the Sky Rim trek, when other trees crashed in the forest. The remembrance brings a sense of completion of another kind of cycle, connecting the last night of this Yellowstone summer with the first.

It has been a full summer, set apart by old trees, long spent, falling naturally in the ecosystem. The end of one cycle and the start of a new one. Each growing out of the last.

Day 10. 8G1 to Trail's End

The final morning of the trip. And the final morning of the summer. Seems it ought to be more of an emotional experience, on this day of fulfilling a long-held dream. But this will not be my last Yellowstone trek. Tentative plans for future trips have already begun to form in my mind. And there's still time to squeeze in at least one more trek this year. Nothing is really ending.

Packing up is easy when an empty food bag leaves ample room for the gear. After shouldering the pack, I notice two men looking around at the far end of the food area. On my way out, I swing by to say hello. They are also nearing the end of a trip, an out-and-back outing from the Lone Star Trailhead down Bechler Canyon as far as site 9B6. Tonight, their last, they'll camp on Shoshone Lake.

"We got the only site available," the younger man says, "and it was only available one night. Every other site was booked as far out as the computer had readouts."

As he is saying this, two other hikers pass on the Shoshone Lake Trail. He pauses to assess their gear.

"Wow," he says to his friend. "His pack is as big as yours."

"I used to be a horse-packer," the older guy explains. "In those days, three horses was a light trip. It has taken a while to go from a four-hundred-pound load to a one-hundred-pound load."

"A hundred pounds for one person?" I ask.

"Divided between us," he says.

"My pack," the younger one says, "just holds my zero-degree sleeping bag and food."

"He *has* a larger pack," his friend says, "but he won't carry it."

"When I carry it on a trip with him," says the younger one, "by the end of the trip, my pack is always ten pounds heavier than it was when I left."

We all laugh at this.

"We cook a lot," says the older one. "I think we have ten pounds of cooking gear."

"We cook bacon every day," the younger one adds.

"But you always think of other things you need," says the older man, "like 'I can't go without a skillet,' and 'I can't go without a dutch oven.'"

Clearly, they're pretty serious about backcountry cooking. We bid each other good journeys, and I head toward the trail junction. The couple that passed earlier is standing there, taking a break. They came in at Shoshone Lake and are headed to Bechler Canyon for two nights before coming back out this way.

My route turns north, crossing the Continental Divide a final time at Grants Pass. The morning is warm and sunny, pleasant hiking weather. As the trail descends through forest, more hikers appear. Three groups in so short a span after seeing no one at all on the long hike yesterday.

Leading this group are a middle-aged man and his twelve-year-old son. I step out of the trail for a water break to let them pass. As they approach, we exchange hellos.

"What kind of car do you drive?" the man asks.

It's a bizarre question to be asked in the backcountry. I answer in the most general terms.

"You've been out here quite a while," he says. "I left a note on your windshield, asking if you want to get together next year for a shuttle hike in the Absarokas, so we can exchange car keys along the route."

Wondering how he knows I've been out for so long, I ask, "What, did you come hiking every day and notice my car?"

"We started this trip over a week ago," he says, "but our stove crapped out, and we had to go back for a few days. When we came back, your car was still here. I told my son, 'That guy's been here a long time.' We were starting to get worried." He takes out a camera. "Will you pose for a picture?"

Though I don't care much for having my photo taken, I don't want to be rude.

"Get in there," he says to his son. "We have a new hero."

"Let me put my water bottle away," I say. "It won't look very heroic being thirsty."

After snapping the photo, the man says they're from a small town just north of Jackson, Wyoming. As we talk, his wife and daughter approach.

"This is the guy whose car we've been seeing," he says to them.

As we exchange greetings, the man takes a long look at my backpack.

"You don't care about pack weight do you?" he says.

"I guess not," I say. "My pack weighed around sixty-five pounds when I started this trip."

"That's what two of our packs weigh," he says to his kids.

"This was a ten-day trip," I explain, "covering about seventy miles, if you count all the side trips."

"By yourself?" he asks.

I answer yes.

"Well *you* can carry all that," he says. "You're a gorilla."

"The first few days, I was a *tired* gorilla," I say.

He explains they are using some of the latest high-tech gear to keep pack weight down, admitting it's quite expensive. "We just got some new ground pads that have large holes in them to make them lighter," he says. "They're quite comfortable."

"They're comfortable if you don't move around while you sleep," his wife says. "I don't like them that much."

"I'm a flopper," I say. "I don't think they'd work for me."

He assesses my gear again. "What do you got there, sleeping bag, ground pad, and tent?"

"Yes," I say.

"Oh, you can get that *way* down," he says.

He's trying to be helpful, but I'm pretty set in my ways. This is the gear I've always carried and probably always will. But he's an ultralight packer, for whom reducing pack weight is something of a religion. And he's out to convert all us nonbelievers. I must seem like an infidel, living a decadent lifestyle, with a three-pound tent, sleeping bag, thick ground pad—without any holes—and a pillow, which they don't even know about. A pillow! That'll send me straight to ultralight backpacking hell.

When I ask about their trip, the man says they are going through Bechler Canyon and out at the Bechler Ranger Station. They're coming back in a few days for an out-and-back trip to Dunanda Falls.

"Which campsite do you have at Dunanda?" I ask.

"We got the good one, right there by it," he says.

"That's where I was," I say. "It's a little far to get water, but it's worth it. When you go down for water, you can follow the creek up to the base of the falls."

We say goodbye and head our separate ways, one journey beginning and one coming to an end, if true journeys ever come to an end.

Headed down from Grants Pass, the trail offers more glimpses of the meadows along the upper Firehole River, still several hundred feet below and a half-mile to the west. When the terrain levels, the meadows come closer, stretching now and again across the trail. A few boggy areas are crossed on boardwalks, one spanning a shallow channel dotted with yellow-green lily pads. In drier stretches, small thermal areas sit near the trail, a few simmering hot springs and gurgling fumaroles. Near one of these, a garter snake lies warming itself on the sun-drenched ground. So many snakes on one trip.

After following the Firehole River for a while, the trail makes a crossing on a sturdy footbridge. A solo backpacker approaches, young, perhaps in his twenties. He says he is headed to Mr. Bubbles, and camping tonight at site 9B9, the one at the base of Albright Falls.

"I camped there three nights ago," I tell him. "It's a great site."

"Do I stay on this trail the whole way or do I branch off somewhere?" he asks.

"Stay on this trail," I say, wondering why someone would walk into the backcountry without being certain of the route.

"I saw a sign that said it was fifteen miles, but I didn't know if that meant from the trailhead or from the last trail junction."

"Do you have a map?" I ask.

"Not a good one."

"You want to look at mine?" I say, taking out my National Geographic map of the Old Faithful area.

"I would *love* to see a map."

I open it and point out our location. "You'll pass this junction with the Shoshone Lake Trail," I say, "but stay on this trail. It's a little bit of a climb going toward Douglas Knob, then it's all downhill to where Mr. Bubbles is, right here."

"Thanks," he says. "What's the bear situation up there? Do they have those things where you can hang your food?"

"Yeah, all the sites have bear poles."

"Good," he says with a grin. "Because I've got some good ol' jerky."

We part ways. He's got a long day ahead of him. It's already after noon, and he's still got twelve miles to go, with a bit of climbing in the middle. But he is young and seemed fit enough.

The last trail junction comes just beyond the Firehole, where another route breaks off toward Old Faithful. A sign says the Bechler Ranger station is now twenty-eight miles away. Lone Star Geyser is only a third of a mile ahead, and the trailhead is less than three miles from there. Nearly done now.

Gaps through the forest offer increasing views of the large, blocky cone of Lone Star Geyser. It is quiet now, without even a wisp of steam rising. A few people are scattered about the area, though it's unclear whether they are lingering after the last eruption or waiting for the next.

A trailside pedestal holds a placard saying the geyser erupts every two to three hours. It has a logbook filled with gleeful notations of recent eruption times. There are also crestfallen messages from some who hiked the three miles in, arrived minutes too late, and felt they didn't have time to wait for the next one.

According to the most recent entry, the next eruption should occur in about an hour. I'm due for a lunch break, and a geyser eruption would be a fitting close to this Yellowstone summer, a steamy exclamation point punctuating the end of my travels.

The day has turned warm, with abundant sunshine. At a log in the shade, I drop my pack and unwrap my last energy bar. Over the course of the hour, the geyser begins to steam and then rumble, casting intermittent splashes of hot water that grow larger with time. A few more people trickle in from the trailhead. A couple sitting near me converses quietly in French. Their strong aromas— his cigarette and her perfume—make an all-out assault on my olfactory senses, which have known nothing but natural smells for ten days. As nonchalantly as possible, I move to a different log closer to the geyser, as though to have a better view.

Two men arrive on bicycles, bringing the overall group size to ten. Someone spots a bison grazing along the bank of the Firehole and several people run over to get photos. A few of them get much too close, sticking their cameras almost in the bison's face. Back in the front country.

The gurgling in the geyser cone increases, and the intermittent jets grow larger, expelling enough water to fill the runoff channel winding across the sinter toward the river. A lone coyote trots out of the forest, passing between the geyser and crowd, unconcerned with either. Instead of chasing the coyote as they did the bison, the people remain still, only snapping photos. The coyote trots on, pausing at the forest edge to scan ahead, and disappears.

More people arrive, with either impeccable timing or admirable luck. Among the new arrivals are two white-haired women, one of them pushing a third woman in a wheelchair. They move into the half circle of observers just as the geyser's full eruption begins.

Lone Star Geyser

In a display of the geothermal power that underlies much of Yellowstone, the geyser erupts in a jet of superheated water and steam, sending a column nearly forty feet high. The top of the plume bends in the breeze, pushed downward briefly by the wind before rising again and drifting eastward. This is repeated through several cycles, tracing a large white squiggle across the blue sky.

After an extended time the eruption subsides, tapering into noisy gurgles of the steam phase. As the crowd remains, still watching the geyser cone, I fade into the shady forest. Only two and a half miles to the trailhead.

On the drive home, though it's two weeks past Labor Day, the roads are still busy. The first wildlife jam appears near the bridge over the Firehole River. Several vehicles in front of me swerve toward the roadside, not getting quite out of the roadway before disgorging scampering folks with cameras and phones.

Their target is a lone bison standing in the river. I ease past the crowd toward the clear roadway beyond. On the bridge, I steal a glance at the bewildered bison, feeling more kinship with the wild animal than with the hectic, hustling crowd.

Beyond the park's west entrance, the homeward route turns north onto Highway 191, which crosses the northwest corner of the park. The last trailhead before the northern boundary is the Dailey Creek Trailhead, the place where my first trip began. Though only two months back, it now seems long ago. With no one behind me, I let off the gas, coasting slowly past the empty parking area, scanning the start of the trail and as much of the Sky Rim as is visible.

My thoughts go back to July, when I was filled with anticipation. What do I feel now? After a long inward look, I realize the feeling on this late September day is one of wholeness. It's a feeling of having fulfilled a long-held dream and found it as rewarding as hoped.

There is also another feeling, one of growth. Now that I've walked across much of the Yellowstone backcountry, all of those places have become part of me. I can now make an instantaneous return with only a thought, to the Sky Rim, the Hoodoo Basin, Thorofare, and the Bechler, and all points in between. From this point onward, no matter where life may take me, I will always be close to Yellowstone. And Yellowstone will always be close to me.

Acknowledgements

I would like to thank Mary Rosewood and Laurie Dahl Rea for offering to read the manuscript and providing many thoughtful comments. Their timely and generous efforts helped make this a better book.

Many thanks are also due to my girlfriend and soul mate, Mari Lindsley. In addition to helping me set up shuttles for three of my treks, she also transcribed the many trip notes I made with a digital voice recorder I carried with me on the trail. She also read the first draft, as well as a later draft, which she read to me aloud so I could hear the flow of the language and catch rough patches I may have read over. For all she does, I am eternally grateful.

Made in the USA
San Bernardino, CA
05 April 2016